THE OPEC FUND FOR INTERNATIONAL DEVELOPMENT: THE FORMATIVE YEARS

The OPEC Fund for International Development: The Formative Years

IBRAHIM F.I. SHIHATA

Said Aissi
Mehdi Ali
A. Benamara
Antonio R. Parra
T. Wohlers-Scharf

CROOM HELM
London & Canberra
ST. MARTIN'S PRESS
New York

© 1983 The OPEC Fund for International Development
Croom Helm Ltd, Provident House, Burrell Row,
Beckenham, Kent BR3 1TT

British Library Cataloguing in Publication Data
The OPEC fund for international development.
    1. Organization of the Petroleum Exporting Countries
    2. Economic assistance
    I. Shihata, Ibrahim F.I.
    338.91'177'01724   HC60
    ISBN 0-7099-2450-X

First Published in the United States of America in 1983
All rights reserved. For information write:
St. Martin's Press, Inc., 175 Fifth Avenue, New York, N.Y. 10010

ISBN 0-312-58616-7
Library of Congress Catalog Card Number 83-40051

Printed and bound in Great Britain

CONTENTS

TABLES

TO my colleagues in the OPEC Fund.
In recognition of seven years of fruitful association.

Ibrahim Shihata

FOREWORD

This book is an attempt to describe the experience of the OPEC Fund for International Development over its first seven years of operations, the period during which I was entrusted with the responsibilities of the office of Director-General. As the first chief executive of this institution, my task was not limited to the management of its day to day business, but included the responsibility of transforming it progressively from a special account of a temporary nature into a fully fledged international agency for development finance. Over those seven formative years the Fund evolved as a major multilateral financial institution and an important instrument of progressive change, to the benefit of developing countries at large. Its philosophy and approaches have presented a welcome addition to development finance, matched only by its wide geographic and sectoral coverage.

Although I was responsible for writing most of the material in this book, other colleagues in the Fund made their contributions. Chapter 1 is co-authored by Mr Antonio R. Parra, Chapter 4 by Mr Said Aissi, Chapter 5 by Mr Abdelkader Benamara and Chapter 6 by Dr Traute Wohlers-Scharf, while Chapter 3 was written by Dr Mehdi Ali. Other Fund staff members whose names do not appear here also contributed to the research for, and refinement of, the book. In particular Mr John Stephens, the Fund's editor, revised the whole text to ensure consistency and readability. The chapters written by myself were patiently typed several times by my secretary Miss U.A. Faustmann with typical efficiency.

By compiling this book before my departure from the Fund, my purpose was to leave on record a history of the Fund's experience and achievement which I hope will prove to be of interest and value to all those involved in the development process. I also wanted to demonstrate that, through the political will of its Members and the dedication of its small staff, the OPEC Fund had been able to achieve over a short period of time what would have remained otherwise mere aspirations. I am confident that after this impressive beginning, the OPEC Fund will remain an exemplary institution in its vital field of activities.

Ibrahim F.I. Shihata
Vienna, June, 1983

INTRODUCTION: THE ROLE OF THE OPEC MEMBER COUNTRIES IN FINANCING THIRD-WORLD DEVELOPMENT*

Dr Ibrahim F.I. Shihata

The subject matter of this book has been my major concern, over the last seven years, since I started my responsibilities at the OPEC Fund as its first Director-General. Although the institution and the job were new, ten years had already passed since I had first been involved in Arab development finance, as adviser to the Kuwait Fund. It is with these seventeen years of personal involvement that I wish to address the important phenomenon that has come to be known as 'OPEC aid efforts'.

There are certain facts about this phenomenon which I have tried to clarify in earlier lectures and publications.[1] As these facts were so different from the prevailing thoughts and images, they remained generally unrecognized until recently, when clear signs brought them home to the Western public. It might be useful to restate the relevant facts I have in mind.

Five Preliminary Facts

First, OPEC countries, which have for some time been thought of as the new rich countries of the world, are in fact a group of developing countries whose relevant economic and social indicators do not place them even among the better-off third-world countries. Not one of them has yet developed a powerful industrial base, an advanced agricultural sector or, with the possible exception of one or two members, any major exports other than oil. They are all food-deficit countries, some relying almost exclusively on imports to meet their food needs. Five of them figure among major third-world borrowers. In spite of the financial surpluses of a few among them, OPEC countries as a group are already reported to be net borrowers from Western banks as their borrowing and withdrawals have started to

---

* Based on an address to the Symposium of Zentralsparkasse & Kommerzialbank on 'The Issues of the Eighties', Vienna, March 19, 1982.

1. See, in particular, Shihata, I., *The Other Face of OPEC*, Longman, 1982.

exceed their deposits. The Western mass media, which had long spoken enviously of the 'excessive wealth' of OPEC, now have a new complaint expressed recently in a major daily under the headlines: 'OPEC applies new pressure to West by borrowing'.[2]

Even when OPEC countries are in surplus, and this is the *second* point, their oil revenues can never be equated with the incomes realized in industrialized or agricultural economies, where revenues are earned from recurrent outputs generated from a permanent, or at least a renewable, productive stock. In fact the so-called surpluses of some OPEC countries have always resulted from the extraction of their depletable natural resource at a rate so fast that it often exceeded financial needs at the time of production. The resulting liquidity should not therefore be mistaken for additional wealth. It is simply a monetary realization of a pre-existing asset. One may easily argue, as I have repeatedly done since the early seventies, that the transformation of a depletable natural resource into cash which cannot be converted immediately into new real investment, and thus real wealth, may make a country poorer rather than richer in the long run. Because of this major difference in the nature of the revenues of OPEC countries and industrialized countries, the GNP of the former cannot be calculated on the same basis as that of the latter. As economists are increasingly recognizing now, an important depletion factor has to be allowed in calculating the GNP of countries whose economies rely heavily on the exportation of a fast-depleting asset, such as oil. Ignoring this point simply results in gross over-estimation of the GNP and of the savings of OPEC countries.[3]

The *third* point I wish to make is that even if the present distorted calculations of GNP are taken as a basis for analysis, the GNP of OPEC countries, though grossly exaggerated, is still quite small when compared with that of the industrialized countries, or even the semi-industrialized countries of the South. The GNP of OPEC as a group, as now calculated, does not exceed 7% of the GNP of the OECD countries. In 1979, Saudi Arabia's GNP was similar merely to that of Austria, and the combined GNP of the six major Arab donor countries (Saudi Arabia, Kuwait, UAE, Iraq, Qatar and Libya, listed

2. The *International Herald Tribune*, February 20-1, 1982, p. 11.

3. See Thomas R. Stauffer, 'Measuring Oil Addiction: Growth Versus Expansion in a Rentier Economy', *Middle East Economic Survey*, vol. 14, Sept. 7, 1981; idem, 'The Dynamics of Petroleum Dependency, Growth in an Oil Rentier State', *Finance and Industry* no. 2, pp. 7-28, 1982, Kuwait.

in order of the size of their external assistance efforts) was equivalent to one half that of the UK, one third that of France, one fourth that of Germany, one sixth that of Japan and one fifteenth (or 6%) that of the US alone!

In spite of their relatively small GNPs, these OPEC member countries in particular have embarked since the sixties on external assistance efforts which are so great that they have exceeded by far not only the record of the truly rich countries of the North, but even the target set by the international community for the aid efforts of those truly rich countries. This leads me to the *fourth* point: the impressive magnitude of OPEC aid.

Official development assistance to the developing nations, the so called ODA flows (see Annex 3 for a list of the acronyms used in this book) of OPEC countries, as defined and calculated by the DAC secretariat of the OECD, was over US$9 billion in 1980 and in the order of US$8 billion in 1981, the last year where data are available. The annual average of such ODA flows in the preceding five years was about US$7.86 billion. Most of such flows are outright grants. In 1980, grants represented 55% of total OPEC ODA flows, while the loans' component included a grant element of 49%. According to the OECD publications, some OPEC countries have been among the world's largest donors in absolute terms, with Saudi Arabia, for instance, coming at the top of the list in 1981 and second only to the US in two earlier successive years (when the United States' GNP was more than 33 times that of Saudi Arabia). According to more convincing figures, which do not take into account US assistance to Israel and Southern Europe, and France's assistance to its dependent territories, Saudi Arabia could be easily established in recent years as the number one world donor in absolute terms.

Since 1975, the list of the ten largest donors in the world has always included three OPEC members. During some years in this period, the ODA of small countries such as Kuwait and UAE exceeded in absolute terms the aid of France or Germany whose wealth, power and external interests are simply beyond comparison with those of OPEC donors. In fact, if one cares to look at the aid performance per capita of the donor countries, one may be startled to see that in 1980, for instance, ODA disbursements reached US$1450 for each inhabitant of Qatar, US$1328 per capita in the UAE, US$849 in Kuwait and US$362 in Saudi Arabia. These figures, one should be reminded, compare with only US$30 for the US, the richest country of the world. To complete the picture, aid from OPEC sources is never used to promote the export interests of the donors, as is often the case in the bilateral assistance of DAC countries.

The *fifth* point I want to emphasize here is that this unprecedented aid performance cannot be taken simply as an attempt by OPEC countries to compensate certain consumers for the financial burden caused by the oil price rises. In fact, these aid efforts have been unrelated to such financial burden in most cases, notwithstanding popular themes to the contrary. The OPEC aid phenomenon started in the early sixties, when the price of oil was, if anything, particularly cheap. Most of this aid has gone to the poorer countries of the world, which account for a small volume of oil imports. Large portions of this aid have been received by countries such as Egypt (until 1979), Syria and Tunisia which are not even oil importers. Hardly any country has received aid from OPEC sources on the basis of the volume of its oil imports (with the exception of the credits extended by Iraq and Venezuela for financing oil purchases in certain countries).

The birth and the growth of the OPEC aid phenomenon, as a whole, did not follow the developments of oil prices, although of course, the increased oil revenues helped to expand and enhance the aid efforts of OPEC members. Separation of the aid issue from the issue of the financial burden resulting from higher oil prices is important in understanding the OPEC aid phenomenon. Although OPEC's main objective is to defend a remunerative price for the oil exported by its members, no one can reasonably claim that the drastic price rises of 1973 and 1979 were engineered by OPEC. If it is illogical for a seller of a commodity to compensate the buyer (why raise the price in the first place?), this becomes all the more so when the price rise results from the interaction of forces not caused by that seller.

The point to be emphasized here is that the sharp changes in the price of oil which have taken place since 1973 were not the work of an international cartel manipulating the market, as was generally, but erroneously, assumed in the West. In point of fact, OPEC, simply, has not been a cartel. Since its inception in 1960 until 1983, OPEC never adopted coordinated production programs aimed at con-trolling prices through production cutbacks, as a cartel technically operates. When an attempt was made for the first time to reach agreement on production ceilings in 1982, some members even argued that such action was beyond the scope of OPEC's jurisdiction.

Under severe market conditions, OPEC countries recently

(March 1983) agreed on a production ceiling and quotas in an unprecedented attempt to influence prices through cartel-like techniques. The only previous instance of coordinated oil output restrictions occurred outside OPEC. Such action, which lasted only for a few months (October 1973 to March 1974), was taken by the Arab producers in a war situation and for a political purpose completely unrelated to the price issue. Since that date, OPEC's agreement on prices has been to a great extent a ratification of market trends which at times resulted in sharp increases in prices, due to the decline in oil supplies, or rather the fear of such a decline, mainly because of political developments in the Middle East. Meanwhile, concerted action was to be noticed more in the behaviour of the major oil consumers than in that of the oil producers. The present decline in oil prices, like the smaller decline in 1975, despite the continued presence of OPEC throughout these periods, should provide the best evidence of the correctness of this thesis.

What is most interesting about the five facts I have just stated is that they are facts, easily documented by established evidence. Yet, they have sounded for a long time as though they were personal views, controversial at best. This merely exemplifies another fact: the world's present information order, much as its economic order, is still largely dominated by the few industrialized countries which also happen to be the major oil consumers.

The Evolution of OPEC Aid

It is also fair to say that the true dimensions of the OPEC aid phenomenon as it stands today may be hard to believe. One may reasonably ask:

(1) if OPEC member countries are not that rich in fact,
(2) if there is no case for compensation for the financial burden resulting from higher oil prices, and
(3) if OPEC countries have nothing to gain financially from extending their assistance, which is completely untied to source;

why, in the first place, do they extend so many billions of dollars every year to other developing nations?

This question, I submit, cannot be adequately answered without tracing back the origins of this phenomenon and understanding the socio-economic and political circumstances in which it has evolved. OPEC aid efforts find their historical origins in the link which ties

Arab countries together and which is generally referred to in the vocabulary of the Middle East as 'Arab Solidarity'. Long before the accumulation of oil wealth, the more able Arab countries extended assistance in the 1930s and 1940s, especially in the form of educational and health services, to their less able neighbours.

In 1957, Egypt and Saudi Arabia undertook to provide what was at the time substantial budget support to Jordan. A year later, Kuwait, which was not yet fully independent, initiated the first attempt to institutionalize aid efforts by creating the Authority for the South and Arabian Gulf. This agency, which is still operating under Kuwait's Ministry of Foreign Affairs, provided social services for the poorer Gulf Emirates and for the Yemens. The precedent was soon followed by a more important step when Kuwait, in the very first year of its independence, established, on December 31, 1961, the Kuwait Fund for Arab Economic Development.

This particular institution, which initiated the historical movement of OPEC development aid, started with a capital of KD 50 million, then equivalent to US$140 million, and with a mandate to finance development projects in other Arab countries. Its capital was soon doubled in 1963 and then doubled again in 1966, to KD 200 million.

In 1967 the heads of all Arab States met in Khartoum, Sudan, immediately after the Israeli invasion of the territories of Egypt, Jordan and Syria. Among the decisions taken at this Arab Summit Conference, two were of great relevance to our subject:

(1) agreement was reached that Kuwait, Libya and Saudi Arabia would provide sizeable budgetary support to the three affected countries 'Until the liquidation of the effects of aggression' and
(2) it was also agreed in principle that a regional fund should be established to finance the development efforts of Arab countries at large.

The *Agreement Establishing the Arab Fund for Economic and Social Development* was finalized the following year. Before that fund became operational in 1972, the Emirate of Abu Dhabi established, in 1971, the Abu Dhabi Fund for Arab Economic Development which closely followed the Kuwait Fund's precedent. Thus, before the so-called oil revolution of 1973 had taken place, inter-Arab aid efforts were an important phenomenon, which was both sizeable (net disbursements of US$1.75 billion in 1973) and institutionalized.

The most important development took place, however, in 1974. In that year, the phenomenon which found its *raison d'être* in Arab Solidarity was to receive a great boost after the significant increase in the oil revenues of OPEC countries. In that single year, the Kuwait Fund underwent two important changes. Its capital was increased fivefold, to the equivalent of US$3.6 billion, and all developing countries, not only Arab countries, became eligible to benefit from it. Similar changes in both respects were adopted by the Abu Dhabi Fund a few months later. Saudi Arabia established the Saudi Development Fund, which started with the sizeable capital of US$4.5 billion, for which all developing countries were eligible. Iraq established its own Iraqi Fund for External Development, with a smaller capital but with the same comprehensive geographical coverage.

To complete the picture, the same year witnessed the creation by the Arab League of an assistance facility for African countries which was soon replaced by the Arab Bank for Economic Development in Africa (BADEA), a regional Arab agency for extending assistance to non-Arab African countries. Saudi Arabia became instrumental also, in the creation of the Islamic Solidarity Fund, which was complemented a year later by the Islamic Development Bank (initial authorized capital US$2.6 billion).

Non-Arab OPEC members were soon to enter the aid scene, with both Iran and Venezuela establishing public investment funds which covered also the extension of development aid on a large scale to developing countries (African and Asian countries in the case of Iran, and Latin American and Caribbean countries in the case of Venezuela).

Libya, which had participated, sometimes substantially, in all the above mentioned regional aid agencies, also utilized its Arab Libyan External Bank for extending development aid to other countries. Algeria and Nigeria created trust funds with the African Development Bank, while Venezuela had a similar arrangement with the Inter-American Development Bank.

The following years witnessed the establishment of the Gulf Organization for Development in Egypt (US$2 billion, now dissolved) by four Arab OPEC members, the Arab Authority for Agriculture Investment and Development (US$562 million, mainly for Sudan) and the Arab Monetary Fund (US$1 billion), as regional institutions.

All OPEC countries, including traditional recipients such as Indonesia and Ecuador, joined forces in 1976 in the creation of the

OPEC Fund whose modest initial resources (US$800 million) were increased more than 400% in less than four years. In fact, the resources of most of the agencies mentioned were substantially increased, especially in 1980 and 1981 when the resources of the Kuwait Fund, the Saudi Fund, the Islamic Development Bank and the OPEC Fund were all doubled. All in all, to date there are fourteen specialized agencies exclusively or mainly financed by OPEC members whose total resources stand close to US$30 billion. Together they account for about one fourth of the annual ODA transfers of OPEC countries, the rest being channelled directly by governments (for the most part) or through other multilateral institutions.

The above developments reveal how the Arab aid phenomenon gradually evolved into a larger phenomenon, involving OPEC countries as a donor group and, in some instances, other third-world countries as well. Seeing these developments from this perspective makes it clear that the phenomenon was not based on any notion of compensation for higher oil prices, but was rather the natural evolution of a trend which started first as an expression of solidarity among the countries of the Arab region. It also explains the often misunderstood concentration of bilateral aid on Arab and Islamic countries, the sympathy for which was in fact the origin and the justification for the wider efforts which constitute today an important landmark in international financial cooperation. It is interesting to note in this respect that while in 1973, beneficiaries of Arab aid numbered 23 countries which were all Arab or Muslim, today the beneficiaries of the OPEC Fund alone have exceeded 80 countries and only 15% of its loans have gone to Arab countries.

Non-concessional Transfers

The role of non-concessional, or commercial, transfers from OPEC to other developing nations is also obviously of great interest. The expansion of such transfers has a greater potential than that of concessional flows.

The so-called recycling issue was presented in standard literature as a 'problem' facing financial institutions after 1974. The problem, of course, was not in the availability of surpluses as much as in the fact that the owners of such surpluses were newcomers from the Third World. Before that date, financial surpluses, like military power and political influence, had been the exclusive prerogative of a few advanced countries which had the financial institutions to lend these surpluses and the industrial capacity to produce and sell capital goods to the rest of the world. These functions were mainly in the hands of Great Britain in the 19th century and until World War I. They gradually shifted to the United States, and at a later stage included also other countries such as Germany and Japan. The unexpected developments of the oil price adjustments in the 1970s dramatically shifted financial surpluses to the accounts of some Arab oil producing countries. These new surpluses were different, however, in that they resulted from the sale of a domestic asset, oil, in such volumes that the return exceeded the import requirements of the oil producers, and did not merely arise from imbalances in external transactions involving reproducible goods and services.

As the new holders of surpluses were not familiar with the functions traditionally performed by the advanced countries, they were unable to translate such surpluses without delay into new real investments. As a result, they found themselves accumulating paper claims on outsiders in the form of deposits with foreign banks, treasury bills of foreign governments, and other foreign financial papers. This in turn raised a challenge for the Western banks, to use the proceeds of these new deposits by 'recycling' them to the deficit regions. It also created a challenge to the owners of these liquid assets to develop their own financial institutions and their capacity to go into direct investments abroad.

Private Western banks were successful in recycling the funds and, despite occasional complaints, made enormous gains in the process. Huge amounts, whch mostly reached middle-income developing countries and enabled them to achieve record growth rates in the 1970s, were by and large the proceeds of deposits of oil exporting countries. In addition, these latter countries lent substantial amounts to the IMF to channel to the deficit countries, thus enabling them among other things, to meet their obligations to their foreign bankers. Seen in a wider perspective, such processes presented a mechanism for the redistribution of income on the international level, real benefits reaching both developed and developing countries in different degrees. The game has been far from the one generally depicted in standard literature, in which only the oil exporters stood to gain.

Meanwhile, Arab financial institutions and joint institutions with other agencies in developed or developing countries continued to grow. A recent list shows that more than half of the 50 largest Arab banks,[4] with total assets exceeding US$140 billion, were established after 1970. Seventeen of these banks have already figured in *The Banker's* list (June 1981) of the world's 500 largest banks, as measured by size of assets. In addition a growing number of investment companies, including those which operate according to Islamic principles, are entering the market. The success of these banks and investment companies has led many of them to play an increasing role in international markets especially in providing finance to developing countries in what is now referred to as 'direct recycling'.

The real challenge lies, however, in converting financial instruments into real resources, or to put it differently, an involvement in new direct investments which appreciate with time and yield more enduring income. There is also a growing concern that such investments should to the extent possible, be carried out in developing countries in particular.

For their part, the four OPEC countries which are likely to continue accumulating surplus funds are fully aware of this challenge. Arrangements have recently been completed for the creation of a large Gulf Investment Corporation to complement the work of the several national, inter-Arab and other multilateral investment corporations financed wholly or partially by these countries. This challenge requires, however, more than merely establishing investment institutions, even if they are highly capitalized. Success requires new policies and the introduction of institutional changes in recipient countries to encourage a greater flow of investable resources to their territories.

It will certainly be advisable if joint efforts are made by both developed and developing countries, including OPEC members, to allow this trend to grow through the establishment of joint investment corporations and the strengthening of financial markets in developing countries. It is gratifying to see that this mutually beneficial trend has already started to prevail.

OPEC members with surplus funds have already expressed their will and demonstrated their readiness to use their wealth for the benefit of the world at large and developing countries in particular. Greater efforts on the part of other countries could and should lead to the orientation of a larger volume of resources towards direct investment in the Third World, with the aim of increasing the real wealth of the world for the benefit of the poorer countries. Such an

4. *IMF Survey*, February 8, 1982, p. 41.

aim, I submit, is worthy of the full support of the industrialized countries themselves, if only because it means an increase in the effective demand for their capital goods and their services and because it will definitely help in checking world inflation. With the recent decline in the revenues of OPEC countries, their ability to continue their aid efforts will be adversely affected. The case for greater cooperation and coordination with traditional donors is now stronger than ever.

1 THE ESTABLISHMENT AND EVOLUTION OF THE OPEC FUND

Dr Ibrahim F.I. Shihata and Antonio R. Parra

The OPEC Fund for International Development is one of seven inter-governmental development finance institutions[1] created exclusively by developing countries and financed to a substantial extent, and in one case exclusively, by four states in the Arabian peninsula.[2] The latter states have come, since 1973, to lead the aid-giving process on the world scene in terms of the proportion of their official development assistance to their gross national product, as reported annually by the Development Assistance Committee of the Organization for Economic Cooperation and Development.[3] The largest among these states, Saudi Arabia, became in 1981 the world's largest donor in absolute terms according to the same source.[4]

The trend in OPEC 'surplus' countries to provide development funds on concessional terms to other developing nations through specialized institutions was started in the Gulf area by Kuwait who established, in the early sixties, two national agencies for this

1. The other six are (in order of their dates of establishment): the Arab Fund for Economic and Social Development, 1968; the Islamic Solidarity Fund, 1974; the Arab Bank for Economic Development in Africa, 1975; the Islamic Development Bank, 1975; the Gulf Organization for the Development of Egypt (GODE), 1975; and the Arab Authority for Agricultural Investment and Development (1976).
2. I.e., Kuwait, Qatar, Saudi Arabia and the United Arab Emirates. They exclusively financed GODE and contributed between 47% and 77% of the capital of the other agencies mentioned in note 1 above. GODE's operations have been suspended since 1979.
3. Source: DAC's annual review *Development Cooperation* from 1974 onwards. Also DAC's *Economic Assistance by OPEC Countries and Institutions*, OECD/82-83, 1982.
4. Ibid., p. 4. According to DAC, Saudi Arabia provided in 1981 concessional disbursements to developing countries in the amount of US$5.795 billion against US$5.780 billion extended by the USA which came second. A large part of the amount contributed by the USA goes, however, to areas not universally considered as developing countries, such as Israel and southern European states.

purpose[5] and led, in 1967, the attempt to create a regional Arab fund. The Arab Fund for Economic and Social Development was created in 1968 and became operational in 1972. The United Arab Emirates established its Abu Dhabi Fund in 1971 on the same pattern as the Kuwait Fund.

The movement was greatly strengthened after the rise in oil revenues in 1973/74 which led to the expansion of the national funds in Kuwait and the UAE, and the creation of new national funds in Saudi Arabia and Iraq, as well as to expansive aid programs by Qatar and Libya. Other oil-exporting developing countries soon joined the movement. Iran and Venezuela entrusted the task to national agencies in charge also of direct investments,[6] while Algeria and Nigeria created trust funds for this purpose within the African Development Bank. By March 1975, when the heads of States of the members of the Organization of the Petroleum Exporting Countries (OPEC) met in Algiers, all but three members (Ecuador, Gabon and Indonesia) had been involved already in the aid-giving process in different degrees and forms. Their total ODA commitment to other developing countries in that year was reported as US$7.690 billion and their actual disbursement as US$6.239 billion or 2.92% of their combined GNP.[7]

By that time, most of the OPEC donor countries had their national aid agencies in operation, and had participated in a number of multilateral aid efforts and institutions.[8] When the participants in the

5. These two are the Kuwait Fund for Arab Economic Development, KFAED, established in Dec. 1961, and the Authority for the South and Arabian Gulf institutionalized in 1966, after having been actually in operation since the fifties. The statutes of KFAED were amended in 1963 and 1966, to double its capital in each case; in 1974 to increase its capital fivefold, and extend its activities to all developing countries (not just Arab countries as before), and in 1981 to double its capital to KD 2 billion (equivalent to about US$7.5 billion).

6. These national agencies are The Iran Organization for Investments and Foreign Assistance, established in 1974, and the Venezuelan Investment Fund, established in 1975.

7. DAC, *Development Cooperation*, p. 224 of the 1977 review and p. 242 of the 1982 review. According to a study prepared by the United Nations Conference on Trade and Development (UNCTAD) the corresponding figures for 1975 were US$8.220 billion for commitments and US$5.607 billion for disbursements, representing 2.69% of the combined GNP of OPEC donors. See *Financial Cooperation for Development*, pp. 14-15, UNCTAD Document TD/B/C 7/31, Vol. I, 1978. Net ODA disbursements from DAC countries have by contrast never exceeded 0.35% of their combined GNP. See, *Development Cooperation, 1982 Review*, p. 199.

8. It should be noted, however, that most of the disbursements, then as at present, were made in the form of direct government-to-government grants or

Algiers Summit considered the issue of strengthening co-operation with other developing countries, the idea of establishing a collective OPEC aid facility spontaneously became the center of discussion.[9] The Summit Conference referred the general issue to a joint committee of OPEC finance ministers where specific proposals for establishing that facility were to be discussed in detail.

The ministers of finance held their first meeting pursuant to this directive in Vienna in mid-November, 1975. They constituted themselves into a formal 'Ministerial Committee on Financial and Monetary Matters' and decided to recommend to their governments the 'Establishment of a new facility for the provision of additional financial support' to other less developed countries (LDCs) 'under the aegis of OPEC'.[10] The ministers, who initially envisaged that members' contributions to the facility during 1976 would total US$1 billion, entrusted to a subcommittee of 'Experts on financial and monetary matters' the task of examining the specific proposals for the institutional shape such a facility would assume. The experts were specifically instructed to discuss possible alternatives and to prepare, on the basis of their findings, a first draft of an agreement for the establishment of the OPEC aid facility envisaged by the Ministerial committee.

The Alternative Proposals

Within the above broad mandate, a wide variety of proposals and options in respect of the form of the proposed facility was reviewed by the committee of experts during the succeeding weeks. These proposals and options reflected in varying degrees the different

loans. Institutionalized development assistance granted through the 14 national and multinational funds created by these countries accounted on average for less than 30% of total annual disbursements. It should also be emphasized that prior to the establishment of the OPEC Fund, there was no multilateral agency providing ODA in which all OPEC members participated as donors.

9. Reflected in the Summit Conference's call for measures that would strengthen OPEC members' cooperation with 'other developing countries in their struggle to overcome under-development'. See, *Solemn Declaration of the Conference of the Sovereigns and Heads of State of OPEC Member Countries,* Algiers, March 4-6, 1975. Published by OPEC, Vienna.

10. OPEC Press Release No. 7-75. Vienna, November 18, 1975. Reproduced in *OPEC Official Resolutions and Press Releases, 1960-1980,* p. 160. The OPEC resolutions and press releases mentioned here are all conveniently reproduced in that volume.

circumstances and outlook of OPEC's small but diverse member-ship.[11]

Chief among the interests at play in this process were the practical constraints felt above all by the Gulf Arab members of OPEC, who had their own national aid agencies and had been contributors to a host of multilateral institutions and arrangements. They foresaw that because of their relative wealth, or rather financial liquidity, they could end up bearing most of the financial burden the new facility would impose, especially if it were to become a long-term proposition.[12] Some of them might also have been particularly uncertain about the implications of a long-term association in an aid-giving process with fellow members who were newcomers in this field.

Caution as to the duration of the facility for these influential members went hand-in-hand with a desire to avoid creating a large bureaucracy, which not only might duplicate the work of existing institutions and constitute a needless drain on members' qualified human resources, but also involve considerable expense and contribute, like all bureaucracies, to its own indefinite existence. These practical issues, balanced against the consensus among members of the need for swift implementation of a facility that would enhance the role of OPEC in the Third World and promote OPEC's solidarity with it,[13] were decisive in determining the character and structure of the new facility.

11. Which comprises Algeria, Ecuador, Gabon, Indonesia, Iran, Iraq, Kuwait, Libya, Nigeria, Qatar, Saudi Arabia, United Arab Emirates and Venezuela.

12. It is important in this respect to note the true economic situation of these OPEC members at the time. Although in 1975, after the major oil price rises, Saudi Arabia for example, had an average annual income per person of around US$5,000 (comparing favourably with that of some industrialized states), it had only very recently and suddenly emerged from a state of dire financial need. In 1970, Saudi Arabia's gross national product per capita was below US$500. Moreover there was, and continues to be, no assurance that this affluence, gained from the exchange of a depleting natural resource for paper assets, was not a temporary and illusory phenomenon; or that it could instead, lead to real economic development, freeing the country from its nearly total dependence on a vulnerable trade in a single commodity. The same, to a lesser or sometimes even greater degree, was true of all OPEC members, whose aggregated gross national product, it should also be recalled, even now amounts to little more than 7% of the equivalent figure for the OECD countries.

13. It is useful to recall the sort of charges that were being levelled against OPEC during the period following the 1973/74 price rises. A typical example of writings which had the appearance of lacking academic accuracy is to be found in Kelly, J.B.: *Arabia, the Gulf and the West: A Critical View of Arabs and Their Oil Pricing*, Basic Books Inc., 1980, pp. 429, 430. For a documented rebuttal, see Shihata, I.: *The Other Face of OPEC*, Longman, 1982, pp. 3-19, 40-59, 201-20.

The proposals put forward, usually in the form of draft agreements, covered the full range of existing institutional approaches to aid-giving, from setting up an autonomous international lending agency along the lines of the traditional multilateral development funds to the creation of a short-term grant account. However, none of these proposals, which also included the possibility of establishing a trust fund with the World Bank or a special account within OPEC itself, gained the degree of general acceptance necessary for implementation.

Option 1: A Multilateral Development Agency. The reasons for lack of general enthusiasm for the idea, which was initially propagated by Iran, of setting up the facility as an independent multilateral lending entity similar to the traditional development finance agencies[14] have already been implied above. Although the facility in this form might have most fully enhanced OPEC's multilateral image, particularly by making possible loans in its own name, its characteristics included a self-perpetuating nature (such an entity would, barring liquidation, have to continue in existence until all its loans had been repaid) and tendencies to generate, on the one hand, a large bureaucracy and, on the other, long-term expectations from potential beneficiaries. An indefinite commitment to multilateral OPEC aid efforts was therefore implied, that some major donors among members were not at that time prepared to accept.

Option 2: A Special Account. A completely different proposal was advanced by Venezuela in October 1975. This envisaged a special account held and administered by one or more of members' central banks, for the purpose of channelling balance of payments aid to LDCs in the form of outright grants. To use the words of the Venezuelan position paper, the proposal consisted essentially of a 'balance sheet where the income item will consist solely of the contributions of member countries and the expenditure item will be

---

14. Proposed as early as August 1974 by the OPEC secretariat following a decision of the XXXIX (Extraordinary) Meeting of the OPEC Conference in April 1974 to 'establish an OPEC Development Fund', a decision the implementation of which was ultimately postponed and transferred to other OPEC fora. See, *OPEC Press Release No. 4-74*, Vienna, April 8, 1974. OPEC took up the matter in 1974 following the lack of response from OECD countries to Iran's original proposal for the establishment of a global fund to be financed by industrialized, OPEC and other countries.

the grants destined to developing countries'.[15] This account would be set up for an initial period of two years. Purely operational matters would be decided upon by an *ad hoc* committee of representatives of the institutions chosen to administer the account, while overall supervision would be exercised by the finance ministers.

Although the facility in this form could have been swiftly implemented at minimal administrative cost, the proposal had its shortcomings. Since the facility's day-to-day administration would have been entrusted to only one or possibly two institutions of member countries, it would inevitably have become identified with those institutions and member countries, rather than with OPEC as a whole. Moreover, most members wished to have the facility's duration flexible, an option better preserved by providing for a lending agency whose repayments could eventually be rolled-over in future operations. If, in addition, aid were to be provided in grant form, the benefits of continuous contacts with borrowers under long-term loans would be lost.

The Venezuelan proposal was also unattractive to several other OPEC countries for a more sensitive reason. This reason lay in the basis on which Venezuela proposed to calculate the level of each member's contribution to the facility on the one hand, and the scope and direction of assistance from the facility on the other hand.

Each member's contribution, Venezuela said, should be determined by multiplying a pre-determined fraction of the price of oil by the member's total oil export volume. In other words, the share of each member's financial participation in the account would equal its share in OPEC's overall exports.[16] Beneficiaries of grants from the account would, on the other hand, be the net oil importing developing countries whose major supply sources were OPEC countries. The amount allocated to each beneficiary would be in proportion to the ratio of its net oil imports to the total net oil imports of all eligible beneficiaries.

This aspect of the proposal of Venezuela (which was itself for

15. Special Account of the OPEC Member Countries: Proposal by the Venezuelan Delegation, dated October 19, 1975 (unpublished).

16. In 1975, a large proportion of total OPEC oil exports was accounted for by a small number of members. Saudi Arabia alone in that year provided 27% of the total, while the three biggest exporters (Iran, Iraq and Saudi Arabia) provided 55%. The smallest producers (Ecuador and Gabon) on the other hand accounted for less than 1% each. This phenomenon became more pronounced later on, when the Saudi share jumped to 40% in 1980 before falling to much lower levels in 1981 and 1982. See *OPEC Annual Reports*, 1980, 1981.

many years the world's biggest oil exporter and is still one of OPEC's major exporters) was for obvious reasons unattractive to the other large producers, whose share in total oil export volume, it could readily be argued, did not necessarily correspond exactly to their relative ability to pay, other factors having to be taken into consideration. Iran, however, agreed at the time that each member should contribute 10 cents (US) for each barrel exported, over a 3 year period.[17]

Needless to say, by linking contributions and benefits closely with oil trade, the proposal seemed to involve tacit acceptance of responsibility by OPEC members for a situation they had always disclaimed. Moreover, in practice the main beneficiaries of OPEC assistance under the proposal would have been the better-off industrializing LDCs with a high level of oil imports. These countries, it has been argued, are less deserving of such assistance than the poorer LDCs.

Option 3: OPEC's Own Special Account. Another possibility considered by the sub-committee of experts was to establish the facility as a special account owned and possibly also administered, by the OPEC organization itself. In this form, it would have been similar to the short-lived Special Arab Aid Fund for Africa (SAAFA) of the League of Arab States, and also the Organization of Arab Petroleum Exporting Countries' (OAPEC) Special Account, both set up in 1974 as direct and short-term responses to the financial problems occasioned by the price rises for African and Arab oil importing countries, respectively.

17. Various similar objective systems of burden-sharing have been proposed and discussed in the subsequent history of the Fund, including relating members' contributions to oil production, oil exports, oil reserves or other oil-related indicators, to macroeconomic indicators such as GNP or current account balance, or to an amalgam of several sets of economic and social indicators. Such proposals have, however, never been adopted by the majority in preference to the existing method of voluntary contributions. Similar discussions, with similarly inconclusive results, have taken place in the context of the International Development Association's (IDA's) replenishments. See, *Discussion Paper on Burden Sharing in IDA* (IDA/RPL/78, May 22, 1978, limited circulation).

While the above objective criteria have never been employed to determine burden-sharing among the OPEC Fund's members, the opposite is true for the determination of eligible recipients' shares in the Fund's resources available for lending. Under the Fund's six lending programs to date, which concentrate mainly on the least developed and most seriously affected countries as defined by the United Nations, allocations have been determined according to selected economic and financial criteria to which certain weights are assigned, with adjustments to ensure wide geographical distribution.

SAAFA was administered by its parent organization until April 1976 when this function was transferred to the Arab Bank for Economic Development in Africa (BADEA). In December of the same year, SAAFA's capital was merged, at Kuwait's suggestion, with that of BADEA. The OAPEC Special Account, which also ceased operations in 1976, was from the beginning administered not by OAPEC but by the Arab Fund for Economic and Social Development.

A similar OPEC Special Account could have been set up by virtue of a resolution of the OPEC Conference of oil ministers, the Organization's supreme authority, establishing the facility as a new specialized organ of OPEC.[18] While from a procedural point of view this would have been a simple matter, it raised a jurisdictional issue. The problem did not relate to OPEC's principal functions, and had after all, been referred for solution to the finance ministers, not the oil ministers who constitute the OPEC Conference; further consideration of the possibility was therefore effectively blocked.

Option 4: A Trust Fund. A fourth option, that of setting up the facility as an international trust fund administered by the World Bank, was put forward by Saudi Arabia in November 1975. Under this proposal, contributions of members would be held by the World Bank as trustee in a special account set up within the Bank for this purpose. The resources of the trust fund would be used to provide soft loans for specific development projects and programs and for balance of payments support. The World Bank would process applications for assistance from the fund, and submit recommendations thereon to a small management committee composed of representatives of

18. See, *The Statute of the Organization of the Petroleum Exporting Countries,* Article 37 (a).

The OPEC Conference has once in the past established a specialized organ pursuant to its Statute. This is the OPEC Economic Commission, set up in 1965 by Resolution VII.50 of the Conference. Its functions are *inter alia* 'to examine the position of petroleum prices on a permanent basis' and 'to formulate and submit to the Conference ... recommendations based on its findings': *Statute of the OPEC Economic Commission,* Articles 3 (3) and 3 (6).

In late 1963, the establishment of 'an inter-OPEC High Court for the settlement of all disputes and differences relating to petroleum matters' (Resolution V.41 of the Conference) as a specialized organ of OPEC was also considered, though never implemented.

The recently-established OPEC News Agency (OPECNA) was created not as a specialized organ but as a special unit within the secretariat, by virtue of an amendment to the OPEC Statute approved in July, 1980 (Resolution LVII.217 of the Conference).

the fund's contributing parties. The committee would decide on the basis of such recommendations, also taking into account OPEC finance ministers' broad policy directives. Administration of the loans provided from the fund would be undertaken by the trustee who would provide quarterly reports on the fund to its contributors.

Loan agreements committing the fund's resources would presumably have been concluded in each case between the trustee and the beneficiary.[19] Repayments of the loans would eventually have been remitted by the trustee to the contributors in proportion to their original contributions to the fund. Saudi Arabia envisaged that the fund's resources would be committed over one year, leaving open the possibility of extending it for a further period.[20]

Such a fund would have been set up by virtue of an agreement with the trustee who would of course, have had to agree to the details. While the proposal underscored the preference of the financially most powerful OPEC member to have guaranteed good management of the fund while avoiding a possible long-term financial commitment, it implied relinquishing a large measure of control over the fund to the trustee. The consequent inevitable dilution of members' identification with it, made the proposal unacceptable to most other OPEC members, who were justifiably anxious to see direct political impact of the new facility on the ultimate beneficiaries.

19. The Saudi proposal did not actually foresee this. It provided instead that such loan agreements would be signed 'on behalf of the facility' by the chairman of the management committee, overlooking the fact that the trust fund as such would lack legal personality.

20. As mentioned previously, the device of a trust fund with one of the multilateral development banks was unilaterally employed by several OPEC members in the mid-1970s, most notably by Algeria and Nigeria with the African Development Bank, and also by Venezuela with the Inter-American Development Bank. See e.g., *Trust Agreement between the Fondo de Inversiones de Venezuela and the Inter-American Development Bank* dated February 27, 1975, reproduced in Muthatika, A.P. , *The International Law of Development*, p. 1833 (1979).

Its attraction lay in making programmed assistance available to other developing countries through existing channels, thus avoiding having to set up a new institution for the purpose, and minimizing the strain on the financial and manpower resources of the donors.

A particularly relevant example is the European Economic Community's (EEC's) Special Account established in 1977 with the World Bank, whereby a number of donors placed a certain amount with the Bank to be administered on their behalf according to terms and conditions negotiated between the EEC and the Bank.

The Kuwaiti Proposal

Established techniques having failed to provide a basis for agreement, the need for innovation presented itself. The representative of Kuwait on the experts' subcommittee submitted a comprehensive proposal which tried to incorporate elements of all the other possibilities so far considered, while meeting the concerns of the major potential donors. The proposal called for the establishment of an 'OPEC special fund' as a special account administered by a joint committee, thus preserving OPEC's name and ensuring its members' control over its operation. This 'special account' would actually consist of a series of accounts, each held within and executed by, a national agency of a member state. Duplication of existing facilities would thus be avoided, and at the same time the special fund's identification with OPEC members would be furthered. The importance of the Kuwaiti proposal, which provided the foundation for a solution, calls for a detailed examination of its provisions.

Under this proposal, the resources of the special fund would be used to benefit developing countries other than the contributing parties in an unusual variety of forms. These forms included: long-term interest-free loans to finance development projects and programs; loans for balance of payments support and for financing purchases from member countries of imports required for development purposes; and guarantees for eligible beneficiaries in their borrowing from other sources for the foregoing purposes.

At this same point in time (late 1975, early 1976) the establishment of an international agricultural development agency to counter a food supply problem that had reached crisis proportions in the poorest countries was being actively discussed in UN fora. With their new cash revenues, OPEC countries were expected to be major contributors to this new agency.[21] They were not however in a position to provide financial backing for the creation of two development assistance agencies simultaneously. This issue was resolved in the Kuwaiti proposal by a provision to the effect that members would be authorized to use part of their contributions to the proposed OPEC special fund for the payment of their contributions to 'an international development institution or facility' whose activities would benefit LDCs on acceptable terms. Collective

21. Eventually established in 1977 as the International Fund for Agriculture Development. See note 32 below and Chapter 7.

contributions from the fund's resources to such an institution could also be authorized.

The OPEC special fund, according to the Kuwaiti proposal, would not be a special organ of OPEC, nor would it have any legal or administrative link with that organization. It would be administered by a single body to be called the governing committee, which would be composed of one representative from each contributing party. The governing committee would lay down general policies for the utilization of the fund's resources, and guidelines and regulations according to which contributions would be administered and disbursed. The governing committee would also be empowered to settle disputes under the fund's constituent agreement and issue interpretations thereon and, by special majorities, to request increases in contributions, amend the agreement, or decide on the fund's termination.

An interesting feature of the Kuwaiti proposal concerned voting in meetings of the governing committee. A quorum of two-thirds of the parties to the constituent agreement would be necessary for such meetings. Each member would, regardless of the size of its contribution to the fund, have the right to cast one vote only. For most matters, decisions would require a two-thirds majority of the votes cast. This aspect of the Kuwaiti proposal was in keeping with the prevailing optimistic idealism of third-world countries at the time, who were advocating the principle of equality in the context of the traditional development finance institutions, where voting was weighted in favour of the major contributors — the industrialized countries.[22]

To organize, coordinate and follow-up the governing committee's work and act as the fund's official spokesman, a director-general would be appointed by the governing committee. He would have a limited number of assistants. The director-general and his assistants would work from the headquarters of the OPEC secretariat, but would not be members of the secretariat's staff. Administrative expenses of the governing committee (whose members would however serve as such without remuneration from the fund) and of the director-general and his assistants would be covered from contributions on a *pro rata* basis according to an annual budget approved by the governing committee.

---

22. For a recent examination of this issue, see Zamora, S.: 'Voting in International Economic Organizations', *American Journal of International Law*, vol. 74, p. 566, July 1980.

Each party to the fund's constituent agreement would designate its 'executing national agency' (ENA) for the purposes of the agreement. The proposal envisaged that this would normally be the party's national agency responsible for external assistance. Each member's contribution would be deposited in a separate account in the name of the fund with its respective ENA. Though not explicitly mentioned in the proposal, each ENA would presumably hold this contribution in trust for its state. The ENA would administer the contribution held by it, in accordance with the governing committee's policies, guidelines, regulations and decisions, and would continue to do so after the fund's resources had been fully committed. Within this framework, the ENA would, in respect of project loans, appraise the projects and administer the loans. Contractually the lender under OPEC special fund loans would always be an ENA. But in extending such loans from the special account held by it, each ENA would explicitly indicate to the borrower that the loan was an OPEC special fund loan, using for this purpose a standard loan agreement approved by the governing committee.[23] Repayments to the ENA of the loan so extended would be credited to the OPEC special fund account held by it. Expenses incurred by ENAs in carrying out these duties would be borne by the ENAs.

In addition to the supervisory/administrative role exercised by the governing committee, the bilateral aspects inherent in the Kuwaiti proposal would have been further offset by providing that the fund's resources in the territories of its contributing parties would be treated as international assets, enjoying immunity from seizure, sequestration, exchange control regulations and taxation.

The Draft Agreement

Except with respect to several points of detail, the structure envisaged in the draft agreement approved by the experts for submission to the ministers was basically that of the Kuwaiti proposal, which seemed to strike a satisfactory balance between members' various concerns.

One such detail which the experts' draft supplied to the Kuwaiti proposal dealt with the technical, financial and economic appraisal of

23. Cf. e.g., *Trust Agreement between the Fondo de Inversiones de Venezuela and the Inter-American Development Bank*, Section 28: 'In the contracts signed by the Trustee as administrator of the resources of the Fund, it shall indicate clearly that it is acting in the capacity of trustee.'

projects or programs submitted to the governing committee for approval. The experts' draft provided that this task could be entrusted not only to members' competent national agencies, but also to 'An appropriate international agency'. This addition was made in recognition of the limited number of national agencies, and to accommodate the Saudi request to this effect. If the governing committee reached a favourable decision on the financing of the project or program so appraised, it would then assign from among the ENAs, the agency or agencies to execute and administer the loan.

Another point of difference concerned the types of financing the experts decided the fund should engage in: the range of direct assistance proposed by Kuwait was narrowed to cover only loans for projects, programs, and balance of payments support. The possibility of using part of the fund's resources to make contributions to other international development finance institutions was dealt with in the experts' draft by a broad and simple provision which appeared to imply that such contributions would primarily be collective.

A third, important, difference concerned repayment of loans. The Kuwaiti proposal provided for repayments to be credited to the OPEC special fund account held by the lending ENA. The experts' draft stipulated that such repayments would, upon receipt, be transferred to the ENA's respective state, thus ruling out indefinite continuity of OPEC multilateral aid operations through the use of recycled funds, and somewhat strengthening the bilateral character of the arrangement.

The crucial role envisaged for ENAs by the experts raised two related issues among members. In direct assistance operations, each ENA would execute its state's respective contribution, lending amounts in its (the ENA's) own name. Despite the safeguards inserted in the draft (that loan agreements would clearly indicate that the loans were OPEC special fund loans), the transaction would at this important point of contact with the beneficiary appear primarily bilateral. It should be remembered that members' widely different abilities to contribute to the facility would have meant that most of its operations would actually have been carried out by the ENAs of a few among them. The second of these related issues arose from the fact that not all OPEC members had institutions capable of administering foreign aid, particularly overseas project assistance. It will be recalled that only four members had institutions specially designed to undertake this task, and of these, two had been established only recently. This raised the possibility that the experts' proposal might in practice either be unworkable, or that the task of conducting the facility's operations (and the associated credit) would go by default to a small number of national institutions or to international development agencies, of a world-wide or regional character.

Finally, the experts' draft also raised the question of the distribution of voting power in the Fund's decision-making organ. As in the Kuwaiti proposal, it envisaged that members would each have one vote in the governing committee, regardless of their degree of financial participation in the facility. In view of the large differences between members' prospective contributions, at least one of the major donors argued that this was a case where ideals would have to yield to practical realities.

THE AGREEMENT ESTABLISHING THE OPEC SPECIAL FUND

Despite the questions just discussed, which were raised in subsequent correspondence especially by Iran and Venezuela, the experts' sub-committee succeeded in indicating the way to a compromise arrangement likely to be accepted by all. The Ministerial Committee met again in Paris at the end of January 1976 to discuss the experts' draft. On that occasion Kuwait submitted a revised draft embodying answers to the above questions, which was finally accepted as the *Agreement Establishing the OPEC Special Fund,* and was signed by all OPEC members on January 28 of that year.[24]

This final text provided for the establishment of the Fund as an international special account, directly and collectively owned by the parties to the Agreement, each in the proportion of its contribution to the total amount of all contributions to the Fund (Article 1.01). This made it possible for loan agreements to be concluded in the names of all the contributing parties by the Chairman of the Governing Committee, acting in this respect as their agent (Article 5.04), a solution which maintained the facility's multilateral character at the most important point of contact with the beneficiaries without, however, creating an autonomous international legal entity.

Contributions would be credited (as in the experts' draft) by each member to a special account established in the Fund's name with its

24. Published in *International Legal Materials,* Vol. 15, p. 1357, November, 1976.

respective ENA (Article 4.03).[25] Unlike the experts' draft, the Agreement provided that the day-to-day administration of the Fund's loans would either be entrusted to ENAs or to 'International development agencies of a world-wide or regional character'. (Article 5.04). In the former case, the ENA would disburse from the Fund's account established in its records, the amount of the loan entrusted to it for administration. In the latter case, the Governing Committee would designate an ENA or ENAs to provide, from the Fund's account(s), the funds needed by the international development agency to meet the financial requirements of the loan (Article 5.07).[26] In both cases, repayments of the loans would be made to the same special accounts from which the funds had been originally disbursed and, on receipt, remitted by the ENAs concerned to their respective states (Article 5.07).

As envisaged in the expert's draft, the Fund would for virtually all intents and purposes be administered by a single organ, the Governing Committee (Article 5.01). However, the final text provided for certain matters to be referred to the 'Ministers concerned', i.e. to the standing Ministerial Committee on Financial and Monetary Matters.[27] These exceptional matters were: proposed amendments to the constituent agreement; disputes between members that could not be settled by the Governing Committee; and the decision to terminate the Fund after all its resources had been committed (Articles 7.01, 8.01 and 9.01). Periodical reports on the

25. This raised the question of ownership of amounts accruing as interest on deposits held in such accounts with ENAs. This problem was subsequently raised by such ENAs as the Saudi Fund for Development and the Central Bank of Venezuela. It was solved to the benefit of the Fund by the general rule that the owner of the principal (in this case the contributing parties collectively, not the ENA) owned the interest. The Agreement clearly stated moreover that the Fund's account with each ENA should be 'Separate and apart' from its own accounts (Article 5.07).

26. For OPEC Special Fund loans administered by other international development agencies, 'A central operating account' was in practice established in 1978 to meet disbursement requirements of project loans, as direct involvement by possibly several ENAs would have been too cumbersome in such cases. This central account, which eventually replaced the ENAs for disbursements of all loans, can in hindsight be seen as an initial step towards the Fund's institutional autonomy.

27. The Agreement did not refer specifically to that Committee, as it had been created by the ministers themselves, without a legal instrument based on a pre-existing international agreement or ratified by subsequent domestic instruments. Finance ministers were not mentioned specifically, on the other hand, as Iran had been consistently represented by the Minister of Interior, and the UAE by the Director of Finance of Abu Dhabi (with the rank of minister).

Fund's activities would also have to be submitted by the Governing Committee to the 'Ministers concerned' (Article 5.11). Placing practically all powers in a single organ represented a departure from the standard pattern in financial institutions and was meant to facilitate the Fund's management and avoid periodic ceremonial meetings.

Voting power in the Governing Committee was distributed according to a unique and simple two-tier formula. Each member would have one vote. The votes so cast would then be related to members' contributions. Thus decisions on most matters would require a two-thirds majority of those present at duly constituted meetings,[28] provided they represented parties to the Agreement contributing at least 70% of the total contributions to the Fund (Article 5.08). A qualified majority of four-fifths of members, provided they contributed four-fifths of the total amount of contributions to the Fund, would be required for any decision by the Governing Committee to terminate the Fund before the commitment of all its resources (Article 8.02). A similar special majority of three-fourths of members representing at least four-fifths of contributions would be required for any decision by the Ministers to amend the Fund's constituent agreement (Article 7.01).

In other respects, the *Agreement Establishing the OPEC Special Fund* was similar to the experts' draft, though one further difference between the two is to be noted. Under the experts' draft (following the Kuwaiti proposal) eligible beneficiaries of Fund financing were to be developing countries other than those contributing to the facility. Under the Agreement, only 'the Governments of developing countries other than OPEC member countries' were eligible (Article 3.01).[29] The reason for this difference is that one signatory to the Agreement (Ecuador) had decided at that stage not to contribute to

28. Under Article 5.08 of the Agreement, a two-thirds majority of members constituted a quorum for such meetings. When the Agreement was revised in May 1980, the required majority was related to contributions in the same way as for most decisions (two-thirds majority representing 70% of contributions). The practical difficulties this more stringent requirement could create were, however, mitigated by a provision in the Governing Board's (as it was then called) Rules of Procedure to the effect that if two-thirds of members were present at a meeting without a valid quorum they could decide to meet as a consultative body of the Board and prepare, for submission to the next Board meeting, their recommendations on pending matters.

29. Of all the multilateral aid agencies financed by OPEC members, the OPEC Fund is the only one with what amounts to a world-wide vocation (apart from members' ineligibility). The other multilateral agencies serve only specific regions

the initial resources.[30] The majority of members felt that assistance from the Fund should be an altruistic exercise oriented towards non-OPEC members. This approach, previously followed by the Arab countries in the agreement establishing BADEA, was deemed, in addition, to ensure a greater measure of impartiality in the administration of the Fund.

The Agreement's Innovative Character

The *Agreement Establishing the OPEC Special Fund* reflected throughout a concern for flexibility, swift decision-making, maximization of use of existing resources, and a receptivity to innovation. A mere glance at the text of the constituent agreements of two agencies with a capital structure similar to that of the OPEC Special Fund, namely the International Development Association (IDA) and the International Fund for Agricultural Development (IFAD), provides an indication of the OPEC Special Fund's unique nature.

The IDA and IFAD constituent agreements are comparatively lengthy documents and regulate many questions in detail. *The Agreement Establishing the OPEC Special Fund* was brief and, beyond laying down a basic structure for the Fund, was confined to providing a broad framework of guidelines within which the Governing Committee could deal with issues as they arose, as it might deem most beneficial to members and recipients of the Fund's assistance.

Assistance could be extended through the Fund in a variety of ways, none given any particular precedence over the others by the Agreement. They included loans for balance of payments support, loans for development projects and programs, and contributions to other international agencies benefitting the Third World (Article 2.02). By contrast, IDA's Articles of Agreement provide that its financing 'except in special circumstances', shall be for specific

or groups of countries. Most of the national aid institutions however, and in particular the Iraqi, Kuwaiti and Saudi Funds, are open to all developing countries, although so far they have limited their activities on the whole to African and Asian countries.

30. After agreement on the first replenishment of the Fund's resources in 1977, Ecuador paid an amount representing its contribution to the initial resources of the Fund in addition to its contribution to the replenishment. It has also participated in the two subsequent replenishments of the Fund's resources.

projects (IDA's Article V.1.(b)). Similarly, IFAD's constituent agreement provides that it shall furnish financing 'primarily for projects and programmes' (IFAD's Article 2). Another obvious difference in this respect is that while IDA can provide financing only 'To further development in the less-developed areas of the world included within the Association's membership' (IDA's Article V.1(a)) and IFAD's resources can only be mobilized for 'Agricultural development in Member States' (IFAD's Article 2), the OPEC Special Fund's loans could, as mentioned above, only be extended to developing countries that were not members of the Fund, an innovation previously introduced in the case of BADEA.[31]

The typical tripartite structure of international development finance institutions (such as IDA and IFAD), consisting of a plenary body, an executive body and executive officers and staff, was avoided to accelerate the decision-making process. Instead, virtually all policy-making powers were vested in a single organ, the Governing Committee, assisted in its work by a Director-General and a limited number of staff.

In its early years the Fund had a very small staff, a unique feature in international agencies, which is still maintained in spite of the continuous expansion of the Fund's operations which cover at present 82 countries and some 40 international agencies. Minimization of the Fund's bureaucracy was in large part made possible by entrusting the appraisal of projects and programs and the administration of loans to other institutions. This also served the objective of avoiding unnecessary duplication of the work of existing development finance institutions. It is worth noting that this feature of the OPEC Special Fund, which was codified in its constituent Agreement, is also to be found in the Agreement Establishing IFAD,[32] which provides that IFAD shall similarly use the services of other international institutions 'for the appraisal of projects and programs presented to it for financing' and 'entrust the administration of loans ... to competent international institutions' (IFAD's Article 7 (2), (e) and (g)).[33]

31. Other examples where contributing members are ineligible to benefit include SAAFA and the OAPEC Special Account. Examples can also be found in the three regional banks (the African Development Bank, the Asian Development Bank and the Inter-American Development Bank) where non-regional members contribute to the resources but stand no chance of receiving financial assistance.
32. Adopted by the UN Conference on the Establishment of an International Fund for Agricultural Development on June 13, 1976, opened for signature on December 20, 1976 and effective November 30, 1977.
33. The similarity is not fortuitous. The two entities came into being at the

Voting power in the Governing Committee of the OPEC Special Fund was related to contributions in a unique manner. As we have seen, decisions on virtually all matters required a two-thirds majority of members present at meetings, with a proviso that the votes cast should represent 70% of the total contributions to the Fund. In both IDA and IFAD, as well as in the other traditional international development finance institutions, a more complex system of voting is used. Each member is assigned a certain number of basic votes, and a certain number of proportional votes determined according to the amount contributed or the number of shares subscribed by that member.[34]

But the most distinctive aspect of the OPEC Special Fund lay in its juridical nature. It was an account, and not a fully-fledged international institution possessing legal personality. It was however an international account, not subject to members' national controls and regulations, enjoying instead a full range of privileges and immunities. It was directly owned and managed on a collective and joint basis by the states contributing to it, and not by OPEC, the organization whose name it carried. There is perhaps no exact parallel for this in the law of international organizations, though it could be likened to the regime of community of property between spouses in some domestic legal systems.[35]

History and Evolution of the OPEC Special Fund

With the completion of ratification procedures by nine member

same time, and in both cases members shared a concern to minimize staffing needs and avoid institutional duplication. Moreover, the draftsman of the Kuwaiti proposal which was the basis of the *Agreement Establishing the OPEC Special Fund,* and the Chairman of the Drafting Committee of the Agreement Establishing IFAD were the same person (Dr Ibrahim F I Shihata). IDA, it can of course be remarked, is a case where in one sense an institution possessing distinct legal personality has been called into being without any such duplication. The World Bank's Governors, Executive Directors and President are *ex officio* Governors, Executive Directors and President of IDA, while the Bank's officers and staff are appointed to serve concurrently as officers and staff of IDA (Articles of Agreement, Articles VI. (2) (b), 4 (b), 5 (a), 5 (b)).

34. Articles of Agreement of IDA, Article VI (3)(a); Agreement Establishing IFAD, Schedule II. However, in the case of Category III members of IFAD (the non-OPEC developing countries) all 600 votes of the members of the category — whose contribution to the Fund is nominal — are distributed equally.

35. See Shihata, I.: *The OPEC Special Fund: A New Approach to International Financial Assistance,* OPEC Fund, Vienna, 1976.

countries, the *Agreement Establishing the OPEC Special Fund* entered into force on May 10, 1976, i.e. little more than three months after it had been signed. The Fund commenced operations in August, 1976 with an initial endowment of US$800 million. By the end of 1977, following a doubling of its resources in August of that year, it had provided 71 loans to 58 developing countries, authorized the contribution, out of its resources, of over US$435 million to IFAD in the names of 12 members, and channelled sizable donations by members to the IMF Trust Fund. Lending operations covered 66 countries by mid-1979.

No less important was the work of coordination and representation that members began to assign the Fund for their international assistance activities. Members' positions were coordinated and unified, and therefore made more effective, through the Fund during the negotiations leading to the establishment of IFAD, and subsequently in IFAD's Executive Board.[36] Similarly, the Fund represented members in the negotiations on the Common Fund for Commodities, declaring in that case their willingness to contribute in various ways up to US$100 million to the projected fund.[37] Lastly, the Fund was, and continues to be, active in coordinating the work of members' aid agencies. The Governing Committee of the Fund was entrusted by the Ministerial Committee in 1978 with such coordination, in lieu of a coordination mechanism, previously created (in

36. These tasks were discharged by the Director-General of the OPEC Fund, who, formally speaking, was present at the IFAD negotiations as representative of Kuwait, and sits for that country on IFAD's Board. In January 1981, after the Fund had become an international agency with autonomous legal personality, its management unsuccessfully proposed that the OPEC Fund should be authorized to become a member of IFAD, which would have put its agency function in that forum on a more formal footing. Had this proposal been accepted, it would apparently have been the first instance of one international organization becoming a full member of another. See, Brownlie, I.: *Principles of Public International Law* (1979), p. 693, note 3.

The possibility is provided for, however, in the *Agreement Establishing IFAD*, Article 3 (1) (b), as it was envisaged at the time of preparing that agreement, that the European Economic Community might wish to join IFAD as a member.

37. Although OPEC countries will contribute to the Common Fund from their own separate resources, the Ministerial Council of the OPEC Fund authorized it, in January 1981, to provide grants to 35 developing countries in order to enable them to meet their contributions to the Common Fund, and further authorized the OPEC Fund to contribute in its own name to the resources of the second window of the Common Fund. The OPEC Fund could not, however, join the membership of the Common Fund, which is restricted to states and 'Intergovernmental organizations of regional economic integration'. See Article 4 of the Agreement Establishing the Common Fund for Commodities, UNCTAD Document, TD/IPC/CF/CONF/25, (1980)

1975) which had not operated successfully after a promising start. To avoid duplication in a field where, by definition it can hardly be tolerated, the Fund opted for joining the pre-existing coordination mechanism among Arab Funds which includes the funds of Iraq, Kuwait, Saudi Arabia and UAE, as well as the Arab Fund, BADEA and the Islamic Development Bank.[38]

Replenishment of the Fund's resources demonstrated recognition of its quick success and growing acceptance among members that the Fund should become permanent. The original assumption on which the *Agreement Establishing the OPEC Special Fund* had been based, i.e. that it would be a 'one shot exercise', was becoming obsolete. That this assumption was no longer valid was reflected in the first amendment to the Agreement, adopted at the same time as the first replenishment was approved in August 1977. The amendment qualified Article 4.01 of the Agreement, which had defined the Fund's resources simply in terms of its initial endowment, by also referring to 'Other contributions' and 'funds received from operations or otherwise accruing to the Fund', as part of its resources.

The indefinite continuity of the Fund was more emphatically assured when in September 1979, before the amortization of any loan had started, the ministers again amended the Agreement to allow loan repayments to be used in future operations.[39] This important development, which emphasized that the Fund would remain a going concern, if not actually a permanent institution, paved the way for setting up a working party, composed of representatives of seven members of the Governing Committee. The working party's mandate was to review the text of the Agreement with the aim of providing the Fund with a more appropriate legal framework for its new status.[40] Preliminary studies led the Governing Committee to recommend to the Ministers in January 1980 that the working party's

38. Since 1980, the Director-General of the Fund has also co-chaired with the chairman of DAC, the annual informal coordination meeting between the Arab/OPEC donor agencies and the DAC donor agencies.

39. The amendment involved deleting the provision in Article 5.07 which stipulated that such repayments would be returned to the donor countries.

40. Meanwhile, Algeria and Venezuela were proposing in another forum, OPEC's Ministerial Committee on Long-Term Strategy, more drastic changes, which would result in converting the Fund into a US$20 billion development bank; US$4 billion would be paid in, and the bank would rely basically on borrowing to finance its future operations. This proposal was not approved by the majority of the ministers of finance when it was brought to their attention during subsequent discussion of the amendments. However, it probably gave a strong impetus to the amendments explained in the text.

guidelines should include *inter alia* the conversion of the Fund into an autonomous agency with an international legal personality. The pace of events however overtook that recommendation. At the end of January, the ministers approved a second US$800 million replenishment, and at the same time introduced three further amendments into the Fund's constituent agreement.

The first amendment (to Article 1.01) transformed the Fund into 'An international agency for financial cooperation and assistance ... endowed ... with an international legal personality' to be called the 'OPEC Fund'. This amendment made it possible for the Fund to provide loans in its own name.

The second amendment (to Article 2.02(b)) similarly authorized the Fund to make contributions and provide loans to other international development agencies in its own name.

By virtue of the third amendment (to Article 5.01) the 'Ministers concerned' became a formal 'Ministerial Council' of the Fund, and the Governing Committee became its 'Governing Board', with the 'Director-General and such staff as shall be necessary for the Fund to carry out its functions' completing the structure.

These amendments were explicitly taken as interim measures pending thorough revision of the *Agreement Establishing the OPEC Special Fund*, a task the ministers referred back to the Governing Board and its working party for their recommendations.

In the working party, which resumed its deliberations immediately, some of the possibilities considered at the inception of the Fund were revived. In particular, Algeria and Venezuela reiterated the proposal that it should have a share-capital structure divided into paid-in and callable shares like the World Bank and the major regional development banks. This would make it possible for the Fund to resort to borrowing to secure additional resources without imposing an immediate financial burden on the donors. Some countries' representatives in the working party also proposed that OPEC members should be eligible for assistance from the Fund, and some argued that membership in the Fund should be open to non-OPEC developing countries. In addition, it was suggested that the Fund should be deprived of its power to contribute to other international financial agencies, since this would tend to dilute the Fund's identity and tie up part of its resources indefinitely. The conclusions of the working party on these and other detailed issues are reflected in the amendments to the Agreement approved by the Governing Board and adopted by the Ministerial Council on May 27, 1980.

The OPEC Fund for International Development

According to the revised Agreement, the Fund would henceforth be known as the OPEC Fund for International Development.[41] Its resources would consist only of 'contributions by member countries and funds received from operations or otherwise accruing to the Fund' (Article 4.01), thus leaving Article 4.01 as it had been amended by the ministers in August 1977, virtually intact. The majority had decided to maintain the existing capital structure in view of the greater measure of freedom allowed by a system of voluntary contributions, and because such a capital structure would enable the Fund's loans to continue to be extended on highly concessional terms. That would not have been the case if the Fund had depended for its resources on the market. With regard to membership and eligibility for assistance, the Agreement continued to provide that membership would be open only to OPEC member countries (Article 1.02) and that, apart from international development agencies, only the governments of non-OPEC developing countries, and in particular the less developed among them, would be eligible beneficiaries of financing provided by the Fund (Articles 3.01 and 3.02).

Despite these provisions, which were meant to enable the Fund to conduct its operations with maximum impartiality, intra-OPEC financial cooperation could be undertaken through the Fund under a separate arrangement by virtue of a new article,[42] (standard in similar agreements) whereby the Fund could be authorized to manage special funds put at its disposal by members for specific purposes. The revised Agreement also broadened even further the activities the Fund could engage in, by including the financing of technical assistance activities, contributions and loans to other international agencies, and loans to developing countries for projects, programs

41. Article 1.01 of the *Agreement Establishing the OPEC Fund for International Development*, as revised on May 27, 1980. References which follow are to the articles of the Agreement as revised, which is published in Arabic, English (original text), French, and Spanish by the OPEC Fund.

42. Article 8.01. 'The Ministerial Council may authorize the undertaking by the Fund of the management of financial resources put at its disposal by Member Countries for specific purposes. The Governing Board shall lay down procedures necessary for the administration of such funds and the terms and conditions upon which they may be administered. The resources of such special funds shall have accounts showing their use, commitment and investment separately from those of the Fund's own resources.'

and balance of payments support.[43]

The amended Agreement kept the distinction between the Ministerial Council and the Governing Board, and, in defining their respective functions, maintained for the latter greater powers than those of a typical executive board in similar agencies. The Ministerial Council, the supreme authority of the Fund, would exercise a broad supervisory role and decide on the most critical matters such as replenishment of resources and amendments to the constituent agreement (Article 5.02). The Governing Board, being responsible for the conduct of the general operations of the Fund, would *inter alia* lay down policies for the utilization of the Fund's resources, issue directives and regulations according to which such resources would be administered and disbursed, and approve assistance operations, all with due regard to equitable distribution of operations among eligible beneficiaries.[44] The system of voting employed for the Governing Committee of the OPEC Special Fund was maintained for the Ministerial Council and the Governing Board. The Director-General, who continued to be the Fund's chief executive, was designated its legal representative (Article 5.01 (iii)). The Fund would also have 'such staff as shall be necessary for [it] to carry out its functions within the framework of an organization chart to be approved by the Governing Board' (ibid).

The role of the Executing National Agencies, which had been pivotal in the *Agreement Establishing the OPEC Special Fund*, contracted to being basically a channel of communications between member countries and the Fund.[45] Provision was also made in the amended Agreement for the determination by the Ministerial Council of the headquarters and legal domicile of the Fund.[46]

43. Article 2.02. With the exception of providing loans to other organizations, all these activities had been previously carried out by the Fund under a broad interpretation of the original provisions of its agreement. As noted above, one of the distinguishing features of the Fund is the variety of operations it is authorized to undertake. This is reflected in the unusually large number of assistance transactions it enters into. In 1981 for example, the Fund had 327 such operations, compared with 260 for the Islamic Development Bank, 265 for the Kuwait Fund, and 227 for the Saudi Fund for Development respectively, the three next-most-active agencies funded by OPEC members.

44. Articles 5.05, 6.02 The regulations which the Board is authorized to issue include financial regulations, regulations on the policy and criteria applicable to each lending program, staff regulations, etc.

45. Article 6.05. Not unlike the 'appropriate authority' to be designated by IDA members to act as their channel of communications with IDA under Article VI.10 of IDA's Articles of Agreement.

46. Article 1.04. At the same time as the revised Agreement was approved, the

An important activity which had already been undertaken by the Fund was codified in an article providing that in cases where collective action by Fund members was deemed appropriate, the Fund could be entrusted by them to act as an agent on their behalf, 'in particular in their relations with other financial institutions' (Article 2.03).

A major amendment introduced in the new agreement empowered the Fund to appraise projects and administer its loans, while maintaining the option that such tasks could continue to be assigned to qualified agencies of member countries or appropriate international institutions (Articles 6.03, 6.04). Under this new mandate, the Fund was to develop its own capacity for project appraisal and project loan administration. These tasks have been cautiously started, while maintaining the practice of benefitting from the services of other institutions, which are made available to the Fund at no cost under simple agreements in the form of exchanges of letters.

A transitional provision stipulated that the Fund could be named in place of the relevant contributing parties in all the loan agreements previously concluded in their names (Article 14.01). This substitution was also affected through simple exchanges of letters with the borrowers under such loan agreements.

While the Fund in its new shape more closely resembled similar institutions, particularly from the point of view of organizational structure, the flexibility and innovative approach which characterized it from its inception were still apparent in the conversion. Some of the distinctive features of the OPEC Fund for International Development, such as the wide and varied range of its functions and the extensive powers of its Governing Board, have been mentioned

---

Ministerial Council decided that this should be Vienna, Austria (where the Fund had been based since its inception) and authorized the conclusion of a headquarters agreement with the Republic of Austria once its negotiated text had been approved by the Board. This headquarters agreement was signed on April 21, 1981 between the Republic of Austria and the Fund and entered into force on May 10, 1982. It is similar to the headquarters agreement concluded on February 18, 1974 between OPEC and Austria, with adjustments to reflect the Fund's nature as a financial institution and the addition of a most-favored organization clause (Article 30) which reads as follows:

> If and to the extent that the Republic of Austria shall enter into any agreement with any intergovernmental organization containing terms and conditions more favourable to that organization than similar terms or conditions of this agreement, the Republic of Austria shall extend such more favourable terms or conditions to the Fund by means of a supplemental agreement.

above. The Agreement also continued to be a brief and flexible document, not unduly burdened by minute and constraining regulation.

Moreover, the very way in which the process of conversion was effected was distinctive. Although the *Agreement Establishing the OPEC Fund for International Development* is a substantially different document from the *Agreement Establishing the OPEC Special Fund,* it is legally only an amendment of the latter, pursuant to Article 7.01 thereof. The possibility of concluding a fresh agreement had been discussed by the Governing Board's working party. It was decided, however, to carry out the changes under the authority of Article 7.01, for once they had so been approved they would be effective immediately, thus avoiding the delays inherent in the conclusion of a new agreement and its subsequent ratifications.[47]

Conclusion

With a third replenishment in early 1981, the Fund's authorized resources reached US$4 billion. By April 1983 the Fund had approved 328 loans, for a total exceeding US$1.8 billion, to 82 countries, for balance of payments support and for projects and programs covering almost all economic sectors. It had also been instrumental in setting up other international organizations benefitting third-world countries, such as IFAD and the Common Fund, and had provided grant assistance in the order of US$200 million to over 40 international organizations and research centers.

This had been done with contributions from a group of developing countries with a combined average annual income per person of hardly more than US$1,000, who depend for their income on the exploitation of a finite natural resource, the pricing of which is volatile and (contrary to popular myth) often subject to factors beyond members' control. Although the present crisis in international oil markets has had an effect on the members' ability to sustain ambitious aid programs, their continued support for the Fund and its mission has been reiterated recently in several forms, most

---

47. Venezuela, however, chose to undertake the ratification process anew as its constitutional law requires legislative approval and presidential ratification for substantial amendments of such treaties to which Venezuela is a party. The revised Agreement received congressional approval in Venezuela on March 16, 1982 and was ratified by the President of Venezuela on May 12, 1982.

notably by the approval in November 1982 of its new US$650 million lending program.

These achievements, and the wide appreciation they have generated, are due to a large extent to the innovative approach used to structure the Fund in a manner which not only suited those states whose financial backing was a prerequisite for its success, but also enabled the Fund's management to act swiftly without undue constraints. Both the *Agreement Establishing the OPEC Special Fund* and the *Agreement Establishing the OPEC Fund for International Development,* were tailored to meet real demands and aspirations, without attempting to create a wider framework which exceeded them, or merely to copy pre-existing structures established for other institutions under different circumstances.

Experience shows that legal institutions and regulations which fail to meet real aspirations or excessively bypass them, run the risk of being constantly violated or ignored. This is particularly so in the international arena, where many international organizations have been involved recently in the issuing of resolutions and the creation of institutions which by far exceed their actual degree of acceptability and consequently remain devoid of real impact. The diplomatic 'successes' often acclaimed in reaching such situations hardly hide the real failure in solving the problems at hand. The experience of the OPEC Fund shows, on the other hand, that a modest but well-conceived and well-structured step can, if pursued within the careful limits envisaged for it, create, in time, the momentum needed for taking further steps towards the ultimate objective. It is hoped that this experience will not escape the attention of those involved in ongoing discussions on the need for introducing a greater measure of order and rationality in international economic and financial relations.

2 THE OPEC FUND'S EXPERIENCE (MID-1976 TO MID-1983): Its Approaches and Procedures, the Magnitude of its Assistance, and its Impact on Development

Dr Ibrahim F.I. Shihata

The performance of international development finance institutions is usually measured by such factors as the number of loans extended yearly, the number of beneficiary countries, the ratio of disbursements to commitments, the ratio of administrative costs to disbursements, and the rate of growth of resources. On all these counts, the performance of the OPEC Fund for International Development has established a new record. A comparison covering all multilateral aid agencies whose operations started at about the same time as those of the Fund, confirms this conclusion.[1]

These quantitative measures may not, however, present a definitive judgement of the performance of an international development finance institution. A more indicative test is to be found perhaps, in the extent to which an institution is fulfilling its objectives. Such a test inevitably raises major issues as to the approaches and procedures followed by each institution, the target beneficiaries (countries, sectors and peoples), as well as the actual impact of the institution on the world scene. In the case of the Fund, the objective was twofold:

(1) to assist the development efforts of non-OPEC developing countries; and
(2) to do this in such a manner as to strengthen the bond of solidarity between them and OPEC member countries, thus serving, to the greatest extent possible, the common objective of establishing a more equitable world economic order.

Instead of copying established practices, initiated by the World Bank and largely adopted by other international financing agencies, the Fund started its work with a fresh outlook. The Fund's constituent agreement reflected this attitude by defining its objectives in broad terms, thus enabling it to do all that its Governing Board deemed necessary in assisting developing countries. As a result, the Fund was the first international institution of its kind to combine balance of payments (BOP) support with project lending, and to add to its direct assistance to governments, the financing of other development agencies which play a particularly important role for the benefit of developing countries. By providing BOP assistance, the Fund was also able to ask each recipient country to deposit an equivalent amount in local counterpart funds to meet the local costs of development projects and programs, thus removing a bottleneck created by the insistence of many existing agencies that they meet only the foreign costs of projects.

In addition, the Fund was the first institution to avoid duplicating the already extensive bureaucracies of established agencies and to benefit, to the maximum, from the facilities of those agencies in support of the beneficiary countries. Furthermore, the Fund demonstrated to the existing international agencies that the financing process could be completed in a much faster way than had hitherto been envisaged. It initiated a dialogue with them on the simplification of lending procedures, a process which has already yielded some positive changes in the approaches of many agencies.

Target Beneficiaries

From the outset, the Fund based its activities on lending programs in which the selection of beneficiaries, the types of loan and their amounts, were based on objective criteria established according to carefully selected data. In so doing, the Fund rejected the 'first come, first served' approach, which is likely to benefit only the more advanced developing countries that need the Fund's assistance to a lesser extent than the poorer countries.

The Fund's Governing Board adopted the approach that its activities, though legally extendable to all developing countries (other than OPEC members), would be limited to the poorer countries and would only reach the high-income developing countries when the Fund's resources allowed. This was particularly interesting in the case of the Fund, as the poorer countries happen to be marginal importers of oil, while the major oil importers among the developing countries are those which, relatively speaking, are economically more advanced. As a result, the Fund's First Lending Program was limited to Most Seriously Affected (MSA) countries, as defined by the United Nations. The Fund then adopted the approach that under each lending program a list of priority countries was established including all the Least Developed Countries (UN definition) all other MSA and Food Priority Countries, and other low-income countries. The Fund's Governing Board, however, maintained a great degree of flexibility by authorizing lending operations in higher-income countries on a case-by-case basis, when the particular circumstances of the country justified such action. Thus, relatively higher-income developing countries, such as Barbados, Jamaica, and Costa Rica, occasionally benefitted from the Fund's loans when they experienced severe financial difficulties.

The Fund's priorities were not only expressed in the choice of recipient countries but extended to the selection of priority sectors for its project loans. The sectors that largely benefitted from the Fund's assistance on a priority basis were the energy and food production sectors. It is particularly interesting to note that in its support of the energy sector, the Fund financed the development of indigenous energy resources in the developing countries, thus emphasizing the fact that OPEC aid, far from being an instrument of export promotion, is altruistic in nature. The political objective of OPEC member countries in helping other developing countries achieve energy independence or lessen their dependence on energy imports, was deemed more important than promoting oil exports to these countries. The Fund's Board also maintained flexibility by providing financial support to projects in other sectors when there were no projects ready for financing in the energy or food production sectors.

Within the above-mentioned country and sectoral priorities, the Fund placed special emphasis on reaching, within each recipient country, the poorest segments of the population. It thus applied its assistance to the electrification of rural areas, supplying water to deprived districts, land reclamation coupled with land reform, lines of credit to national development banks designed to benefit only small businesses, farmers and artisans, as well as other projects whose obvious beneficiaries were the poorer peoples of the recipient countries.

Impact on the World Scene

With its 328 direct loans reaching 82 developing countries and its grants to several UN specialized agencies, international agricultural research centers and other research and scientific institutions, the Fund has clearly made its presence felt as a recognized source of international development finance. Although the amount of each loan or grant was often small, the Fund's repeated performance (on average, one loan every week; some countries have already received seven loans from the Fund) enabled it to develop close links with most developing countries and to generate a great measure of good will in the Third World.

More importantly, the Fund has enthusiastically pursued its role, not merely as a development finance institution, but as a policy instrument for forging closer links between OPEC member countries and other developing nations, and for serving the developing countries as a whole in their struggle for the establishment of a more just international economic order. For instance, the Fund played an instrumental role in the establishment and evolution of the International Fund for Agricultural Development (IFAD). It also played an important role in the negotiation of the *Agreement Establishing the Common Fund for Commodities* and is presently providing financial support to enable this Fund to come into existence. It has already offered to pay the contributions to the Common Fund of thirty five developing countries and declared its preparedness to provide, in due course, a sizable grant to that Fund's second window. In addition, the Fund was instrumental in the creation of the Centre for Research on the New International Economic Order, and is closely following the on-going dialogue on North-South relations and the role of OPEC member countries in respect thereof, as reflected in the Fund's publications, especially its Occasional Papers series. By acting collectively, through the Fund, in certain international fora, OPEC member countries have obviously been able to play a more effective role for the benefit of the group of 77 as a whole.

In its attempt to have OPEC aid efforts fairly reported, the Fund held detailed discussions with the Organization for Economic Co-operations and Development on its reporting system for OPEC aid flows. These discussions resulted in a noted improvement in the DAC's reporting of Official Development Assistance from OPEC sources, as evidenced by its most recent publications. Meanwhile, the Fund arranged with the United Nations Conference on Trade and Development's secretariat the establishment of a UN reporting system on financial flows among developing countries, which proved to be fairer to OPEC donors. The Fund also publishes papers in different languages analysing OPEC aid efforts.

In all its activities, the Fund has maintained close cooperation and coordination with the bilateral and multilateral aid agencies of OPEC member countries. It is now active with several of them, e.g. in the co-financing of projects and programs, mutual representation in international fora, joint research activities and coordinated information activities. Through such cooperation, the impact of the OPEC aid phenomenon as a whole is enhanced.

Highlights of the Fund's Operations

By the end of March 1983, the Fund had approved 328 loans consisting of 163 BOP support loans, 158 project loans and 7 program loans. In addition, 77 grants had been approved in support of technical assistance, food aid, research and other activities. Of the loans, 175 had been fully disbursed and 117 were under active disbursement. The ratio between the disbursed amount and the total amount of all signed loans was 62.2%. Disbursement of effective loans had reached 69.93%.

Loans allocated to Africa numbered 176, bringing total commitments[2] on that continent to US$767.31 million; 93 loans had been allocated to Asia, where the level of commitments had reached US$755.19 million; and 46 loans had been allocated to Latin America, where US$182.335 million had been committed.

BOP support loans that had been fully utilized numbered 146; 12 had been half disbursed, and 4 were to be declared effective shortly. Of the total amount of US$671.37 million committed for BOP assistance, at the end of March, 1983, US$386.55 million had been allocated to Africa, US$173.97 million to Asia and US$110.85 million to Caribbean and Central American countries. The equivalent of US$428.597 million in local counterpart funds had financed the local costs of 171 development projects and programs in 54 countries. Of this amount, 35.8% had been committed to the agriculture sector, 27.2% to energy projects, and 15.2% to the transportation sector.

On the same date, from a total of US$985.965 million committed for project financing, US$361.76 million had been allocated to Africa, US$552.72 million to Asia, and US$71.485 million to Latin America and the Caribbean: 52.6% to the energy sector, 14.4% to transportation, 12.0% to agriculture, 8.8% to national development banks, 6.6% to industry and the rest to public utilities, communications and urban development. A total of 27 project loans had been fully utilized, 100 were under active financing and 19 had still to be declared effective.

The total sum committed to program loans was US$47.5 million. The purpose of such lending is to support specific programs which are most concerned with the rehabilitation or improvement of plant, an industry or a sector. The programs serve a clear development objective. Under program loans, the Fund finances imports of goods and/ or services agreed upon by the borrower and the Fund.

Under its grant program, the Fund has allocated US$32.87 million to UNDP-assisted projects related to food production, energy, education (vocational training centers), and health. US$25 million has been approved for the International Emergency Food Reserve which is jointly administered by the World Food Program and FAO. US$8.17 million has been committed in support of agricultural research centers supported by the Consultative Group on International Agricultural Research (CGIAR). An additional US$18.89 million has been provided to finance technical assistance projects in the areas of energy, food production, education, telecommunications, and health, under the auspices of other international agencies and centers. Moreover, US$1.28 million has been allocated to research and other intellectual activities which serve the Fund's objective of supporting developing countries in their economic and social development. About 90 per cent of this amount has already been committed for specific purposes, i.e. fellowships, workshops seminars, training, etc. Overall, the sum of about US$86 million has been committed in the form of grants, other than grants related to the Common Fund and IFAD.

US$861.142 million has been committed to IFAD's resources, of which US$263.52 million has been paid in cash and US$217.363 million, including a special grant contribution made by the Fund, paid in the form of a promissory note. The sum of US$435.5 million was committed to IFAD's initial resources, and US$425.6 million was allocated to the first replenishment of its resources. All IFAD's initial resources have already been approved by that agency for loans and grants benefitting agriculture and rural development.

US$110.72 million was transferred to the trust fund administered by the International Monetary Fund (IMF), representing the profits accruing to seven OPEC members from the IMF gold sales. This amount was in turn, used through the IMF to provide additional BOP assistance on concessionary terms to eligible developing countries.

US$83.56 million in grant form has been allocated to assist the projected Common Fund for Commodities, sponsored by UNCTAD, through a contribution to its second window (US$46.4 million) and by meeting the subscriptions of low-income developing countries (US$37.16 million) to its capital.

Technical Assistance

Shortly after the commencement of the OPEC Fund's activities, its Governing Board, in the spirit of furthering cooperation among developing countries, approved in August 1977 a grant program involving the amount of US$20 million to technical assistance projects assisted by the United Nations Development Program. Following the implementation of that first program, another allocation of US$20 million was approved in June 1979. The second technical assistance program was carried out in cooperation with UNDP as well as with other international organizations. A third grant program was approved in January 1981 with an allocation of US$50 million to cover the period 1981-82. UNDP was to use the proceeds of the grants for specific regional and global projects chosen jointly with the OPEC Fund. Such projects were designed to promote technical cooperation among developing nations, to encourage and coordinate developmental studies and programs, and to increase technical and scientific knowledge. The regional ventures thus undertaken benefit a wide segment of the developing world — about 72 developing countries in Africa, Asia and Latin America — and are related to such diverse fields as energy, food production, health, planning, and training.

Further details of the technical assistance projects financed under the above-mentioned programs are given in Chapters 3 and 5. These projects go beyond the mere preparation of studies and plans. In each case, the Fund sought specific results of obvious advantages to the countries concerned. Two cases serve as relevant examples. Before financing the UNDP/FAO-sponsored Red Sea Fisheries Project, the Fund insisted that the project should include the establishment of pilot villages for small-scale fishermen to benefit from the results of the studies and surveys, rather than limiting the project, as was originally planned, to the studies and surveys. In another context the Fund declined a request by the UNDP to finance an additional study for identifying projects in the Suez Canal region, preferring instead to finance the implementation of a Vocational Center identified under a previous UNDP study.

Socio-economic Impact

The co-financing of a total of 6250 megawatts of generating capacity has been completed through 51 energy projects undertaken since

1977. Hydroelectric projects totalling about 13,818 million cubic metres of reservoir capacity and other power projects allowing for the creation and rehabilitation of 48,470 km of transmission lines have also been financed. Development of oil and gas fields in India and Bangladesh, co-financed by the Fund, will result in the production of 240,000 barrels a day of oil and 160 million cubic feet of gas per day. Oil and gas exploration is being financed by the Fund under two projects in Tanzania, while gas development projects are being financed in Bangladesh and Thailand.

Nine projects have been co-financed for the provision of irrigation facilities for 177,100 hectares of rural land and 470,000 tons of fertilizers. An estimated total of 30,000 ha of land will thus be re-forested and about 7.1 million people in the rural areas will have been assisted.

Twenty road projects have been co-financed for the construction, upgrading and improvement of about 27,680 km of roads serving an estimated population of 15.4 million. Four railway projects have been co-financed for the rehabilitation of more than 400 km of railway so increasing the yearly tonnage carried by the systems by about 300,000 tons.

Five airport projects have been implemented and have con-siderably affected the economies of the developing countries concerned, especially in the commercial and tourism sectors.

Eleven lines of credit to national development banks have enabled them to provide sub-loans to small and medium-scale enterprises in the manufacturing, agriculture and artisan sectors.

Successes and Constraints

The positive achievements of the Fund are the result of a number of factors, including in particular:

(1) The continued support it receives from its member countries as evidenced by the repeated replenishment of its resources and the exemplary attitude of its members in using the Fund as a collective instrument of common policy rather than as an instrument of the national policies and interests of particular members.

(2) The harmony and mutual confidence which has prevailed between the Fund's Governing Board and its management, and the fact that Board members are professionals with long

experience and responsibility in the aid business in their respective countries.

(3) The great network of relationships which the Fund has succeeded in establishing with existing aid agencies of OPEC member countries and other international and regional aid institutions. Within this framework of cooperation, the Fund has been able to benefit from the services of these agencies, thus achieving great economies of time and cost.

(4) And last, but not least, the diligence and dedication of the Fund's carefully selected staff who, despite their extremely limited number, have managed to cope with the responsibilities of the task and carried out their jobs swiftly and efficiently.

The Fund's success may, however, be adversely affected in future by the fact that it lacks a well-defined and predictable system for receiving additional resources. The timing and amount of each of the replenishments has been decided on an ad hoc basis. Some members of the Fund have suggested that this problem could be overcome by authorizing the Fund to borrow. A change in its capital structure would endow the Fund with callable capital, on the strength of which it could resort to borrowing. The same objective might also be served if replenishments of the Fund's resources were effected at intervals which were known and agreed upon beforehand. Such an arrangement would not only help the Fund to plan its activities properly, but would enable it to continue providing its assistance on concessional terms.

As the Fund aspires to play a more instrumental role in the development efforts of a large number of countries, it realizes that it will have to face greater challenges in the future. A meaningful expansion of the Fund's involvement in the energy field alone would require the gradual strengthening of its capital resources and building a strong institutional capacity in the identification, preparation and appraisal of energy projects. It is strongly hoped that the positive factors which enabled the Fund to reach its present stage of growth, will enable it to meet new challenges and to gain greater stature in the future, to the satisfaction of both the countries which created it, and the countries for whose benefit it was established.

Notes

1. By the end of 1982, the OPEC Fund was committed to 318 loans and 94 grants. The loans benefitted 82 countries, the loan's disbursements to 'actual' commitments ratio reached 65%, while administrative costs remained below 1% of annual disbursements. See also page 44 for corresponding figures to the end of March 1983.

2. 'Approved' means approved by the Fund's Governing Board.
'Commitments' refers to loans and grants for which the respective legal instruments have been signed.

3 AGRICULTURE AND ENERGY IN THE OPEC FUND'S ACTIVITIES
— A Sectoral Perspective

Dr Mehdi Ali

Since its inception in 1976, the OPEC Fund has proclaimed agriculture and energy as the economic sectors of highest priority in its assistance programs. These policy declarations have been closely followed in practice. By the end of 1982, agriculture and energy had received the Fund's highest levels of assistance, as shown in Table 1.

Over the past three decades, world agriculture has undergone dramatic change. During this period, the sector rapidly increased its reliance on scientific research, industrial technology, chemical fertilizers, and machinery. As a result, agricultural production and marketing were revolutionized, and agricultural output doubled in comparison with earlier periods. However, the winds of radical

Table 1: The OPEC Fund's Assistance (1976-82) in the Agriculture and Energy Sectors (in US$ million)

	Agriculture	%	Energy	%	Others*	%	Total	%
Project loans	151.8	16.5	457.6	49.8	310.1	33.7	919.5	100
BOP & Program loans	294.0	41.5	156.3	22.0	259.1	36.5	709.4	100
LCF utilization	149.72	35.5	116.64	27.7	155.44	36.9	421.8	100
Grants	63.0	62.4	20.1	19.9	17.9	17.7	101.0	100
Total	658.52	30.6	750.64	34.9	742.54	34.5	2,151.7	100
Contribution to IFAD	865.5	100	—	—	—	—	865.5	100
Grand total	1,524.02	50.5	750.64	24.9	742.54	24.6	3,017.2	100

Note: * Includes transport, industry, national development banks, water supply and sewerage, health, education, and telecommunications.

change which originated in the industrial countries have not yet swept the vast agricultural fields of the developing world. The obstacles are simply too many and too diverse: climate, technology, institutions, management, and policy. The performance of agriculture in developing countries has therefore been diverse, both within and among the various regions and countries.

Rapid growth in population has sharply reduced any gains made in agriculture. For example, while agricultural output in all developing countries increased at 3% per annum during the 1960s and 70s, the increase in per capita output was only 0.4% per annum during those decades. That average conceals sharp differences; growth ranged from 1.4% per annum in South East Asia and 0.6% per annum in Latin America, to virtually nil in the least developed countries. In South Asia as a whole, output barely kept pace with population growth. In Africa, per capita output grew at 0.2% per annum during the 1960s, and dropped by 1.4% per annum during the 1970s.[1]

Absolute poverty also continued to be concentrated in the rural areas of developing countries. According to IFAD, the proportion of people living below the poverty line in developing countries is about 50%,[2] the bulk of them in rural areas. About one quarter of these people are landless, which makes them highly vulnerable to natural calamities, and difficult to reach with development assistance.

Modest improvements in agriculture, rapid population growth, and general underdevelopment, have resulted in the continuing dominance of agriculture in the economies of developing countries. Agriculture still provides a livelihood for about 70% of the population, and accounts for 30% of merchandise export earnings. Agricultural exports are the dominant category of exports for over two-thirds of developing countries.

High dependence on agriculture has made the economies of developing countries particularly vulnerable both to internal and external changes. Agricultural exports finance imports essential for their growth; although good export performance increases their access to international capital markets, it also makes their economies highly susceptible to fluctuations in those markets. Also, the pervasive role of agriculture in the structures of these economies suggests that poor agricultural performance will be reflected immediately in poor performance in the rest of the economy. This is particularly the case in the sub-Saharan African region, where poor agricultural performance in the 1970s sharply reduced overall economic performance.

High dependence on agriculture is also a source of serious concern for the future of the economies of developing countries. The expected increase in the demand for food in these countries has profound implications for their prospects for economic growth.

At the present time, about 8% of the food consumed in these countries and 9% of agricultural products available to them, are imported. Only a few countries would be able to increase these percentages without facing serious balance of payments difficulties. For the rest, any increase in demand for food would have to be supplied largely from their own agriculture. Since these are the poorest countries, with weak agriculture, it is questionable whether they can grow the majority of this increased food demand without substantial external assistance.

The central role of agriculture in the economies and prospects of developing countries has been recognised by the OPEC Fund since its inception in 1976. It has therefore paid particular attention to the development of agriculture. It must be stressed however, that although the Fund attaches high priority to agriculture, it has remained highly responsive to the development needs of the other sectors of the economies of the recipients of its assistance. Relatively high levels of assistance have been channelled to other sectors, such as energy and transport, according to the sectoral priorities of the recipient countries. However, the Fund's assistance to the agriculture sector has been the highest among all the economic sectors. Moreover, if assistance to the International Fund for Agricultural Development (IFAD) extended by OPEC member countries through the OPEC Fund is included, the share of agriculture in the Fund's assistance is a multiple of the levels of other sectors.

The Fund's assistance to agriculture has gone far beyond its loans and grants. It has also included an active role in the establishment, and subsequently in the management, of IFAD, the promotion of trade among developing countries particularly in agricultural commodities, and finally, support for agricultural research and related institutional work.

The OPEC Fund's critical role in the establishment of IFAD is explained fully in Chapter 7. During the negotiations, differences existed both within OPEC countries, and among the rest of the developing countries. In the midst of stormy debates, the Director-General of the OPEC Fund was often the one who unified these divergent views and emerged as the spokesman of the developing countries. Also, as chairman of the drafting committee of the *Agree-*

ment establishing IFAD, he was instrumental in shaping the structure and the direction of that organization. As a member of IFAD's Executive Board, he played a prominent role in determining IFAD's lending strategies, the level of its operations, and its future outlook. By the end of 1982, US$429.6 million, including a special US$20 million grant, had been contributed by the OPEC Fund to IFAD. This sum constituted 52% of the US$886.0 million pledged by OPEC countries to the initial resources and first replenishment of IFAD.

Agricultural Project Loans

Direct project loans are the Fund's most important contribution to the development of the sector. Through this form of assistance, the Fund influences certain developmental objectives within the sector, or lends its support to the efforts of the particular government to reach targets within the sector.

Following the principles explained in Chapter 1, the Fund co-finances agricultural projects that are appraised by other institutions. However there has already been one exception, namely the OPEC Fund's own appraisal in February, 1982, of the Crop Intensification Program for Rice in the Socialist Republic of Vietnam.

It must be stressed that appraisal by others does not imply a passive role for the Fund in the definition of the project, and in formulating its developmental objectives. The financial contribution by the Fund in co-financing the project, leaves the door wide open for the Fund's technical staff both to review the project appraisal and initiate a dialogue with borrowing government and appraising agency. Such a dialogue covers various aspects of the project, particularly the items to be financed by the Fund, and whether the project falls well within the overall objectives for development of the sector. It is through these interactions that the Fund ascertains the suitability of the project for reaching targets or for promoting the overall objectives of the sector.

Under this form of assistance the Fund, up to December 31, 1982, committed about US$151.8 million to agricultural projects in developing countries. The subsectors financed by the Fund include nearly all aspects of agriculture: irrigation, drainage, forestry, livestock production, crop intensification, and agro-based industries. Financing such a wide range of activities reflects the Fund's objectives of broad financing to enable applications of new technologies, promotion of various policy changes, and increases in agricultural production to raise the living standards of rural populations. Details of the Fund's project loans in the agriculture sector are given in Table 9, in Annex 2.

Finally, the Fund's agricultural project loans have covered a wide geographical area. About 50% of these loans (US$76.65 million) went to Asian countries, 36% (US$54.25 million) to African countries, and 14% (US$20.888 million) to Latin American countries.

All project loans extended to agriculture are concessional. Their terms are in Table 2. In earlier periods, all the types of loans in Table 2 were extended on softer terms. However low interest rates have occasionally been applied for loans to middle-income countries.

BOP and Program Loans

Program loans and balance of payments (BOP) support loans have considerable advantages over project loans when considered from the point of view of transfer of resources to recipient countries. They are easier to prepare and implement, and consequently they are characterised by much shorter preparation and disbursement periods. As a result, resource transfers under these loans take place within a considerably shorter time than under project loans.

Table 2: Terms of OPEC Fund Loans (up to December 31, 1982)

	Project loan	Program loan	BOP loan
Service charge, %	0.75	0.75	0.75
Commitment charge, %	0	0	0
Rate of interest, %	0	0	0
Grace period, years	5	5	3
Maturity period, years	20	15	10

Note: From January 1, 1983, the maturity periods became 17, 10 and 8 years respectively, for project, program and BOP loans, and for all three types, the service charge became 1%.

BOP loans represent the opposite extreme of project loans, in terms of the time required for both their preparation and implementation. Preparation of a BOP loan by the OPEC Fund requires close scrutiny of the country's balance of payments position and its prospects. If the proceeds of the loan are used for the importation of food, the Fund has to be satisfied that this process will not have an adverse impact on the country's agriculture sector.

BOP loans are disbursed in two tranches: the first immediately after the loan has been declared effective, and the second immediately following the receipt of invoices by the Fund for utilization of the first tranche.

If the Fund's requirements for declaring the loan effective are met within a short time, and if arrangements for importation are completed, full disbursement can take less than six months. This quick disbursement is of particular benefit for the importation of food and other agricultural inputs. Time is critical in such cases, particularly in emergencies.

In view of their quick disbursement, the terms of BOP loans are understandably harder than project loans. However, the Fund's BOP loans still remain highly concessionary, as Table 2 shows.

Program loans fall between the two extremes of project and BOP loans, in terms of the time required for their preparation and implementation. A program loan becomes necessary when the development requirements are difficult to package under a project. For example when spare parts or rehabilitation works are required for a large number of irrigation schemes, or for agricultural machinery stations scattered all over a country. Another example is the import of fertilizer and pesticide, needed by a large number of farms in different regions and falling under different institutional arrangements and organizations. Under such circumstances, a program designed to meet the specific objectives is the only appropriate form of assistance.

The list of goods to be imported by the recipient country under the program loan must have prior approval of the OPEC Fund. Before approving the loan, the Fund, in turn, has to be satisfied that the design of the program will meet the development objectives, as outlined by the authorities.

The OPEC Fund's program loans differ from other loans in that they finance specific goods and services, required for specific development objectives, and agreed upon beforehand. They should not be confused with World Bank structural adjustment loans. Largely because of their novelty, the Fund has thus far financed only a limited number of programs, particularly in agriculture. There have been few appraising agencies and co-financiers who shared with the Fund, the same concepts and approaches concerning these loans.

The terms of the Fund's program loans are slightly softer than those of its BOP loans, due to their slower disbursement, as Table 2 shows.

Up to the end of 1982, the Fund had extended 166 BOP and program loans, of which 96 financed the import of food and agricultural inputs amounting to about US$294.0 million. The amount just quoted compares with only US$156.0 million for BOP loans in the energy sector.

The Fund's BOP and program loans used for financing food and agricultural inputs have been received by a large number of countries spread all over the globe. About 59.3% (US$174.4 million) went to African countries, 21.5% (US$63.3 million) to Latin American countries, and 19.2% (US$56.3 million) to Asian countries. Details of these loans are given in Table 10 in Annex 2.

Local Counterpart Funds

Local counterpart funds (LCF) are another form of assistance generated by the Fund's BOP and program loans. Recipients of such loans, it may be recalled, are required to deposit equivalent amounts in local currency in their central banks, to finance development projects or programs mutually agreed with the Fund.

Through this mechanism, the Fund has been able to mobilise local financing for a large number of projects. During 1976-82 the Fund approved the utilization of LCF equivalent to US$421.8 million, of which about 36% went to the agriculture sector. The projects financed covered all aspects of the sector including irrigation and drainage, forestry, rural development, and agro-industries. Details are in Table 11, Annex 2.

A summary of the LCF approved by the Fund and the share of agriculture in it, is given in Table 3. It shows that during 1976-82, US$149.7 million equivalent of LCF were utilized for financing agricultural projects. This compares with about US$116.6 million equivalent of LCF utilized for energy projects (Table 1) during the same period. Agriculture was thus the recipient of the greatest amount of LCF financing, which, geographically, extended over about 30 countries.

Assistance through Grants

The Fund has extended outright grants to the agriculture sector, some of which have been channelled through UNDP for the financing of regional projects, including the grants mentioned under the next two headings.

Fisheries in the Red Sea and the Gulf of Aden. Two grants, amounting to US$7.6 million are to contribute to the development of fisheries in these areas. Through these grants, a large vessel is to be chartered, and six small vessels purchased, for surveying the fish stock and developing improved fishing methods. The objective is to implement a comprehensive fishing program which would also involve training. The participating countries are: Jordan, Egypt, Sudan, Ethiopia, Somalia, People's Democratic Republic of Yemen, Yemen Arab Republic, and Saudi Arabia.

The Caribbean Regional Food Plan entails the cooperation of 13 governments of the Caribbean community. The program provides

Table 3: LCF Approved by the Fund, and the Share of Agriculture

Year	Total LCF approved for utilization (US$ million equivalent)	LCF approved for agriculture (US$ million equivalent)	% share of agriculture in total LCF
1977	89.80	28.50	31.7
1978	90.08	33.62	37.3
1979	21.80	9.60	44.0
1980	53.60	17.45	32.6
1981	59.50	14.30	24.0
1982	107.08	46.25	43.2
Total (1977-82)	421.86	149.72	35.5

Source: OPEC Fund for International Development, annual reports, 1976-82.

the technical and financial assistance needed to set up the Caribbean Corporation as a viable and efficiently organized commercial institution in charge of formulating, evaluating and implementing agricultural projects. It also involves assistance for the management and training requirements of a regional livestock program. A third aspect of the program is technical assistance for carrying out pre-investment studies for agricultural development geared towards food production. The Fund's grant amounted to US$2 million.

Research Grants. A number of research centers sponsored by the Consultative Group on International Agricultural Research (CGIAR) have received grants, emanating from the Fund's recognition of the crucial role of research in the agricultural development of the developing countries. The basic objective of the CGIAR centers is to increase the quantity and improve the quality of food production in developing countries through research, training, and the provision of technical assistance to national and regional research programs. By the end of 1982, nine CGIAR centers had received about US$8.17 million in grants from the OPEC Fund (See Table 12 in Annex 2).

Of the above amount, about US$ 6.0 million was allocated to four centers:

*The International Center for Agricultural Research in the Dry Areas (ICARDA), located in Aleppo, Syria, whose objective is to improve the agricultural systems and major food crops of the drier regions of western Asia and North Africa;

*The International Rice Research Institute (IRRI) in the Philippines, which conducts research in increased rice production and provides assistance to national research institutions;

*The West Africa Rice Development Association (WARDA) in Monrovia, Liberia. This center was set up in order to achieve self-sufficiency in rice production in the West Africa region in the shortest time possible through the selection and promotion of improved varieties of rice, and research, training and dissemination of information; and

*The International Service for National Agricultural Research (ISNAR), which is to provide assistance to the developing countries in national research planning, organization and management in putting agricultural science to work.

These centers can contribute significantly to improving the pre-carious food situation in the developing countries. Their assistance to national research institutions will help further extend the capabilities of the latter in dealing with local conditions by developing suitable varieties, and in training national researchers and scientists. Moreover, in 1982, the Fund also approved six grants totalling US$ 2.2 million to various CGIAR research centers.

UNIFSTD. The Fund also extended two grants, to agriculture and energy respectively, channelled through UNIFSTD, the United Nations Interim Fund for Science and Technology for Development. UNIFSTD was established in December 1979; it helps to promote the development of the scientific and technical capacities of developing countries. The OPEC Fund's agricultural grant in the amount of US$ 61,500 will help to support the Sago Starch Hydrolysis and Fermentation Project in Papua New Guinea.

Largest Single Grant. The largest single grant ever extended by the Fund was US$ 25.0 million, to the International Emergency Food Reserve administered jointly by the Food and Agricultural Organ-ization (FAO) and the World Food Program (WFP). The proceeds of this grant covered the cost of purchase and transportation of food supplied from developing countries and met the emergency needs of the poorer developing countries as agreed with the Fund's management. The grant was approved in June, 1981, and disbursed in two tranches, US$ 10 million in 1981, and US$ 15 million in 1982.

IFAD. Another large grant, amounting to US$ 20 million, was extended to IFAD in January, 1982. Its purpose was to enable IFAD to complete its first replenishment, as explained in Chapter 7.

By the end of 1982, the total amount of grants extended by the Fund to the agriculture sector amounted to US$ 63.2 million. They covered a large geographical area, reaching all continents, and they are listed in Table 12 in Annex 2.

Assistance to the Common Fund for Commodities. Establishment of the Common Fund for Commodities, and the OPEC Fund's supporting role, are described in Chapter 7. Of the 18 commodities that the Common Fund will eventually cover, two-thirds (i.e. twelve commodities) are agricultural, so its work will have a big impact in the agriculture sector.

The *Agreement Establishing the Common Fund for Commodities* was adopted by the United Nations Negotiating Conference in June 1980, and was opened for signature at the United Nations head-quarters in New York on October 1, 1980. By the end of 1982, 86 countries, among which were 9 OPEC member countries and the European Economic Community, had signed and/or ratified the Agreement. The Agreement will enter into force after it has been ratified, accepted or approved, by at least 90 countries accounting for not less than two-thirds of the total subscriptions to the 'directly contributed capital' and not less than 50 per cent of the target for pledges of voluntary contributions to the 'Second account'.

The functions of the Common Fund are to contribute through its first account to the financing of stocking of certain primary commodities, and through its second account to the financing of measures other than stocking. The objectives of the Common Fund are:

(1) 'To serve as a key instrument in attaining the agreed objectives of the Integrated Program for Commodities' adopted by the United Nations Conference on Trade and Development; and

(2) 'To facilitate the conclusion and fuctioning of international commodity agreements or arrangements, particularly concerning commodities of special interest to developing countries'.[3]

The OPEC Fund has expressed its full support for the objectives of the Common Fund. This was reflected in the Ministerial Council's decision in January 1981 to approve 35 grants totalling US$ 37.16 million, to cover the subscriptions to the capital of the Common Fund of all the 31 Least Developed Countries and four other low-income developing countries, namely Burma, Djibouti, Mauritania and Sierra Leone.

In addition, the Fund approved the extension of a voluntary contribution totalling US$ 46.4 million to the Common Fund's second account, thus bringing the Fund's total financial contribution to US$ 83.56 million. This amount, however, does not include the individual contributions of OPEC member countries totalling US$ 16.41 million, which will be made directly by the countries concerned.

The countries which had, up to February 1983, taken advantage of the Fund's offer number 25, of which 24 are defined as LLDCs and one as a Most Seriously Affected Country. Each grant was concluded after the country concerned had signed the *Agreement Establishing the Common Fund for Commodities.*

Assistance through Promotion of Trade

Unlike most development institutions, which have confined their activities to project assistance through loans, the OPEC Fund has ventured into a wide range of activities. In addition to its various types of loans and well diversified technical assistance program, the Fund has provided assistance to promote economic cooperation among developing countries.

In response to the Fund's call for solidarity among developing countries, and in support of its US$ 25.0 million grant to WFP for the International Emergency Food Reserve, the Government of Argentina in 1981 agreed to give concessional selling terms (i.e. a price rebate on the cif cost), for food purchased from that country under the Fund's grant. The Government of Argentina also expressed readiness to enter into the same arrangement with those developing countries which decided to use the OPEC Fund's BOP loans for the importation of foodstuffs from Argentina. Following Argentina's offer, other food-exporting developing countries such as Burma made similar offers. They expressed willingness to cooperate with the WFP and offered concessional terms for any food purchases from their countries under the Fund's grant to WFP. When it received the first US$ 10.0 million instalment of the Fund's grant in November 1981, the WFP proceeded to finalize arrangements for purchasing foodstuff from Argentina and Burma. As a result, WFP purchased from Argentina 8,000 metric tons of bread wheat in bulk for Mauritania and Pakistan, and from Burma 13,000 metric tons of bagged rice for Bangladesh. Preferential trading arrangements similar to these two examples are being considered by other food-exporting developing countries.

Future Role of the OPEC Fund

Development of agriculture will remain a priority over the coming decades. According to recent estimates by the end of this century world population will surpass 6 billion people. At that time, therefore, the world food requirement could be double its present level. Consequently, additional production of food has to be planned and organized to meet the needs of the rapidly growing population, particularly in developing countries. Massive investment is required in agriculture, with the introduction of modern and appropriate technology on a large scale, and numerous policy and institutional changes. Substantial transfers of resources, which are far beyond the domestic resources of developing countries, are therefore necessary.

Moreover, for most developing countries, agriculture plays an essential role in the national economy, and thus determines the pace of development in the rest of that economy. However, as economic development proceeds, the role of agriculture in an economy diminishes. Therefore, investment and cost-reducing technologies and innovations become essential for accelerating the growth of the agriculture sector. Cost reducing and other gains in productivity then stimulate the rest of the economy through lower prices for agricultural products and related commodities, and through labour leaving agriculture for more productive employment. Hence, if the economies of developing countries are to develop, they will require heavy investment in agriculture over the coming years.

The preceding discussion highlights the efforts made by the Fund in developing such a vital economic sector. It also highlights the fact that agricultural development in the Third World over the coming years will require substantial external financing. For these reasons, the OPEC Fund, which has always been responsive to the needs of developing countries, will continue to accord agriculture a high priority. This policy has already begun under the Fund's Sixth Lending Program for the years 1983 and 1984, which places particular emphasis on the poorest developing countries whose economies are dominated by agriculture, such as the sub-Saharan African countries. African countries will receive 55% of the total allocation under the Sixth Lending Program, compared with only 46% under the Fund's Fifth Lending Program of 1981-82. Barring any radical change in the Fund's current philosophy and orientation, agriculture will continue to remain one of its high-priority sectors for far longer than the period covered by the Sixth Lending Program.

THE ENERGY SECTOR

Energy, particularly commercial energy, plays a key role in shaping the future direction and growth of the economies of developing countries.

Commercial Energy. During 1950-74, average annual commercial energy consumption in developing countries increased at a rate of 6.9%, compared with a world average of 5.0%. During 1975-80, the corresponding rates of increase were 3.6% and 2.5%. The reason for this fast growth was the development of the modern sector, which is the main consumer of commercial energy. The commercial energy consumption of developing countries is expected to rise by more than 80% during the 1980s, compared with GNP growth of about 70%, and compared with a rise of 30% to 40% for developed countries.[4]

According to the latest World Bank estimates, the investment requirements of the developing countries' energy sector will increase from US$ 25 billion in 1980 to an annual level of US$ 54 billion during 1985-90, at 1980 prices.[5] The resources required are clearly far beyond what can be generated by the economies of the developing countries themselves. Substantial external resources will be required if developing countries are to develop viable energy sectors, and avoid deterioration in the living standards of their peoples.

Non-commercial Energy. Despite the rapid growth of the modern sector over the past half century, the economies of developing countries have remained essentially traditional, and non-commercial energy continues to play a significant role. Non-commercial energy (e.g. the use of wood, charcoal, plant and animal waste, solar, wind and water power) currently provides over half the total energy production of oil-importing developing countries.

A major problem facing developing countries is that non-commercial energy sources are dwindling at a rapid pace, due to an accelerated rate of deforestation. This problem is so serious for a number of countries that it has become known as the 'other energy crisis'. It is estimated that, at the present rate of deforestation, most developing countries will run out of trees in a few decades. Deforestation is also causing other problems, such as the soaring price of firewood, hardship to the rural poor (who have to spend much time searching for an increasingly dwindling supply of firewood) and erosion of the soil, in some cases turning forests into desert as is the case in the Sahel countries.[6]

This situation calls for immediate remedial action, such as implementation of massive afforestation programs and the introduction of efficient wood burning equipment (e.g. stoves) to rural areas. These programs however, require substantial resources which necessitate external assistance.

New and Renewable Energy. The exhaustible nature of commercial energy, particularly oil, is of serious concern. Alternative, non-exhaustible energy sources have to be sought. To highlight the urgency of the matter, the UN General Assembly convened a conference on New and Renewable Sources of Energy in August 1981 in Nairobi. Other international regional conferences on the issue have since been held, among which was a seminar hosted by the OPEC Fund and the governments of Nordic countries, in Helsinki in October 1981. All these gatherings, and the studies which have since emerged, have highlighted the need for massive efforts, particularly in developing countries, to promote the development of new and renewable energy sources.

Here again, although many developing countries are endowed with numerous forms of new and renewable energy, they seriously lack the financial and technical knowledge to carry out the above-mentioned efforts.

Recognizing the critical role of energy in the development of third world economies and the urgency of the issues involved, the OPEC Fund, since its inception, has accorded energy a high priority in its lending and technical assistance program.

Project Lending

The energy sector has been benefitting from an increasing share in the Fund's project lending, rising from US$ 32.2 million in 1977 to US$ 103.5 million in 1981 and US$ 140.3 million during 1982. Energy was thus the largest recipient of the Fund's direct project assistance during the period 1977-82. Amounts of project loans to the energy sector are listed in Table 4.

Despite the Fund's continued emphasis on energy financing, its overall doubling of lending in 1981 was not matched by a doubling or even a sharp increase in lending to the energy sector in that year. In fact, lending to the energy sector in 1981 was only 6.2% over 1980, and the share of the sector in project lending in 1981 dropped below the percentage for 1980. The reason was the absence of a large number of readily-available energy projects to absorb such an abrupt

Table 4: The OPEC Fund's Project Lending to the Energy Sector

Year	US$ million	% increase	% share in total project lending
1977	32.2		36.2
1978	25.8	− 19.9	22.0
1979	58.3	83.3	42.1
1980	97.5	67.2	63.7
1981	103.5	6.2	50.1
1982	140.3	35.6	30.3
1977-82	457.6	—	49.8

increase in lending in one year. To avoid delaying the transfer of resources to developing countries, the Fund did not hesitate to finance other readily-available non-energy projects. However, in 1982, there was a sharp increase in the Fund's financing of energy projects, amounting to about 36% above the 1981 level, reflecting a rise in the number of energy projects readily available for financing. Although project lending to the energy sector was the highest ever in 1982, the sector's share of project lending remained lower than the peak of 1980.

Terms of project loans to the energy sector have been highly concessionary. For details see Table 2. All forms of energy have been financed under the Fund's project loans. Conventional electrical power projects account for a large portion, but other forms of energy (e.g. oil, gas, and coal projects) have been assuming an increasing role. This reflects the Fund's quick response to the changing energy needs of developing countries.

All energy projects assisted by the Fund have been appraised and co-financed by other agencies. The Fund has not yet developed an appraising capacity especially for energy projects. Projects and co-financiers are listed in Table 13 (Annex 2).

Balance of Payments Support Loans

In order to alleviate the serious financial difficulties facing developing countries in the mid-1970s, the Fund began its first operations with a major program of quickly-disbursing BOP loans. This however, was in addition to the project loans extended by the Fund in 1977. In subsequent years, the Fund continued its practice of combining the developmental aspect of its operations through its project loans, and the financial aspect through its BOP loans. Moreover BOP continued to play a significant role in the Fund's operations, accounting for about 45% of lending operations up to the end of 1982. This makes the OPEC Fund the only institution that combines the roles of the IMF and the World Bank, though naturally on a much smaller scale.

As regards energy, a good part of the Fund's BOP loans (estimated at 25%) has been used for financing this sector. This has taken the form of financing the import of gas, oil, oil products, and other imports required by the energy sector such as machinery and equipment. Total amounts of BOP loans used for energy up to December 31, 1982, reached about US$ 156.3 million. Table 14 in Annex 2 provides a breakdown of BOP loans utilized for the energy sector.

Local Counterpart Funds

The Fund has used the LCF mechanism to support the financing of 171 projects and programs in 54 developing countries for a total amount of about US$ 428.6 million equivalent. A significant portion of this assistance has been directed to energy projects. Up to the end of 1982, 23 energy projects received LCF financing amounting to about US$ 116.6 million. For details see Table 15 in Annex 2.

Technical Assistance

The Fund's technical assistance grant program in the energy sector aims largely at promoting regional cooperation among developing countries. Through this program, the Fund has financed a number of regional energy projects, including regional offshore prospecting in East Asia (US$ 2.0 million) and the Central American Energy Program (US$ 1.5 million). The UNDP has been the executing agency for these two projects.

In East Asia, surveys and studies have been completed to assess hydrocarbon and non-hydrocarbon energy resources in the coastal and offshore areas of the region. The Central American Energy

Program, which covers six countries in the region, is nearly complete. The project has assisted in strengthening energy institutions, assessing oil resources, carrying out a study on electrical interconnection for the region, and setting up pilot plants for testing non-conventional sources of energy.

The Fund has extended grants also to other inter-governmental organizations. A grant of US$ 5.0 million was extended to OLADE in support of its extra-budgetary program on alternative sources of energy. Also a grant of US$ 868,000 was approved for four technical assistance projects administered by the United Nations Interim Fund on Science and Technology for Development. Two of these projects are in the energy field. They are the Wood for Energy Program in Honduras, and a biogas and solar energy development project in Lesotho. In April, 1982, a grant of US$ 5.0 million was approved to finance the West African Economic Community's Solar Energy Regional Center.

In addition to the grants mentioned above, in 1980, the Fund was among the first donors to announce its support for the UNDP initiative to establish an Energy Fund for Exploration and Pre-investment Surveys. It pledged a grant of US$ 6.0 million representing 10% of the resources required as voluntary contributions over the first three years. The Energy Fund's objective is to help finance pre-investment surveys as well as exploration and demonstration projects in the energy sector. The Energy Fund's first scheme comprises two components: petroleum surveys concentrating on low-income countries with per capita GNP of less than US$ 500; and the financing of pre-investment assessment of non-petroleum energy resources.

Details of the OPEC Fund's technical assistance grants to the energy sector are in Table 16 of Annex 2.

Issues of Energy Financing

It would not be quite accurate to use the mere amounts of the OPEC Fund's energy financing as indicative of the Fund's role in the energy sector in developing countries. The Fund has neither considered itself to be, nor has played the role of, a major financier of energy in developing countries. Instead, the Fund, since its inception, has been a catalyst in mobilizing sources of finance for both energy and non-energy sectors.

In this catalytic role, the Fund has demonstrated considerable flexibility and speed in processing requests for loans, and in meeting the priorities of developing countries. As a result, it has, on occasion, been called on to fill a financial gap left by other co-financiers. This has resulted in saving projects from imminent delays and the consequent higher costs. Developing countries have, also, on occasion, relied on the Fund to be the first institution to provide assistance for a project, and thus encourage other co-financiers to follow suit. Quick response of the Fund in both cases has proved instrumental in mobilizing resources for developing countries. Consequently, the Fund's role in financing energy has gone far beyond the amounts of finance that it has provided, and its impact should be measured by the opportunity cost to the recipient country, had the Fund not been able to participate in the projects concerned. Nevertheless, the energy sector has had the greatest share of the Fund's project loans, amounting to 49.8% of its total project lending.

New and Renewable Energy (NRE) Sources. The OPEC Fund was one of the first development institutions to emphasize the importance of NRE. For example, in 1979, the Fund and the Nordic governments began discussions on sponsoring the seminar on the subject mentioned earlier, which was held in Helsinki in October, 1981. It followed the UN Nairobi conference of August 1981 on the same subject, and was attended by the Chairman of the Nairobi conference, representatives of the co-sponsoring governments, developing countries, and international and regional development institutions.

The main objective of the Helsinki seminar[7] was to provide a forum for exchange of views on:

(1) financial policies and needs with regard to the development of NRE sources in developing countries;
(2) scope and possibilities for technical cooperation; and
(3) possible models for cooperation among developing countries, financial institutions, and the Nordic countries.

The seminar also provided an opportunity for the participants to review the outcome of the Nairobi conference. The Fund presented three papers at the conference, two of which it has since published.[8]

Participants highlighted, among other things the need for more pre-investment studies on NRE sources in developing countries, and for strengthening the capacity of developing countries' institutions in the identification and preparation of NRE projects. The seminar also called on international development institutions to adopt new attitudes regarding the appraisal of NRE projects. In particular, due regard had to be given to two factors: the advantage of uninterrupted supply from an indigenous source; and the additional advantage of continued supply from a renewable resource.[9] Recognizing the importance of this call, the OPEC Fund commissioned a study with the Center for Research on the New International Economic Order, to deal with appraisal criteria for projects of this type. The Fund also published a paper dealing with the problems of evaluation of NRE projects in Latin America.[10]

Participants also emphasized the importance of research in the field of NRE, and the need for strengthening research institutions in developing countries. The Director-General of the OPEC Fund proposed the establishment of an international non-governmental research center for fuelwood, with particular emphasis on research on afforestation of sub-Saharan African countries. To give the proposal momentum, he later put it forward again during the joint meeting of DAC members and OPEC/Arab aid agencies held in Paris during June 10-11, 1982. In his capacity as Co-chairman of the meeting, he proposed setting up a committee to review the proposal. A committee was duly formed and held a separate meeting on the matter. All participants at the meeting supported the proposal, particularly those of the World Bank and the Nordic Governments. The OPEC Fund is currently following up the proposal with the DAC member countries, and may host a meeting in 1983 to review the progress made.

In addition to these efforts, the Fund's actual financing of NRE has rapidly accelerated in recent years. By the end of December 1982, the Fund, through its project lending, had financed about 22 hydro-electric projects with assistance totalling about US$ 140.0 million. Moreover, nearly all the energy projects financed by local counter-part funds generated under the Fund's BOP loans have been hydro-electric projects, about 13 projects in all and assistance totalling about US$ 50.0 million equivalent. See Tables 13 and 15 of Annex 2.

Energy Financing and OPEC's Energy. It may be argued that financing energy projects in developing countries runs counter to the interests of OPEC member countries. This issue is often raised when there is surplus oil in the world market, a situation that is faced today,

with consequent decline in the oil income of OPEC member countries. Moreover, many OPEC countries have embarked on large
investment programs at home, and are now facing serious financial
difficulties.

OPEC member countries have never linked their aid to their oil
supply position, nor have they attempted to tie their aid, so that it
benefits their own economies. These principles were explained in the
introductory chapter, but perhaps should be mentioned briefly again
in this context. OPEC aid, as has been made clear, is simply an
expression of the will of the OPEC member countries to assist other
developing countries who are in need. It began in the early 1960s,
before the upward adjustment in oil prices of the mid-1970s. The
current decline in oil income of OPEC member countries has not
resulted in a marked reduction in OPEC aid to fellow developing
countries, or to their energy sectors.

OPEC countries are well aware that any increase in the oil supply
of other developing countries will have a minimal impact only, on the
world oil supply situation. Therefore, any increase in the energy
supply of other developing countries is considered a welcome
addition to their own strength, and to that of the rest of the Third
World.

However, the ability of OPEC countries to assist their fellow
developing countries is certainly a function of their external financial
position, which is closely linked to their oil revenues. While the
current decline in oil revenues may weaken the ability of OPEC
countries to continue to provide aid on a substantial scale, it will by no
means affect their decision to assist in the development of the energy
sectors of other developing countries. The obvious corollary is that
third-world countries have a strong vested interest in supporting
OPEC member countries in their efforts to achieve a healthy and
solid economic and financial position.

In formulating its Sixth Lending Program for the period 1983-84,
the Fund reiterated its desire to continue to be responsive to the
priorities of developing countries. Therefore, as long as energy
development remains a priority sector in a number of developing
countries, it will continue to be a major recipient of the Fund's
assistance over the coming years.

Notes

1. *World Development Report, 1982*, The World Bank, p. 90.

2. *Annual Report, 1982*, IFAD, p. 25.

3. *Annual Report, 1982*, The OPEC Fund for International Development, p. 39.

4. *World Development Report, 1980*, The World Bank, p. 15.

5. Ibid., p. 7.

6. Ali, Mehdi, *Financing the Energy Requirements of Developing Countries: The Role of OPEC Aid*, OPEC Fund pamphlet series no. 17, December 1981, p. 7.

7. *Annual Report, 1981*, The OPEC Fund for International Development, p. 27.

8. Paper no. 1 is reference 6 above. Paper no. 2 (unpublished) was entitled 'The Changing Energy Scene of the Seventies: A Look at the Developing Countries'. Paper no. 3 is: Mackillop, Andrew and Al-Shaikhly, Salah, *New and Renewable Sources of Energy: Evaluating Selected Technologies*, OPEC Fund pamphlet series no. 21, 1982.

9. Ministry of Foreign Affairs of Finland, *Seminar on the Financing of New and Renewable Energy Sources in Developing Countries*, organized by the OPEC Fund and Governments of Denmark, Finland, Norway, and Sweden. Helsinki (October 22-24, 1981). State Printing Center, 1982, p. 123.

10. de Valle, Alfredo, *Cost-benefit or Technology Assessment? Problems in the Evaluation of New and Renewable Energy Projects*, OPEC Fund, pamphlet series no. 22, 1982.

4 THE OPEC FUND AND AFRICA
— A Geographical Perspective

I AFRICAN DEVELOPMENT AND THE ROLE OF THE OPEC FUND   *Said Aissi*

Nowhere have the Fund's first years of activity been more challenging than in Africa; sometimes they have been rewarding, but often frustrating. This appreciation is not unique to the OPEC Fund; it is indeed shared by most development agencies of similar mandate. A number of specific characteristics give the continent a standing apart, particularly those characteristics which have come to be recognized as indicators of relative poverty.

Africa accounts for 21 of the 31 Least Developed Countries, 28 of the 45 Most Seriously Affected Countries, and 26 of the 43 Food Priority Countries. Beyond this clear expression of the state of poverty of the continent, a number of indicators show that in the 1970s its economic situation deteriorated, auguring more challenges, more frustrations but, hopefully, some satisfaction. Growth indicators, productivity measurement — in the essential area of food — and the financial situation of the continent illustrate the gloomy performance of the last decade:

*GNP per capita declined on average by about 0.3 per cent per annum in the low-income countries and 0.5 per cent per annum in the middle-income countries, compared with an increase in the 1960s of 1.6 and 1.9, respectively.

*per capita agricultural production declined by 1.1 per cent in the low-income countries and 0.4 per cent in the middle-income countries.

*the volume of exports declined by 4.5 per cent for the low-income countries and 3.5 per cent for the middle-income countries.

*the current account deficit rose from US$ 1.5 billion in 1970 to US$ 8.0 billion in 1980; and *partly reflecting these deficits, the level of indebtedness of the continent rose from US$ 6.0 billion to US$ 32.0 billion, carrying the debt service ratio from 6 per cent to 12 per cent between 1970 and 1979.

Although self-explanatory, these indicators are more meaningful when contrasted with the vast potential that the African continent is known to command. Especially so when compared with countries at similar levels of development in Asia and Latin America where performance has, in most cases, been more impressive than that of African countries. So what are the peculiarities of the African continent which seem to hamper its economic growth?

Most of them arise from historical background and physical environment. Most African countries south of the Sahara underwent long periods of colonization, which, on the whole, bequeathed social and economic structural imbalances that had to be faced after independence. Not least of them were artificially defined borders, ethnically heterogeneous populations, ill-health, widespread illiteracy and dismally inadequate infrastructure. This heritage was generally so taxing, that substantial resources were devoted to building national loyalties and creating a sense of nationhood. Not surprisingly, these often daunting tasks had their setbacks, which delayed even more the time when resources, human and other, could be fully devoted to the construction of sound economies. Another factor characterizing Africa is to be found in the largely hostile climate which creates ecological obstacles of a magnitude unknown in the other continents.

After twenty years, the African continent still seems to be endeavouring to overcome its burdensome heritage of history and nature with varying degrees of success. In the lives of nations, twenty years is indeed a short period, but set in a world of rising expectations, enhanced by easy communications with the developed world, it seems exceedingly long for the creation of basic living conditions and the satisfaction of the average citizen's minimal demands.

Whilst it is undeniable that some progress has been achieved on all fronts, and in particular great strides have been made in the areas of education and medical care, nonetheless, the gap in social and economic development between the African continent and the other continents persists in most areas of comparison. The one single factor that has maintained this gap unrelentingly is undoubtedly the continuous growth of population. Between 1960 and 1979, population rose by 63 per cent. During the last decade the population growth rate slowed down in Asia and Latin America; but in Africa rose to 2.7 per cent on average, depriving its people of the fruits of the economic growth achieved, and increasing the already difficult task of governments of providing basic living conditions.

The governments of Africa and the international development agencies concerned with the fate of the continent, have in the past few years, demonstrated their awareness of present conditions. But more important, they have also come to realize that the trends are not towards improvement but towards further deterioration. Hence, the commendable efforts to explain the situation in Africa, and the pleas for effective and concerted action.

The OPEC Fund's contribution to the debate has been facilitated by the close ties that exist between OPEC member countries and the African continent, and by the intimate understanding of the problems of the continent shown by the Fund's staff who have experienced similar problems in their own underdeveloped native countries.

The Fund's attempts to assist African countries in meeting their development problems will be reviewed in detail in this chapter. However, to help understand the rationale behind some of the policies the Fund has pursued, first the economic context of the continent will be analysed, outlining the internal and external factors facing the developing African countries.

The Economic Context

Most observers now agree that Africa is undergoing a deeply-rooted economic crisis, of a nature and magnitude not experienced any-where else in the world. Whilst it is agreed that the degree of crisis varies from country to country, it is also recognized that some instances of relative prosperity that emerged in the last two decades have also been caught in the web of slow economic growth, unsatisfied basic social demands, and above all, poor prospects. In explaining and often justifying this economic crisis, the reasons most often cited (apart from the harsh physical realities of sub-Saharan Africa) are extreme dependence on external factors and severe internal constraints.

Dependence on External Factors

Most African countries developed during the colonial period as sources of raw materials and primary products for industries located generally in Europe. Hence, primary products represent about 80 per cent of the continent's exports. These proportions rise to almost 95 per cent if primary processing is included. These exports represent some 20 per cent of Africa's combined GNP. Even more telling is the fact that most African countries depend on one or two commodities, the fates of which have a direct and immediate impact on the country as a whole. Examples of such dependence abound. To cite only a few: copper accounts for about 95 per cent of Zambia's export earnings; iron ore accounts for about 85 per cent of Mauritania's export earnings and 70 per cent of Liberia's; coffee accounts for 80 per cent of Burundi's earnings; groundnuts account for 90 per cent of the export earnings of Gambia; sugar accounts for 90 per cent of Mauritius's export earnings.

In the period 1970-80, the prices of most of these commodities registered negative annual average growth rates, amounting to: — 18.7% for copper; — 13% for iron ore; — 3.5% for groundnuts; and — 1.3% for sugar. Among all the commodities cited above, only the price of coffee increased (+3.9 per cent). Statistics for 1981 and the first half of 1982 do not bring any relief, as the overall average of prices for primary commodities (other than oil) declined sharply. As a result of this lasting downturn, commodity prices are currently lower in real terms than at any other time in the last three decades.

At the same time the prices of African countries' imports, essentially machinery and other manufactures (which had a 75% share of the continent's merchandise imports in 1978), either were maintained or increased. Another factor which affected the oil-importing countries of the continent was the relative increase in oil prices over the decade. While this factor is undoubtedly important, its spectacular and sometimes dramatic effect should not blur the realities. Analyses made by the United Nations Conference on Trade and Development,[1] of the price increases of one developing country's imports, show clearly that the contribution of manufactures to the deterioration of the import price index was consistently greater, except for the years 1974 and 1979/80. Increased prices of manufactures accounted for over 90 per cent of the unfavourable variation of the import price index of developing countries in 1975 and 1978 and between 58 per cent and 81 per cent in the years 1971, 1972, 1974 and 1977.

Generally commodity price changes resulted in a deterioration of the terms of trade in the 1970s of — 1.5 per cent per annum, compared with a rate of growth of 3.4 per cent per annum in the 1960s.

The extreme dependence of the African economy on exports is clearly illustrated by these economic effects of the ongoing depression in the traditional markets for African raw materials and primary products. Furthermore, restrictions, quotas and substitutions by man-made products have also had their impact, further proving the vulnerability of African exports.

Not surprisingly the combined effects of increased import bills and weak demand for African exports[2] led to a sharp deterioration in the trade balance of the African countries. The enlarged deficit in current account that followed is illustrated by comparison with GDP: the current account deficit was 2.4 per cent of GDP in 1970; in 1980 it is estimated at 9.2 per cent.

For a long time the current account deficit of African countries was, by and large, compensated by Official Development Assistance. However, since 1975 these flows of ODA have not matched the growth of current account deficits, and have amounted to only half of current account deficits. African countries have therefore been forced to revert to commercial loans at ever increasing costs, aggravated by sharp increases in interest rates.

Development of the balance of payments problem has added another factor of dependence. Response to growing pressure on the balance of payments differed from country to country, due presumably to the amount of pressure exerted internally and externally in favour of policy changes. But over a period of time, three basic strategies emerged.

The first and most easily-administered measure, was to reduce the rate of growth of imports and in many cases, actually reduce the volume of imports. The second generalized measure was to seek an increase in the net flow of capital to sustain essential and minimum imports, and in some cases to finance additional investments required for basic structural adjustments.

The third measure was to attempt to increase exports. This last measure was evidently the least successful. Countries found themselves unable to expand export volumes owing largely to the depressed state of world demand, and unfavourable weather which adversely affected output in the agricultural African states. Another factor which has tended to limit availability of production for exports and which needs to be more seriously considered, is the ever increasing demand of the African populations for a quantitatively and qualitatively greater supply from national markets.

In a perverse sense, the first two measures have indeed been more successful. Their long-term effect is now fully apparent.

Political bureaucracies were — quite understandably — averse to reducing imports of socially and politically sensitive commodities, and the brunt of the reductions fell on agricultural and industrial imports, leading to under-utilization of existing industrial capacity and below-optimum utilization of agricultural potential.

Recourse to borrowing has been the most common strategy of African countries, for their relatively nascent economic development limits their choice of adjustment measures.

ODA to the oil-importing countries of Africa nearly tripled between 1970 and 1980. Nevertheless, it covered only half of the current account deficit for the period 1975 onwards. While most African countries are not considered sufficiently credit-worthy for private capital,[3] nonetheless, commercial loans to Africa have doubled since 1973. The cost of these loans partly explains the large increase in debt service ratio — alluded to above — from 6 per cent in 1970 to 12.4 per cent in 1979.

The Internal Constraints

The objective analyst of the African scene will undoubtedly recognize that a considerable amount of attention has been directed to the external factors hampering the growth of African economies. Discussion of the internal factors, on the other hand, has generally been met with suspicion and distrust by African leaders and opinion makers. This atmosphere has certainly a great deal to do with the unyielding attitude of the economic partners of the developing countries, towards the numerous attempts made to establish a more realistic — if not more equitable — economic order. It is also greatly influenced by the often unrealistic economic and political adjustments that precondition the assistance provided by financial agencies.

The adoption of the Lagos Plan by African states had introduced a new impetus to these discussions and set a healthy framework for action. Since the adoption of this plan, a number of studies have reinforced it,[4] with, in particular, a balanced view of the internal factors which contribute to the stagnation of African economies. The central position given to agriculture by the plan goes beyond the sterile debate in which, for too long, the advocates of industry opposed those of agriculture.

The fact of the matter is that agriculture is at the heart of African economies. It provides a livelihood for more than 80 per cent of the population of the continent. Its share of GDP varies between 30 and 60 per cent; and it provides about 60 per cent of the export earnings of the non-oil-exporting countries. More importantly, agriculture is recognised as the sector which is capable of providing employment for a rapidly increasing work force, and the sector with the greatest potential for growth.

In recognising the pre-eminence of the agricultural sector in African economies, its contribution to the overall economic crisis is made even more evident. Statistics over the past two decades provide a clear illustration of the stagnation in this sector. Total food production rose by only 1.5 per cent per year in the 1970s, 0.5 per cent less than the 2 per cent achieved in the 1960s. This performance, unsatisfactory as it is, appears dismally low when population growth is taken into account. Given that population growth in the first decade was an annual average of 2.5 per cent, and in the second decade 2.7 per cent, food production per person at best stagnated in the first, and actually declined in the second decade.

Exports of agricultural produce have stagnated at the level of the 1960s and as a consequence, sub-Saharan Africa's share of world trade in these commodities has not increased substantially, whilst the share of Africa as a whole has actually declined. Imports, on the other hand, have increased each year, resulting in a new drain on scarce foreign exchange resources, and adding a major constraint to development financing.

Significantly this decline has occurred over a period when the agricultural sector was allocated considerable amounts of financing. More than in any other sector, the internal policies pursued by the different states are the primary cause, since statistical evidence shows that the effects of external factors on the sector have been minimal or non-existent in the case of sub-Saharan countries.

There now appears to be general agreement on the negative factors which have adversely affected at least this sector. They may be summarized as follows:

*fiscal and pricing policies which tended to discourage growth of production;
*over-valued rates of exchange which — when used as a lever for economic management — tended to discourage exports, conceal inefficiencies, and support local production beyond reasonable cost;

*inefficient physical control and management of scarce resources
— such as foreign currency — leading to misallocation of
resources;
*bureaucratization of the economy through proliferation of
parastatals and state monopolies, with unclearly defined objectives and undefined standards of management.

While recognizing these internally-created stumbling blocks, a
number of other factors also have to be appreciated:

*In their great majority, the African countries are in their post-
independence formative years. Lack of experience, and above all
lack of qualified manpower, are unique handicaps;
*the capacity of any country to adjust to sharp changes in its
economic environment is a function of its economic base and the
level of sophistication of its institutions. Not many African
countries could claim much for those attributes;
*the expectations of the population of Africa for better living
conditions, enhanced by recent improvements in health and
education, are rising at such a pace that the nascent economies of
Africa may not be able to respond fully to them. In particular,
expectations in education and social welfare may well divert
resources from other more productive uses;
*a number of problems encountered by African states are also
encountered by other countries of the developing and developed
worlds. The major difference is that the African states do not
enjoy broadly-based economies; their room for manoeuvre is
much more limited, so their capacity to adjust to rapidly changing
situations — internal and external — is that much less.

The OPEC Fund's Contribution to the Development
of Africa

All development agencies — national and multilateral — have recognized the particular circumstances of the sub-Saharan African
countries, and efforts have been made to allocate more resources to
them. However, it must be recognized that the problem is not just a
matter of aid. For, however considerable it may be, aid alone will not
compensate for the internal and external factors just described, which
constrain the development of African economies.

To break what appears to be a vicious circle, it is felt that a clear commitment from the economic partners of Africa to help alleviate the burden of the external factors, will provide a lead for the African governments to address the major issue of internal adjustment. Some of these adjustments often require large resources which have to come from outside the countries, or they may take time to bear fruit, but a number of them may be dealt with in a relatively short time framework. Government action on some of these internal adjustments, and the easing of some of the external factors by the economic partners of Africa, would form the basic elements of a concerted plan of action in which development finance institutions would play a major role. More and more evidence points today to the fact that such an understanding is gradually being reached, but meanwhile the need to give high priority to the African continent is fully recognized.

Like most other development institutions involved, the OPEC Fund has designed its operational programme to reflect this recognized priority that African countries legitimately claim. The OPEC Fund's operations in Africa are reviewed from three points of view: their magnitude, the form they take, and their socio-economic impact.

Magnitude of Operations

The Fund's direct commitments to African countries amounted at the end of January 1983 to US$ 854.17 million, of which US$ 377.05 million took the form of balance of payments support loans, US$ 415.21 million represented project/program financing and lines of credit, and finally US$ 61.91 million were extended as grants.

In addition to these direct operations decided by the Fund's Governing Board and directed by the Fund's management, the Fund assisted the African continent indirectly through its contribution to the International Fund for Agricultural Development and the International Monetary Fund's Trust Fund. These contributions were made to the institutions as such, but it is felt appropriate for the sake of completeness, to consider an appropriate share of these institutions' operations in Africa as an indirect contribution of the Fund.

In respect of IFAD, the OPEC Fund has contributed, in the name of its member countries, US$ 865.5 million and, in its own name, US$ 20 million in the form of a special grant. This total amounts to more than 40 per cent of IFAD's resources. The proportion of IFAD's operations in Africa which can thus be credited to the Fund amounts to US$ 165.5 million, of which US$ 158.30 million is in the form of loans for project financing and US$ 7.20 million that of grants. As regards the IMF Trust Fund, US$ 110.7 million of profits from the sale of gold by seven of the member countries were credited to the OPEC Fund, and subsequently extended in the form of balance of payments support loans by the Trust Fund. The proportion of IMF Trust Fund commitments to the African continent representing the Fund's credit thus amounts to US$ 42.40 million.

To sum up, the total magnitude of the Fund's direct and indirect operations in Africa amounted to over 1 billion US dollars at the end of January, 1983.

Form of Operations

Unlike a number of other development institutions, the Fund has long recognized the need to adapt to particular requirements and circumstances. The Fund did not start with a set of rules and with preconceived policies. On the contrary, simple guidelines have apparently sufficed to give the Fund its personality and overall philosophy, whilst operational policies have tended to develop pragmatically from examination of each case. After six years of practical experience the Fund's conceptual framework may be said, albeit, with the necessary generalisation, to have developed into five methods of assistance: institutional support; balance of payments support; program or sector support; project support; and finally lines of credit to national development banks.

As stated above, this framework has developed from experience. In practice each method encompasses elements of another method. For example any form of assistance in foreign currency implies an impact on balance of payments; furthermore, each method, whether using foreign exchange or local currency, implies institutional support and sectoral support. With this reservation in mind, the five methods are further described.

Institutional Support. The Fund has granted support to agencies such as UNDP, UNICEF, and UNWRA. Whilst the financing provided by the Fund was justified by, and tied to, programs or projects, it is undeniable that the Fund's support was also greatly influenced by the nature and objectives of these institutions. Other examples include grants to agricultural research centres such as WARDA and ICARDA, whose objectives coincide with the Fund's concern for the development of agriculture in Africa. This type of financing is not limited to existing institutions. Indeed, it has helped to establish new institutions, the necessity for which is evident. Such is the case of the Common Fund for Commodities or the West African Economic Community's Solar Energy Centre. The total commitment of the Fund in the form of grants for institutional support amounted to US$ 62 million at the end of January 1983.

Balance of Payments Support. This type of financing is designed, above all, to alleviate financial difficulties, especially imbalances in external payments. The vulnerability of sub-Saharan African countries' balance of payments situations has been explained earlier. It is therefore not surprising that 44.14 per cent of all the Fund's direct operations in Africa, amounting to US$ 377.05 million, have taken the form of BOP support loans. The total number of these operations amounts to 102, of which 91 have been fully disbursed, and the remainder are in the process of disbursement.

Balance of payments support is in practice used to finance the importation of essential commodities to meet immediate needs or to serve developmental objectives. Statistics available to date show that about 70 per cent of the Fund's financing by this method in Africa has been used for the procurement of foodstuffs and oil products, and about 22% for the procurement of equipment and spare parts. By its very nature this method of financing has helped African governments in their efforts to reduce balance-of-payments current account deficits. It has also helped, at least temporarily, to rebuild the foreign exchange reserves of the beneficiary countries. As this method of financing has been extended in the form of concessional loans with a large grant element, it has helped to improve the structures of external debt of the recipient countries, and to that extent, improved their capacity to borrow further.

An important feature of a balance of payments support loan is that the recipient government sets aside local counterpart funds equivalent to the loan proceeds. These counterpart funds usually represent the proceeds generated from the domestic sales of imports financed by the loan. This requirement has contributed to increased investment in sub-Saharan Africa. The legal agreement for this type of loan provides that within a reasonable period of time, the Fund and the beneficiary country agree on the specific allocation of these local counterpart funds. By the end of January 1983, a total of US$ 165.5 million equivalent in local currency had thus been mobilized for the financing of 94 projects in sub-Saharan Africa.

Program or Sector Support. This method of assistance is intended for developmental undertakings at sectoral or enterprise level, particularly in relation to programs of rehabilitation or schemes for fuller utilization of existing productive capacities. Such financing is generally more flexible than project financing, and more specific than balance of payments support. It has a short gestation period, as its immediate objectives are to create conditions that favour more efficient use of productive capacities.

Considering its flexibility, it is somewhat disappointing that this type of financing has not been widely taken advantage of, by the African states. This is due partly to the influence of other development agencies who deal only at project level, and partly to the importance given to new projects as opposed to improving the performance of existing investments. It is also undeniable that in a number of instances, balance of payments support could be used to achieve similar results, albeit at a higher cost, in so far as the Fund's program financing is more concessional than balance of payments support. So far only three program loans totalling US$ 19 million have been extended to three sub-Saharan countries.

Project Support. This method of financing, in the form of loans, is the most prevalent. It ties the funds to a precise developmental undertaking and covers all sectors. The Fund has so far financed 62 projects in sub-Saharan Africa, with loans amounting in total to US$ 321.96 million. Compared with BOP and programme loans, these specific operations, sometimes involving large amounts, require a longer preparation period and long drawn out consultations between the financiers and the beneficiaries.

The Fund's characteristic philosophy in respect of projects is markedly influenced by its concern not to freeze funds for projects insufficiently prepared, nor projects in their early stages of preparation. As a result, the Fund has generally entered into commitments only at the later stages of preparation. In so doing, it has been able to select those projects which have gone beyond the feasibility stages; it has thus often been able to act as the financier of last resort. In the context of Africa, where the number of projects seems to have mushroomed recently (in direct relation to the proliferation of offers of technical assistance grants by industrial countries), this standpoint has appeared salutary in so far as a number of ill-prepared projects have never reached the stages where the Fund would normally take up the project.

This is not to infer that the Fund never intervenes in the earlier stages of project preparation; but in no case has the Fund frozen available financing to nurture the projects it has itself initiated. On the contrary, its philosophy has been to make funds available to projects that are most likely to be implemented without delay, irrespective of their initiators. This point may appear over-emphasized but the concern is justified by the number of projects which have been waiting for their financial gaps to be closed, due to the large number of uncoordinated actions by development agencies in Africa. In this respect, it is hoped that, in the absence of greater inter-agency coordination, the African states will ensure that fewer projects are presented for co-financing, thus pooling available resources and ensuring their rapid implementation.

Under the envelope of project financing, the Fund has not limited itself to financing new productive facilities as the term 'project' might imply. In point of fact such financing has often served as a vehicle for concessional funding of activities incidental to the project, such as technical assistance and studies (feasibility, sectoral, tariff, organizational, managerial, etc). This practice has by-passed deep-seated prejudice against the financing of seemingly non-productive developmental activities. In the same way, the Fund has taken, especially in the context of Africa, a more liberal view of a project's scope and content allowing, where justified, the inclusion of recurrent costs with investment costs. Similarly, although the Fund would normally finance only the foreign exchange costs of projects, it has often agreed to include indirect foreign costs (i.e. goods and services procured locally which were known to have been imported previously). Furthermore, and in recognition of the weak economies of African states, where savings are minimal, the Fund has also agreed to finance local costs. This practice often permits completion of projects, and so brings greater relief to the governments concerned. Another aspect which characterizes the Fund's activities in Africa is its preparedness in principle to provide complementary financing where costs have exceeded estimates, thus recognizing the particularly difficult conditions for implementing projects on the African continent.

Lines of Credit to National Development Banks. The introduction by the Fund of this new *modus operandi* illustrates its resolve to assist in the development of small-scale enterprises, in Africa in particular.

So far 10 lines of credit have been extended to 9 countries on the continent. The case for such financing, especially in Africa, needs no explanation. Suffice it to recall the need Africa has to expand the employment base; expand managerial capacity; substitute for imports; develop services; and encourage local enterprises. Suffice it also to recall the system of land tenure in the small African states, and the case for reaching small and medium-sized undertakings is made, and with it the case for lines of credit.

In extending this type of financing, the Fund considers the programme and the strategy of the national development bank, and ensures that they agree with the Fund's own philosophy. The capacity of the national bank to implement its strategy is also evaluated. In so doing, the Fund ensures that the following conditions are met: suitable capital structure; sound liquidity position; well balanced portfolio; adequate provisions and reserves; satisfactory interest-spread; and, above all, capacity to appraise projects and to administer the sub-loans generated by the Fund's financing.

These are the key factors upon which the Fund bases its decisions to finance national credit institutions. Despite its limitations in terms of resources and institution-building capability, the Fund attempts to maximize the benefits derived from its loans by identifying the needs of the beneficiaries of the line of credit, before reaching a decision. Moreover, credit eligibility guidelines, expressed in terms of ceilings (normally determined by the size of asset holdings) are drawn. This step ensures that only beneficiaries who do not have access to capital from other sources receive assistance through the Fund's lines of credit. As the Fund's lines of credit are extended to national development banks through governments, and are generally free of interest, the interest earned by the local institution is deposited in an account after withholding a minimum spread allowance. This income is then used by the development bank, after consultation with the Fund, to subsidize interest rates on sub-loans to some of the beneficiaries (often in the agriculture sector) and also to finance some of the technical assistance needs of the development bank and its borrowers.

This procedure has enabled the Fund to assist small-scale enterprises that would not otherwise have had access to credit, because of the traditional lending policies of other financial institutions.

To date the Fund has made available US$ 74.25 million in loans to national development banks in Africa, which has enhanced considerably their capacity to assist in the development of small and medium-scale enterprises.

The Socio-economic Impact of the Fund's Activities in Africa

The nature, the magnitude and the complexity of the problems encountered by sub-Saharan Africa in its efforts to extricate itself from the entanglements of economic underdevelopment, preclude any significant results in a short period. The Fund's own impact on these problems is to be viewed in the same perspective. However, whilst recognizing that neither the size of the Fund's operations on the continent nor its relative youth presuppose a major impact, it is, nonetheless, important to ascertain at least the relevance of its operations to the problems diagnosed. The Fund's operations in Africa are therefore now examined from the dual view-point of policies pursued, and the actual concrete achievements of the financing made available.

One of the most striking features of the Fund's operations in sub-Saharan Africa is the relatively large share of balance of payments support financing. More than 44 per cent of the Fund's direct operations benefitting African states have been directed towards the importation of essential commodities, so easing somewhat, the pressure on the foreign exchange requirements of the beneficiary countries. Indeed since 1977, the year in which the Fund practically commenced its loans,[5] the most prevalent and constraining economic problem of Africa has been that of continuous balance of payments deficits. In recognition of this, the Fund allocated up to the end of January 1983, nearly 57 per cent of its worldwide balance of payments assistance to the African continent.

This financing helped to provide essential inputs for development, such as energy (oil products), equipment, spare parts, and agricultural inputs, without which the production facilities of the countries would have been incapacitated. Nonetheless, to emphasize the developmental character of its BOP assistance, the Fund insisted, with notable success, upon channelling equivalent amounts of local savings to development projects. At the end of January 1983, a total of US$ 165.5 million equivalent in local currencies had been mobilized for the financing of 94 projects in a variety of sectors, notably agriculture, industry and transportation.

In the other major area of the Fund's financing, namely project and program, the Fund has given priority to the enhancement of countries' productive capacities. The energy, agriculture and industry sectors have absorbed 68 per cent of this type of financing. In the energy sector, the Fund has been involved in 22 projects. The great majority of them are concerned with developing renewable sources of energy. The case for such projects does not require advocacy. But two points must be made: Africa's energy potential is largely untapped and its future requirements of this basic commodity are tremendous. The need for such projects thus goes beyond the justification, often given, of replacing imports of oil. In agriculture, the Fund has been involved in four projects, of equal importance for the development of food and cash crops. Africa's potential for agricultural production has been largely established for both self-sufficiency and for exports. The Fund's involvement in this sector would certainly have been greater were it not for the existence of IFAD, to which the Fund has contributed considerably. Finally, in the area of industry the Fund has contributed to 13 projects, increasing the continent's ability to process locally its raw materials and reap maximum benefits from its natural endowment.

Another sector vital to the development of a country, namely transportation and communications, has benefitted greatly from the Fund's project and program financing. The transportation and communications infrastructure of the continent has for a long time seriously hampered the development of new areas. The Fund's allocation of 29 per cent of its direct project and program financing underlines the importance of the sector. The Fund has been involved in 14 road projects, four railway projects, two airport projects, one port and one telecommunications project. In the case particularly of road projects, emphasis was given to the penetration of hitherto under-developed areas with the objective of triggering their development, and to inter-state linkages facilitating economic integration.

In all these areas of project and program financing, the Fund has emphasized completion of on-going projects as well as rehabilitation of existing facilities, thus consolidating previous investments, and ensuring by the same token, a high return from the funds made available.

Another aspect of the Fund's operations has been the encourage-ment given to small and medium-scale enterprises through lines of credit extended to national development banks. Agricultural, industrial and service enterprises have benefitted from this type of financing. This relatively recent trend bears out the importance attached by Africa to encouraging small entrepreneurs, so that they can play a part in the development of their countries. The multiplica-tion of small-scale enterprises becomes a necessity as the economic apparatus of such countries grows. In the particular case of the nascent economies of Africa, the development of small and medium-scale enterprises will prevent bottlenecks and will contribute to the mobilisation of national savings for economic development.

Like all other development finance agencies, the Fund is naturally deeply concerned that resources should be effectively utilized. The risks of sub-optimal utilization of the resources extended by the Fund are high, in so far as the costs to the beneficiary countries of the financing extended appear so low. Rather than question the merits of concessionality, the Fund's management has emphasized the need for cost-effectiveness and efficiency of utilization of its fundings. Careful screening of projects, cross-examination of their appraisals and constant follow-up of their implementation, in conjunction with loan administrators and other co-financiers, are some of the cautionary measures taken by the Fund to hedge against such risks.

However, these measures do not make up for the technical and administrative shortcomings of a number of the executing agencies the Fund has been dealing with. To confront this problem the Fund has systematically given special attention to the institutional aspects of its operations, in the form of direct grants or as a component of project financing. Particular emphasis has been given to assistance for project supervision and for transfer of technology. In this respect the Fund has insisted on the direct involvement of a country's own nationals in the preparation and implementation of the project. Evaluation of the executing agency has also invariably included an analysis of its capacity to run the project after it has been commissioned. The Fund's concern for proper utilisation of the capacities created by projects has led to a number of initiatives, such as assistance in the management of completed projects, and encouragement of evaluation of projects a few years after their completion. A practical illustration of such concern is the continuous follow-up of projects after the Fund's financing has been completed.

The results of such efforts await the test of time, particularly in view of the constraints or instabilities in the beneficiary countries, where social shifts and changes follow closely on economic progress. The Fund has endeavoured merely to maintain simple lending procedures. Its efforts to spare its borrowers many of the difficulties, delays and duplications inherent in the process of co-financing by several donors, are largely recognized.

In the preceding text, the Fund's work for the continent of Africa in general and sub-Saharan Africa in particular, has been viewed as that of a financial agency providing development finance. This is the Fund's own vision of its role in the partnership deal it has struck with its beneficiary countries, which may well be a reaction to the seemingly unceasing talk of the development of Africa and the relatively ineffectual actions that follow. Whilst this attitude has its merits, it would be unjust to ignore the Fund's contribution to exposing the problems of the developing world in general and the poorer countries in particular.

It has been said that the Fund is a development agency of the developing world, not just another agency 'recycling petrodollars' or some other compensatory facility. In fact, it is only one of a constellation of agencies funded by OPEC member countries, to express their solidarity with other developing countries. The performance of the Fund is intimately tied to the performance of the whole group, for their philosophy is a common one and their organizational ties are strong. Observers of the 1970s have termed the decade that of energy. Objective observers have gone beyond the product and analysed the deeper message of OPEC: that of a new economic order which recognizes the true value — and not just the price — of exhaustible raw materials. The OPEC Fund's contribution to this message is the most rewarding achievement it could claim. No major international gathering and no important and serious debate on the economic order have taken place without the Fund registering its views, and taking action to support those views. Advancement of the cause of the poorer countries of the world lies naturally with the international community in its entirety, and the OPEC Fund's voice and programme of action is only a small fraction of the total effort, but the mere presence of the Fund is in itself a full reward.

In its short history, the OPEC Fund has evolved into a major source of concessional development finance for the poorer countries of the world, especially those of the African continent. In a little more than six years of operations, the Fund has extended to African countries 102 balance of payments support loans which, besides financing import of essential commodities, have generated local counterpart funds which have so far (January 1983) helped to finance the local costs of 94 projects. The Fund has also extended 62 project loans, 3 program loans and 10 lines of credit to African countries. In addition, the Fund has provided 22 grants for development purposes to 11 different institutions active in Africa. The total amount hence committed on the continent directly by the Fund, at the end of January 1983, was US$ 854.17 million. When added to the indirect contribution to the development of Africa through the IMF Trust Fund and IFAD, this amount exceeds US$ 1 billion.

While considerable in absolute amounts and timely in its delivery, the Fund's assistance could not by itself be considered sufficient. Nor could, for that matter, any amount of aid be sufficient to alleviate all the economic problems of Africa. The Fund's contribution is viewed as one of the enabling factors which the African states can rely upon to tide over their financial difficulties.

While this general philosophy is — for obvious reasons — the only practicable one, the fact that for a number of African countries aid is the only possible source of financing for development, must not be ignored. The Fund's bias in favour of the group of most seriously affected countries and least developed countries stems from recognition of this reality.

The priority given by the Fund to the continent of Africa in its operational program is a practical application of this principle. Up to the end of January 1983, 45 per cent of the Fund's world-wide commitments went to Africa. In line with this trend, the on-going sixth lending program allocates about 54 per cent of its total amount to the sub-Saharan African countries. The priority given, and the attention paid by the Fund to those countries is further illustrated by the following facts relating to the region:

*largest beneficiary of the Fund's overall operations
*highest aid per capita
*largest number of countries benefitting from the Fund (45 out of 82)
*largest number of operations (177 out of 318)
*most favoured terms of lending
*largest number of projects initiated by the Fund
*first loan ever made by the Fund

The Fund's role has nonetheless not been limited to the financial assistance it has provided. The policies it has pursued and the procedures it has followed, have been designed to respond to the particular requirements of the continent. Moreover, the Fund has defended all the legitimate claims of its countries in international fora, so much so that the Fund is unequivocally identified with them and their major claims. The Fund can claim also to have assumed a responsible attitude in giving its support wherever needed and in whatever possible form, but only in cases well justified and where the countries concerned had exhausted internal resources and possibilities of self-reliance, for the Fund considers itself a partner in development rather than a lender of money.

II SUPPORTING SUB-SAHARAN AFRICA:
THE NEED FOR CONCERTED STRATEGY
Dr Ibrahim F.I. Shihata

Among attempts to contribute to progress in solving the problems of development outlined in the foregoing text, was a two-day meeting entitled 'Aid strategy for sub-Saharan Africa' organized by the OPEC Fund and held in Vienna in February 1982. Major donor institutions participated in the discussions at this meeting. An introductory address was given to the meeting by Dr Ibrahim F.I. Shihata, Director-General of the OPEC Fund. It forms the concluding section of this chapter, and is reproduced below.

The world aid community seems at last to have given priority attention to the economic problems in Africa. Such attention is long overdue. Sub-Saharan African countries are facing an economic crisis of unprecedented proportions following a depressing decade of poor economic performance. The average GDP growth rate figure of 1.6% estimated by the World Bank for sub-Saharan countries during the 1970s, stands in stark and disappointing contrast to the modest achievements of the previous decade (1960-1970) when GDP grew at an average rate of 4.1%. As a result, sub-Saharan Africa experienced in the 1970s actual declines in per capita output. In agriculture, the backbone of African economies, output per capita experienced a record decline. On the whole, Africa's economic performance was much worse than that of any other developing region. There is no indication that this situation will improve in the foreseeable future without exceptional additional efforts.

Africa's economic ills have been recently outlined in a variety of major reports and studies all of which are familiar to this audience.[6] Having gone through these reports, I feel that there is a virtual consensus among them that sub-Saharan Africa has enormous resource potential in agriculture and minerals, but that the region is nevertheless handicapped by the lack of the other requirements of development: investment capital, technology, trained manpower, viable institutional frameworks, established infrastructure, helpful domestic policies and political stability.

In response to these development constraints, there are basically two proposed solutions prevailing in the literature: fundamental changes in domestic policies and substantial increases in development aid. Regarding the former, the World Bank report specifically recommends more suitable trade and exchange rate policies for African countries, more realistic pricing policies, increased export incentives particularly in the agricultural sector, improvements in education and health care, and adequate policy response to the population problem. On the issue of increasing external aid, the World Bank recommends the doubling of aid to the region in real terms by the end of the 1980s from US$ 4.9 billion to US$ 9.1 billion.

The underlying assumption behind these prescriptions is that additional financial flows coupled with the improvement of domestic economic policies represent the key to solving Africa's problems. While we agree that these factors are of great importance, we believe that they are not the only essential considerations. Furthermore, these prescriptions are regrettably not likely to be implemented in the near future. Hence, it may also be useful to emphasize other relevant factors of equal importance to Africa's quest for economic progress and to look for the implementation of more practical steps in the meanwhile.

For instance, it is clear that externally generated factors relating to the worsening of terms of trade, rising interest rates, escalating inflation, and increasing protectionism in industrialized countries have, in varying degrees, had adverse effects on sub-Saharan Africa. Such external factors can hardly be countered merely through the adoption of more sensible domestic policies. Within the region, there is also a need for comprehensive reforms that go beyond economic policies to reach the administrative, educational and population policies in particular. These reforms should aim, above all, at introducing a better formation, organization and utilization of human resources. In the absence of significant progress in this area, we submit that a narrow focus on the improvement of strictly economic issues may not succeed in creating an encouraging climate for investment and development and could, moreover, lead to adverse social consequences.

Role of Donors

That said, the purpose of this meeting, as we see it, is not to reach agreement on Africa's development problems and the ideal ways of coping with them. Such a task is definitely beyond the reach of this practically-minded gathering. We believe that our primary concern should be what we, as donors, ought to do in response to Africa's urgent needs. How can we be more responsive and effective than we are at present?

While we share the hopes of all those concerned with helping Africa and recognize the existence of formidable external forces, we feel that efforts should be concentrated on the more realistic steps which donors may take in the immediate future. In this respect three areas readily present themselves: (a) policy reforms of individual donors, (b) greater coordination among donors and (c) creation of appropriate new institutional frameworks for channelling additional capital flows to sub-Saharan Africa.

With regard to reforms in policies of donors, I would like to underscore the point that the OPEC Fund is not in a position to advise, let alone lecture the other institutions present, all of which are more experienced and probably better equipped. We can only speak of our modest efforts to devise policies and to streamline our activities in order to produce more satisfactory results. Here, I shall briefly touch upon some aspects of our operational policies which could prove relevant in the ensuing discussions:

First, in our lending activities, we do not follow the policy of 'first come, first served' which is likely to favour the better-off countries. Rather, we devise periodic programs which deliberately favour the poorest countries both in the allocation of funds, in extending technical assistance grants, and in the follow-up and monitoring of projects.

Second, we do not limit our assistance to project aid. We also assist in program financing and balance of payments support, while requiring in both cases the generation of local counterpart funds to be used for agreed development purposes.

Third, it is our policy to give priority to project completion over the financing of new projects. This in turn leads us to accept the financing of cost overruns (when justified), of recurrent costs (in the initial stage of project operation) and of local costs.

Fourth, we try to pay special attention to the institutional aspects of the projects we finance and of the ability of the borrowers to carry out these projects as agreed, even if it means financing such aspects as part of the financing of the project involved.

Fifth, we aim at simplification of lending procedures to facilitate quick disbursement of committed funds, and we deliberately fight what we consider as 'excessive professionalism' on the part of the staffs of some donor agencies.

Sixth, our only conditionality, beyond the technical conditions required for the success of the projects financed, is that funds be used by the recipient country for the agreed purpose and are not diverted to other uses. We feel that the involvement of project financiers in the overall macro-economic policies of the recipient governments which are unrelated to the project at hand, may exceed the limits of their function, and could lead to conflicting advice by different donors which would be harmful to the countries they intend to assist.

Seventh, we value a close working relationship with other donors and do not hesitate to rely on the project appraisals made by them and to appoint them as loan administrators on our behalf, thus saving time and cost.

On the issue of greater coordination among donors, it is important to understand and accept what it presupposes, and what it requires of donors. For us in the OPEC Fund, we take it to pre-suppose mutual confidence among donors based on the complementarity of their individual aid objectives. To bring such a complementarity into greater realization, it would be helpful if the various donors developed some common ideas, if not a concerted aid strategy, particularly in relation to: (a) flexible lending criteria, (b) mechanisms for quick disbursement, (c) simplification of co-financing procedures with a view to shortening the lending process and eliminating unnecessary and cumbersome procedures, and (d) joint action to encourage regional cooperation among neighbouring recipients especially when it is a prerequisite for the sound implementation of projects, as is often the case in the energy sector. All these areas of potential cooperation could be effected through the development of closer working relationships and responsive mechanisms for inter-institutional collaboration.

As for institutional innovations, a host of suggestions have been made for the establishment of new institutional frameworks, which could have important bearing on sub-Saharan Africa. For instance, an energy affiliate at the World Bank, 'Shelter Afrique' at the African Development Bank and a food facility for the Sahel at the Islamic Fund have all been suggested as possible mechanisms to cope with problems confronting the developing countries and particularly the poorer among them.

It is beyond the scope of my remarks here to probe the pros and cons of each of these newly proposed institutional frameworks. Instead, I would like to take this occasion to emphasize, once again, the need for the creation of a multilateral investment corporation to allow the investment of surplus funds in developing countries on the basis of making profits and distributing dividends, to the mutual benefit of the shareholding governments and the host countries. Such a project-oriented and profit-making corporation should find ample opportunities for investment in sub-Saharan Africa. It should be a mechanism of sufficient size and importance to marry investment funds and investment opportunities which currently remain unrealized in many African countries, within a framework that guarantees the security of these investments. The ownership of such a corporation could be shared by OPEC countries, African and other developing countries, and public agencies in the industrialized countries (which could be authorized to sell part of their shares to the private sector). It would present a departure from the typical approach of creating non-profit-making development funds but could work closely with the several funds which exist at present. In fact, there is nothing which logically prevents the implementation of the proposed energy development agency in this form as well.

This proposal is mentioned primarily to emphasize that the lack of enthusiasm in traditional donor circles for increasing their aid efforts at present, though unacceptable, should not stop us from considering other possibilities for channelling resources for the financing of new real investments in Africa. On the contrary. There are also good reasons for the attempt to find ways for investing the surplus funds of some developing countries where a good return is assured in other developing countries, rather than keeping such funds in unproductive 'placements'.

The present problems in sub-Saharan Africa are a challenge to all of us involved in the development process. It is of the utmost importance that we clarify our concerted response to the urgent needs of Africa in a manner commensurate with the dimension of that challenge.

Notes

1. UNCTAD, *Trade and Development Report, 1981.*
2. Coffee, cocoa, cotton and copper constitute about half of the exports of the African countries other than oil.
3. In 1980, 10 developing countries, all outside sub-Saharan Africa, accounted for 70 per cent of the total lending by international commercial banks.
4. Among them the World Bank study, *Accelerated Development in Sub-Saharan Africa.*
5. The first loans extended by the Fund were signed on December 23, 1976.
6. For example, reports of: CILSS/Club de Sahel; FAO, *Agriculture 2000*; the UN Economic Commission for Africa's Lagos Plan of Action; OECD, *Development Review, 1980*; BADEA's study, *Development Prospects in West Africa's Sahel and the Role of Arab Aid*; and the most comprehensive of all, the World Bank's report, *Accelerated Development in Sub-Saharan Africa: An Agenda for Action.*

5 THE OPEC FUND AND THE LEAST DEVELOPED COUNTRIES: AN ORIENTATION TOWARDS THE POOR

I THE OPEC FUND'S ASSISTANCE TO THE LLDCs   *Abdelkader Benamara*

The Least Developed Countries (LLDCs) are characterized by severe impediments to development: a low level of per capita income; a high proportion of the population depending on the agriculture sector and living largely at subsistence level; a low degree of manufacturing activity; a vulnerable and unstable export sector; and very limited skilled manpower and administrative capacity. They include 31 countries comprising a population (mid-1980 estimate) of 276 million, which constitute a target group for the Fund's assistance.

In recent years, economic performance in these countries has at best stagnated, if not worsened. From 1970 to 1979, real gross domestic product increased at an annual average rate of 3.1%. Real per capita GDP, on the other hand, rose by only 0.7% during the same period, owing to a population growth rate of 2.4% per annum. This past trend does not augur well for the development prospects of the LLDCs, unless serious measures are adopted to deal with the bleak economic and social situation prevailing in these countries.

Financial Transfers to the LLDCs

Most of the LLDCs are heavily dependent on foreign assistance. Their economic development cannot rely on the mobilization of their domestic resources alone. Total investment in the LLDCs, according to UNCTAD, amounted to about US$ 60 billion over the period 1970-79. Part of it was made possible through an estimated net inflow of external aid of approximately US$ 38 billion, or over 60% of the total. In this external assistance effort, OPEC member countries played a significant role.

According to OECD, net disbursements to the LLDCs by OPEC member countries in the period 1974-81 totalled over US$ 5.7 billion in concessional aid alone, an annual average of about US$ 715 million. With their general policy of concentrating their efforts on the poorest nations, the OPEC member countries have achieved appreciable results in that direction.

OPEC aid to the LLDCs

Net disbursements of ODA from OPEC member countries to the LLDCs represented about 10.5% on average of the total OPEC concessional assistance to the developing countries during the period 1974-81 (see Table 5). Of this total amount, the share of multilateral aid allocated to the LLDCs was substantially smaller than that of bilateral aid. Between 1974 and 1981, 85% of OPEC aid was extended by bilateral sources, and the rest was provided through multilateral agencies (Tables 17 and 18 in Annex 2 give the details). details).

OPEC member countries provided 0.21% on average of their combined gross national product yearly during the period 1974-81, in the form of concessional assistance to the LLDCs. In comparison, the developed countries that are members of the Development Assistance Committee of the OECD, directed only about 0.06% of their aggregate GNP in aid to the LLDCs. This is one twelfth of the 0.7% target which the International Development Strategy for the Second UN Development Decade suggested as ODA to be extended to all the developing countries.

Table 5: ODA from OPEC Member Countries to the LLDCs, 1974-81 (net disbursements)

| | LLDCs | Overall OPEC aid | Share of LLDCs in overall OPEC aid |
	(US$ million)		(per cent)
1974	417	4,579	9.1
1975	665	6,239	10.7
1976	714	6,098	11.7
1977	935	6,067	15.4
1978	601	8,130	7.4
1979	655	7,691	8.5
1980	899	9,043	9.9
1981	826	7,750	10.7

The minimum of 0.15% of GNP proposed by UN General Assembly Resolution 35/36 to be allocated as ODA to the LLDCs by the first half of the 1980s (to be increased by up to 0.20% during the second half of the decade) has thus already been surpassed by OPEC member countries.

With respect to the adequacy of the overall financial flows channelled so far to the LLDCs, OPEC member countries recognize that there is need for additional resources. Although they themselves have exceeded the targets proposed, they continue to give all due consideration to measures aimed at enhancing financial assistance to the developing countries, with special emphasis on the LLDCs. Proposals to that effect have been put forward within the framework of OPEC's long-term strategy.

The OPEC Fund's Assistance to the LLDCs

One of the specific provisions in the Fund's constituent agreement stipulates that special attention be paid to the needs of the less developed among the eligible developing countries. Since its inception, the Fund has reserved a large share of its assistance for the LLDCs. Particular efforts have been, and continue to be, made to reach these countries, where economic and social conditions are notably harsh. Aware of the enormous difficulties and the arduous development task with which the LLDCs are confronted, the Fund has treated this group of countries on a priority basis.

Loans. The Fund has so far provided about US$ 670 million in direct aid to the LLDCs in the form of balance of payments support and development project and program financing: Thus, 83 BOP support loans totalling US$ 304.02 million (see Table 6) and 62 project and program loans in the amount of US$ 365.54 million have been extended to 30 LLDCs. The total amount committed to the LLDCs in the form of direct loans, represented, up to January 19, 1983, 38.4% of the total loan amount of US$ 1,743.335 million extended by the Fund. All loans to the LLDCs have been provided free of interest, and in most cases with long maturities and grace periods. Owing to these soft terms, the grant element or concessionality of the loans has been significantly high.

As shown in Table 19 in Annex 2, 40.4% of all project loans to the LLDCs were directed to the energy sector. This emphasis encourages the LLDCs to rely on their domestic sources of energy by developing and utilizing them efficiently, thus reducing their

Table 6: The OPEC Fund's Total Direct Loans to the LLDCs to
January 19, 1983 (amounts in US$ million)

Country	Project	BOP	Program	Total
Afghanistan	3.55	3.75	—	7.30
Bangladesh	83.00	38.90	7.00	128.90
Benin	18.60	6.50	—	25.10
Botswana	4.00	3.00	—	7.00
Burundi	12.00	6.20	—	18.20
Cape Verde	1.50	6.05	—	7.55
Central African Republic	5.10	1.75	—	6.85
Chad	2.45	2.40	—	4.85
Comoros	3.00	2.00	—	5.00
Ethiopia	—	4.80	—	4.80
Gambia, The	—	9.15	—	9.15
Guinea	11.00	10.85	—	21.85
Guinea-Bissau	—	8.65	—	8.65
Haiti	7.50	3.15	—	10.65
Laos PDR	4.00	2.15	6.50	12.65
Lesotho	3.00	5.90	—	8.90
Malawi	1.80	—	—	1.80
Maldives	1.88	3.42	—	5.30
Mali	13.45	28.05	—	41.50
Nepal	39.70	4.15	—	43.85
Niger	—	16.75	—	16.75
Rwanda	2.35	9.20	—	11.55
Somalia	8.16	25.05	—	33.21
Sudan	20.45	33.45	—	53.90
Tanzania	32.00	20.45	—	52.45
Uganda	15.00	4.55	5.00	24.55
Upper Volta	4.50	27.75	—	32.25
Western Samoa	—	5.35	—	5.35
Yemen AR	27.05	2.25	—	29.30
Yemen PDR	22.00	8.40	—	30.40
Total	347.04	304.02	18.50	669.56

dependence on imported fuel. A number of LLDCs have potential
for increasing their energy self-reliance. Chad and Sudan have
proven oil reserves; Afghanistan and Bangladesh have natural gas
reserves. Coal exists in Bangladesh, Botswana, Burundi and
Tanzania. Hydroelectric potential is quite significant in the LLDCs:
according to the 1980 World Bank study, *Energy in the developing*

countries, 20 LLDCs account for some 24% of the hydroelectric power potential in all the net-oil-importing developing countries. Many LLDCs have a remarkable potential in biomass, geothermal and wind energy sources as well.

The Fund has extended financial assistance to hydroelectric power projects in Laos, Nepal and Rwanda: power distribution systems in Bangladesh, Nepal, Tanzania, Yemen AR and Yemen PDR; and a gas project in Bangladesh which included a well-drilling program and the construction of gas gathering and conditioning facilities. In Tanzania, two projects for hydrocarbon exploration have benefitted from the Fund's loans. The Fund has also extended loans for thermal power projects in Bangladesh and Mali. The project in Mali consists of the construction of a thermal power plant at Mopti/Sevare which will use rice husks as fuel. Finally, the Fund recently provided financing for a fuelwood development project in Benin to help alleviate an acute shortage of energy for domestic uses.

The second largest share (32.7%) of the Fund's project lending to LLDCs has gone to the transportation sector and its related infrastructure. This sector is a very critical one in the LLDCs, constituting a major bottleneck which impedes economic progress. Its problems are related to weak institutional frameworks, shortages of spare parts, lack of equipment, and inadequate repair and maintenance facilities. The Fund has financed the construction and rehabilitation of roads in Afghanistan, Benin, Botswana, the Central African Republic, Comoros, Malawi, Mali, Sudan, Upper Volta, the Yemen AR, and Yemen PDR. Emphasis has been placed on institution building, and on consolidation, expansion and rational development of the highway sector.

The Fund has also participated in airport projects in Bangladesh, Botswana, Lesotho, Maldives and Nepal; provided financial assistance for an inter-island transport system in the Maldives; and contributed to the expansion of the Comoros' main port, Mutsamudu.

The agriculture sector has received 10.4% of the Fund's total direct lending. In Bangladesh, the Fund has financed the local production of fertilizer. It has been involved in rural development projects in Benin and Burundi; in forestry development in Nepal; in irrigation in Chad; and in sugar production in Burundi and Somalia. Direct lending to the agriculture sector by the Fund is supplemented by lines of credit to national development banks, whose proceeds are partially earmarked for that sector. A large portion of the Fund's

BOP support loans has also been used to import foodstuffs, equipment and spare parts essential to the agriculture sector. In addition, local counterpart funds approved so far for use in financing the local costs of agricultural projects and programs have amounted to the equivalent of US$ 60.7 million. The Fund has also contributed to IFAD as explained in Chapter 7.

To help ensure an adequate supply of safe water and basic sanitation, the Fund has helped finance projects in the public utilities sector in Burundi, Haiti, Somalia and the Yemen PDR. Lines of credit have been made available to Benin, Haiti and Uganda through their national development banks and their proceeds have been made available to small farmers, artisans and small agricultural and industrial enterprises. Cape Verde received a loan to be used in the upgrading of its telecommunications system. Guinea benefitted from the Fund's assistance in its efforts to rehabilitate and promote industrial enterprises; and a loan was provided to Tanzania for the building of an integrated pulp and paper mill.

Besides engaging in project financing, the Fund has extended program loans to Bangladesh, the Lao PDR and Uganda. In Bangladesh, the proceeds of the loan served to finance imports of rock phosphate and finished fertilizers. In Laos, two loans were provided, which were used for the purchase of spare parts and plant for the construction of reservoirs that are part of an agricultural rehabilitation and development program in the Vientiane Plain. In Uganda, the loan supports the rehabilitation program being under-taken by the Government in order to revive the economy.

A large share of the Fund's loans, about 38%, has been allocated to the LLDCs (see Table 7). The target of 30% of total aid suggested by the UN Conference on the LLDCs has therefore been exceeded. The absolute amount of BOP support totalled US$ 304.02 million up to January 19, 1983, compared with US$ 347.04 million for projects and US$ 18.50 million for programs. The large sum provided for BOP assistance reflects the importance given to such assistance to the LLDCs, as they often find themselves short of much-needed foreign exchange.

Mobilization of Local Counterpart Funds. Supplementary resources used by the LLDCs in support of their social and development efforts consist of local counterpart funds generated under the Fund's BOP support and program loans. The amount mobilized is used, upon agreement with the Fund, in the financing of the local costs of

Table 7: The OPEC Fund's Lending Operations in the LLDCs
Relative to Total Lending Activities, to January 19, 1983

	Total US$ million	LLDCs US$ million	as per cent of total
Project financing	1,033.965	347.040	33.6
BOP support	661.870	304.020	45.9
Program financing	47.500	18.500	38.9
Total	1,743.335	669.560	38.4

development projects or programs in the recipient countries. These funds are particularly helpful for the LLDCs when their limited capacity to mobilize domestic savings is considered Local counterpart funds have to date been utilized by 28 countries in the group of LLDCs, and the equivalent of about US$ 172 million has been approved by the Fund for the partial financing of 85 projects and programs (see Table 20 in Annex 2).

Technical Assistance. Technical assistance constitutes an integral element of the Fund's activities. In the case of the LLDCs, this assistance is particularly essential to development. The Fund is involved in the financing, through grants, of technical assistance programs which have benefitted a large number of LLDCs. These programs, designed to meet the development requirements of the recipient countries, are to promote technical cooperation and foster economic integration among developing countries. They embrace nearly all sectors and cover a wide geographical area, as the following examples indicate:

*Hydrological forecasting system for the Niger River Basin (US$ 5 million). This program covers West African countries of which six are LLDCs, namely Benin, Chad, Guinea-Bissau, Mali, Niger and Upper Volta. As early as 1963, the nine countries concerned entered into a joint agreement establishing the River Niger Commission to encourage, promote and coordinate studies and programs related to exploration and development of the river basin's resources.
*Development of the Red Sea and Gulf of Aden Fisheries (US$ 7.64 million). Five LLDCs — Ethiopia, Somalia, Sudan, the Yemen AR and the Yemen PDR — are involved in this program

aimed at ensuring a rational exploitation through comprehensive planning of the fishery activities in the area.

*Desert Locust Emergency Assistance (US$ 1 million) was set up to help contain the spread of locusts in many Asian and African countries, and to strengthen national and regional capabilities for controlling locust invasions.

*The International Research Center for Diarrhoeal Disease in Bangladesh (US$ 1.6 million). The Center was established in order to undertake research, training and dissemination of information about one of the most lethal groups of diseases in the developing world. The activities of the Center promote the development of advanced health care methods and improved public health programs.

*The Onchocerciasis (river blindness) Control Program for West Africa (US$ 2 million), has as its objective, control of the spread of this disease in the Volta River Basin in West Africa.

*Nine research centers supported by the Consultative Group on International Agricultural Research (US$ 8.17 million). The basic objective of the centers is to improve food production through research, training, and the provision of technical assistance to national and regional research programs.

*Programs of labor-intensive public works in Burundi, Nepal and Tanzania (US$ 1.3 million). Initiated in 1975 by the United Nations Development Program, the programs benefit the poor unskilled labor force in the rural areas by creating employment.

*The Agency for the Safety of Aerial Navigation in Africa received a grant of US$ 1 million. Its objectives are (i) to ensure the safety and regularity of all civil aviation activities in the airspace above the territories of the member countries; (ii) to increase the member countries' capacity in the area of telecommunications administration; and (iii) to expand training facilities. The Fund's grant is to help finance a program designed to rehabilitate and improve the telecommunications equipment in five countries, of which three are LLDCs, namely Mali, Niger and Upper Volta.

*US$ 5 million was provided to the West African Economic Community (CEAO) for the partial financing of its Solar Energy Regional Center. The CEAO aims at promoting trade relations between its six member countries, three of which are LLDCs — Mali, Niger and Upper Volta. Other LLDCs, members of the Permanent Inter-State Committee for Drought Control in the

Sahel (CILSS) are also involved in the establishment of the Center. They are Cape Verde, Chad and the Gambia. The role of the Center is that of a catalyst for industrial production and a promoter of industrial projects involving renewable energy.

*Part of the proceeds of a grant of US$ 25 million committed to the International Emergency Food Reserve, which is jointly administered by the World Food Program and the UN Food and Agricultural Organization, was used to purchase foodstuffs for Bangladesh, Ethiopia, Somalia and Tanzania. The foodstuffs originated in food-exporting developing countries that agreed to offer concessional terms.

In addition to the above operations, the Fund has contributed to the Rural Water Supply and Sanitation Program of the United Nations Children's Fund (UNICEF). It has extended grants to assist UNICEF's activities in three African countries most in need, namely Benin, Cape Verde and Sudan. A total amount of US$ 3 million has been approved for the three LLDCs. The proceeds of the grants will cover the foreign exchange expenditures of UNICEF-sponsored water supply and sanitation programs. The Fund has also approved grants in the amount of US$ 501,600 to assist projects in two LLDCs sponsored by the United Nations Interim Fund for Science and Technology for Development. One project in Lesotho will help in the development of domestic energy resources, i.e. solar energy and biogas production. The second project in the Yemen AR aims at increasing the domestic consumption of local crops, such as sorghum, millet and maize, and thus at reducing the large imports of wheat.

Other Assistance to the LLDCs. The LLDCs have benefitted not only from the resources described thus far, but also from the assistance extended by multilateral organizations to which the Fund has contributed. These are mainly the International Fund for Agricultural Development (IFAD) already mentioned, the Trust Fund administered by the International Monetary Fund (IMF), and the Common Fund for Commodities.

A number of LLDCs have received aid from IFAD, whose objective is to expand food production, alleviate rural poverty, and ameliorate the nutritional standards of the poorest segments of the population in developing countries. IFAD's cumulative total lending to the LLDCs amounted to US$ 482.3 million by the end of 1982. This sum constitutes 32.3% of all IFAD's loans to developing countries, which totalled US\$ 1,492.2 million during the same period. In addition, IFAD provided technical assistance grants to developing countries totalling about US\$ 63 million, part of which benefitted the LLDCs. OPEC member countries, which have contributed through the Fund a large sum to the initial resources of IFAD, have also recently made pledges to the first replenishment of that agency. By the end of 1982, over US\$ 861 million had been allocated to IFAD, including a special grant contribution of US\$ 20 million made by the Fund. This grant enabled IFAD to reach its replenishment target and conclude the first replenishment process.

OPEC representatives in IFAD's governing bodies have always stressed that priority should be given to the LLDCs in IFAD's activities. The agricultural sector is predominant in the LLDCs and is estimated to be the source of income for more than 80% of the population. Its performance has been very poor as a result of numerous factors, such as a lack of basic physical and financial inputs, namely fertilizers, pesticides, credit, etc.; a deficient infrastructure with respect to transport, distribution and marketing; and lack of incentives offered to producers. These problems need to be addressed seriously, as the overall economic and social development of the LLDCs depends upon the growth achieved in the agriculture sector.

The IMF Trust Fund. Irrevocable transfers have been made to the Trust Fund administered by the IMF of the profits realized by seven OPEC member countries (US\$ 110.7 million) from the sale of the IMF's gold. The Trust Fund was established in May 1976 for the benefit of eligible low-income developing countries (LLDCs in many cases) and assists them with their balance of payments difficulties by providing highly concessional assistance. All LLDCs that are members of the IMF qualify for Trust Fund loans. Loan disbursements to these countries totalled SDR 141.54 million in 1979, SDR 174.3 million in 1980, and SDR 2.12 million in the first three months of 1981. The final loan disbursements were made in March 1981 and the Trust Fund was terminated in April 1981.

The Common Fund for Commodities. The Fund's role as coordinator of the OPEC member countries in the establishment of the Common Fund for Commodities was itself a commitment in support of the LLDCs. The common fund proposal was the main element of the Integrated Program for Commodities adopted at UNCTAD IV in

Nairobi in 1976, and represents a step towards the implementation of a New International Economic Order. The developing countries, among them the LLDCs, will play a role in the management of this new institution, which is aimed at improving the prevailing market structures for internationally-traded commodities. Through its First Account, the Common Fund will finance buffer stocks and inter-nationally-coordinated national stocks. Its Second Account, on the other hand, is intended to finance measures other than stocking, and to promote related coordination and consultation. OPEC member countries have agreed to cover, through the Fund, the subscriptions to the Directly Contributed Capital of the Common Fund of each of the LLDCs and four other developing countries. The contribution of the Fund for that purpose totals US$ 37.16 million, out of which US$ 32.94 million benefits the LLDCs. The contribution is in the form of grants. A large number of grant agreements have already been concluded between the Fund and the LLDCs. By the end of 1982, 22 LLDCs had taken advantage of the Fund's assistance in the total amount of US$ 23.72 million. In addition, the Fund has pledged a voluntary contribution of US$ 46.4 million to the Second Account of the Common Fund, which is designed to benefit the poorer countries in particular.

Action in the 80s

The economic and social problems facing the LLDCs are not unique to this group of countries. They also exist to a certain extent in the other developing countries, the difference being one of degree rather than of nature; these same problems are chronic and more serious in the LLDCs. It is recognized, however, that particular measures should be adopted with respect to the poorer countries with the most critical and overwhelming needs. In global discussions, more emphasis could be placed on their specific characteristics and preoccupations, not losing sight of realistic possibilities and expectations.

Essentially, renewed efforts by the international community need to be combined with those of the LLDCs, both at the national and regional levels. A determined and concerted action should provide the basis for a quickened pace of development in the LLDCs.

Concerning external financial and technical assistance, larger amounts are needed. Countries starting from a very low level of development are faced with a difficult task in their efforts to educate and train personnel, accumulate capital, and install and operate productive facilities. External help through soft loans, grants and investments, which assists in providing supplies, equipment and technical services, can alleviate the strains of the early stages of development. External aid, correctly timed and in adequate amounts, may make it possible to derive tangible results, although it is realized that such aid by itself cannot solve the problems of the LLDCs.

It is to be stressed that the Fund is well aware of the crucial role which external concessional assistance plays in helping the LLDCs in their social and economic development. It intends to continue to provide such aid and expand it, and special emphasis has been placed on the LLDCs in all of the Fund's lending programs.

Besides external aid, other measures related to the existing structures and practices in the world economic system, whether in the areas of trade, primary commodities, energy, food, money and finance, transfer of technology etc, are required. New mechanisms, procedures and incentives in favour of the LLDCs can advance the mobilization and more efficient use of available resources. It is hoped that the specific mandate received by the UN Conference on the LLDCs to 'finalize and support' the new Program of Action for the 1980s will meet these countries' expectations. More importantly, the agreed program should be followed by serious action. A larger measure of regional cooperation is also needed among the LLDCs if they are to maximize the utilization of their limited resources. It is fair to call on the LLDCs to exert greater efforts towards furthering such cooperation while aspiring to increased support from other countries.

II THE NEED FOR COMMITMENT*
Dr Ibrahim F.I. Shihata

Of all existing international development finance institutions, the OPEC Fund for International Development can be most appropriately identified as a fund of the Third World, an energy fund, and a fund of the poorer countries. It is this latter characteristic of the Fund, and indeed of OPEC aid in general, on which I wish to elaborate.

Even before such terms as the Least Developed Countries and the

* This section is based on an address delivered by the Director-General of the OPEC Fund, Dr Ibrahim F.I. Shihata, before the United Nations Conference on the LLDCs which was held in Paris from September 1-14, 1981.

Most Seriously Affected Countries were coined by the United Nations, OPEC donors had concentrated their assistance efforts on the poorest developing countries. The countries included in the two groups I have just mentioned have in fact received about 50% of OPEC aid in general and 73% of the assistance directly provided by the Fund. According to DAC, OPEC donors gave, during the period 1974-81, an average of about 10.5% of their total net aid disbursements to the LLDCs as a group. But this refers only to direct assistance from OPEC countries and institutions, and does not include the indirect aid channelled through other multilateral agencies. This level of assistance to the LLDCs is, at any rate, equivalent to about 0.21% of the total gross national product of OPEC donors. In comparison, the target sought by the Group of 77 for official development assistance to the LLDCs has been set at the lower level of 0.15% of the donor's GNP. It may be added that the DAC countries during the same period, gave the equivalent of only 0.06% of their GNP to the LLDCs.

Concentration of OPEC countries' assistance efforts on the world's poorest nations naturally led to the result that their assistance bore no relationship to the volume or cost of oil imported by the recipient countries. As is well known, more than 70% of the Third World's oil imports are accounted for by eight developing countries, most of which are semi-industrialized. The 31 LLDCs account for no more than 4% of the oil imported by developing countries. Thus, if OPEC aid were tied to the cost of oil imports, the LLDCs would have received far less in aid from OPEC sources. In fact, this group of countries received in the period 1974-81 about US$ 5 billion in direct grants and soft loans from OPEC countries. This amount exceeded the incremental cost of their oil imports over the same period. This, I should add, has taken place in spite of the fact that the volume of oil imports of the LLDCs increased by an annual average of 5% in this period.

What I have just mentioned is by no means intended to suggest that enough has been done to help the LLDCs in their development efforts. I shall be the first to call for greater assistance in this area, from all those who are in a position to extend it. I meant simply to underline two facts which until now have not, unfortunately, been clearly established in the minds of the public.

The first is that OPEC countries' assistance to the LLDCs represents, in relative terms, more than other donor groups have given, and even exceeds, by more than 150%, the projected target for aid to the LLDCs established by the United Nations.

The second is that OPEC aid efforts to the LLDCs as a group, have surpassed in volume any additional cost the recipient countries may have incurred as a result of the increase in oil prices, despite the steady rise of the volume of their oil imports.

As developing countries themselves, OPEC countries realize the extent of the needs to be met, and the tremendous efforts which have yet to be exerted both by the LLDCs and their sources of external assistance. The liquidity which some of the OPEC countries have at present is not to be mistaken as a sign of added income, as it merely represents another form of their mineral wealth, which is fast being depleted. Yet they are using a generous part of it to assist other developing countries and will obviously continue to do so as long as they can afford it.

To our knowledge, no international development institution has put as much emphasis on the LLDCs in its operations as the Fund; 145 loans totalling US$ 670 million have so far been extended by the Fund to these countries, representing more than 38% of its total lending. The Fund's grant programs are also designed to benefit the poorest countries. We are happy to see the same philosophy prevailing in the other international institutions which receive significant financing from the Fund, such as the International Fund for Agricultural Development.

In the Fund's programs of operations, all the LLDCs are included in the priority list of recipient countries. I would like to take this opportunity to assure the governments of those LLDCs of our continued readiness to participate in the financing of their development projects and programs. As before, the Fund will continue to exert maximum flexibility in dealing with the LLDCs, both in considering the types of financing to be extended and in devising the rules and procedures to be followed. It is a regrettable fact, however, that the LLDCs themselves do not always make use of the resources made available to them including those of the Fund.

I would like to conclude with a few remarks which should be taken merely as the view of the management of the Fund, derived from its own modest experience:

(1) We do not share the view, which seems at present to be gaining ground in certain Western circles, according to which first, the poor nations are to be blamed for their poverty, and second, the present international economic system allows for enough 'social mobility'

among nations. On the contrary we believe that the developing countries which have managed to achieve some measure of prosperity under the present system have done so in spite of the system, and not thanks to it.

(2) We do agree, however, that development starts at home. While we call for a new international economic order, we must ensure that new domestic economic orders are being introduced, whereby a greater discipline in the economic management of developing countries is coupled with a more equitable distribution of income and a more serious dedication to developmental objectives.

(3) We also believe that the poorest countries of the world should not take their present population growth rates as an irreversible trend, and should more clearly realize the tragic aspects of the demographic dimension, if left unchecked. This dimension should not be treated as merely a health problem, as is often the case in developing countries. It should receive the attention it deserves at the national level as a challenge of the highest political order.

(4) Furthermore, we feel that the financial problems of developing countries differ in their causes and magnitudes from one country to another, and cannot, therefore, be subject to uniform solutions. Most of the suggestions considered at present for easing the financial burdens of developing countries, such as greater access to capital markets and the elimination of trade barriers in manufactures, may indeed be of little or no relevance as far as the LLDCs are concerned. For these countries, we believe that it is necessary:

  *to ensure a greater flow of external resources on the softest possible terms; and
  *to ensure that such resources, together with the little domestic savings that can be mobilized, are used in the most effective manner.

To that end, the LLDCs are best advised not to fall prey to the vicious circle of international conferences issuing elaborate and often unrealistic plans of action. They may better concentrate on business-like discussions with interested sources of assistance on the ways and means of increasing the volume, effectiveness and complementarity of such assistance, taking into consideration that additional capital, though necessary, cannot alone solve complex development problems. Politically stable systems run by dedicated individuals and assisted by well-managed institutions have proven to be more important in the development process than ready access to abundant funds and natural resources.

(5) The development process as experienced in the developed countries, with its patterns of excessive consumption and its oil-based technologies, simply does not, in our view, suit present conditions in the LLDCs. It must give way to new development patterns which promote less wasteful consumption and greater energy efficiency.

(6) External sources of development assistance should realize the need for special treatment of the LLDCs. This special treatment may best be reflected in:

   *devising simpler procedures for lending to them;
   *giving greater attention to technical assistance, especially in project identification and preparation, and in the process of institution-building;
   *providing greater assistance and closer supervision in the execution of projects; and
   *taking a more flexible attitude in meeting the recurrent and local costs of development projects and programs.

(7) Last, but not least, we feel that, as they aspire to greater cooperation from external sources, the LLDCs should prove, through their own domestic action and regional co-operation among themselves, that serious indigenous developmental efforts are being exerted and deserve to be supported.

The greatest incentive to the donors is indeed to see the positive results of their assistance, and its impact in helping the recipient countries achieve a greater measure of self-reliance. The best achievement of all for the LLDCs is to prove, through their serious efforts and dedication, that this unfortunate name which the world community has given them is a misnomer, and that, although financially weak at present, they are reliable partners in the struggle toward world prosperity.

6 INNOVATIVE FORMS OF COOPERATION: THE OPEC FUND'S APPROACH

Dr Ibrahim F.I. Shihata and Dr T. Wohlers-Scharf

I INSTITUTIONAL COOPERATION AND CO-FINANCING WITH OTHER DONOR AGENCIES

In some ways, the establishment of the OPEC Fund at a late stage[1] proved to be an advantage, particularly in relation to the diversity of its operations and the innovations it has pioneered. On the one hand, the Fund operates under more liberal articles of agreement than most of those governing older donor agencies; on the other, it has no long-established policies which might otherwise have proved to be barriers when introducing, or even testing, new ideas.

The Fund's areas of cooperation with other agencies can be classified in three broad categories:

1. to support new institutions and to develop new aid policies that will contribute to changes in international economic relations;
2. to establish dynamic working relationships with all major international development finance institutions, including especially those of OPEC members; and
3. to co-finance projects and programs with other sources of development finance, that is with other donor agencies, but now also with an orientation to cooperate with commercially-motivated institutions.

The Fund's philosophy of development is based on the conviction that development must start at home through domestic discipline and efforts. Although external assistance is necessary for many LDCs, it should not be considered as an endless process, but as support during

1. In terms of years of operations the OPEC Fund for International Development is the youngest international development finance agency, with the exception of IFAD whose constituent agreement was finalized at the same time as the initial agreement establishing the Fund.

a transitional period leading eventually to mutually beneficial economic cooperation. Given the inequities of the present world order, balanced economic growth in LDCs can only be achieved — beyond the problems of finance — through processes of change. Therefore, the Fund is promoting new institutions, and developing and testing new concepts. The main objectives of all these endeavours are to provide the prerequisites of progress by enlarging the institutional infrastructure which is essential for more constructive and successful international collaboration.

One of the many examples of this conceptual approach is the participation of the Fund in the creation of IFAD, as discussed in Chapter 7. Another is given by the Fund's task of coordinating the position of OPEC countries in the negotiations, and by providing financial support, for the establishment of the Common Fund for Commodities (see also Chapter 7). Grants by the Fund have also been made to finance a number of the United Nations Development Program's (UNDP) and the Latin American Energy Organization's (OLADE) regional technical assistance projects. The most recent institution-building endeavours of the Fund include two initiatives early in 1983: supporting the establishment of the International Development Law Institute (IDLI), to be set up in Rome, and the African Center for Fertilizer Development (ACFD), to be set up in Harare, Zimbabwe.

The Fund established, in a short period, dynamic working relationships with most major development finance institutions. These relationships covered a wide range of activities, surpassing the usual exchange of information, mutual attendance at annual meetings, etc, to culminate in the pooling of resources for the financing of development projects. Inter-institutional cooperation was thus particularly important in relation to co-financing activities.

Coordination with Other Development Organizations

The emergence and rapid rise of OPEC aid and OPEC donors in the 1970s made coordination of the aid policies of the group desirable, if not mandatory. The heads of states of the OPEC countries, at the summit meeting in 1975, declared their intention of intensifying and coordinating their aid programs. This has been partly achieved through the Ministerial Council and the Governing Board of the OPEC Fund.

Close ties with other OPEC/Arab institutions are exemplified by the coordination meetings, which since the mid-1970s, have taken place twice a year at the director-of-operations level and less often at the head-of-agency level within the framework of the Coordination Secretariat of Arab Development Funds. The Secretariat was established prior to the creation of the Fund and the Fund preferred to join its efforts rather than duplicate them, in an area which, by definition, defies duplication. The Fund hosted these meetings several times and contributed, together with other agencies, to the harmonization and simplification of operational procedures, the exchange of information on new projects, joint appraisal and supervisory missions, etc. These coordinated procedures have enabled the Fund, as well as the Arab aid agencies, to broaden the geographical coverage of their activities, to accelerate their assistance activities, and to economize on staff resources.

OPEC/Arab donor agencies have coordinated their aid policies not only among themselves, but also with other international and regional donors. Since 1978, OPEC/Arab agencies have met annually with DAC member countries and their respective donor agencies for an informal exchange of information, and to discuss possibilities for improved cooperation. Since 1980, these meetings have been co-chaired by the Director-General of the OPEC Fund. The 1983 meeting was held at the Fund's new headquarters premises in Vienna, and, for the first time, major commercial banks were invited to join in the discussions.

OPEC/Arab aid agencies have also started to hold meetings with the Commission of the European Economic Communities, the European Development Fund and the European Investment Bank. A growing number of OPEC/Arab aid agencies have followed the Fund in taking part in the high-level conference of the Club du Sahel, which attempts to harmonize the aid policies of donors towards the Sahel region. From 1983 onwards, there will also be coordination meetings between OPEC/Arab aid agencies and the IBRD, following the first meeting to this effect hosted by the OPEC Fund.

With regard to cooperation with international and regional organizations, the OPEC Fund's representatives have attended regularly the annual meetings of the World Bank Group, the IMF, the three regional development banks (IDB, AfDB and ADB) and some of the subregional agencies such as the Caribbean Development Bank. Such attendance provided opportunities for close contacts which yielded fruitful results, without being preceded by the typical 'framework cooperation agreements' which are often entered into by other agencies. The Fund has also participated in a number of meetings involving various donors including the United Nations Conference on New and Renewable Energy Sources, held in Nairobi in 1981 and the United Nations Conference on the Least Developed Countries, held in Paris in the same year. All of these meetings provided an opportunity for expressing the Fund's views and policies on development issues and for promoting its flexible approach to development financing.

A special feature of the Fund's cooperation is its close relationship with the national development agencies of its member countries. According to the *Agreement Establishing the OPEC Special Fund*, each OPEC member country designated a national institution to act as its executing national agency. Most OPEC member countries which have national institutions for development assistance designated these institutions as their executing national agencies. Thus the Fund developed, almost automatically, a close relationship with Arab donor agencies, paving the way also for close cooperation in co-financing activities.

Co-financing and Loan Administration

Co-financing (i.e. joining with other organizations to finance development projects or programs) is an area of cooperation of particular significance to the Fund, which has relied extensively on this technique from the start of its operations. Nearly all of its projects, with a few exceptions, are also co-financed by other sources.

The Fund's Agreement reflected the intention of cooperating with other development finance institutions by utilizing their appraising and loan-administering facilities. Thus the Fund was able to benefit in an optimum way from existing facilities, while maintaining flexibility and accelerating development performance. Under the original agreement, projects to be financed by the Fund had to be appraised by an appropriate international development agency, or an executing national agency, or another agency of an OPEC member country. Once a project had been approved for financing, the Governing Board again entrusted an executing national agency, or an international development agency of a world-wide or regional character, with the administration of the loan. Before the amendment of the agreement on May 27, 1980, both procedures were mandatory. Since that date, the Fund has had the power to appraise and administer project loans directly along with the possibility of entrusting such tasks to other agencies.

The Fund's Governing Board also gave clear priority to the co-financing of projects, on a joint or parallel basis, with either inter-national, regional and/or national development finance agencies. The Fund's experience was that it could expand its activities much faster in this way, while keeping down its own costs and the size of its staff. Through co-financing arrangements, the Fund extended, within less than seven years, concessional finance to about 170 projects and programs in more than 80 countries.[2] Many of these projects involved more than one co-financier, allowing a choice in selecting the administrator of the loan. Even in cases where the Fund was the sole external co-financier, it was possible to entrust the tasks of loan appraisal and/or loan administration — at no cost to the Fund — to other international development institutions.

The advantages of co-financing were not restricted to the Fund's savings in time and cost. Often such arrangements facilitated, or even made possible, the implementation of projects that otherwise might have been postponed *ad infinitum*, or only have been financed later at substantially higher costs for the developing country concerned.

By providing the required complementary finance for a project — which is often only a small fraction of the total cost of the project — substantially larger amounts are deployed for developmental purposes. Furthermore, co-financing brings about closer and continuous contacts among the various sources of external develop-ment assistance, which may lead later to other financial packages for the same, or other recipients.

Through such international financial interactions, more-recently-established agencies have benefitted from the experience of longer-established institutions, and the latter may have learned to appreciate the more flexible ways of the former, possibly with mutually positive impacts on their policies. Such positive aspects have already been demonstrated, in the experience of the Fund, especially in the early stages of loan negotiations and in the details of the lines of credit jointly extended to national development finance institutions.

Recent Trends and Future Areas of Cooperation

Given the present financial position of OPEC countries, the finite basis of their wealth, and their continuing commitments to South-

2. The above figures do not include the 42 technical assistance projects and 32 intellectual grants for research and studies, as well as 171 projects and programs financed through local counterpart funds generated under the Fund's balance of payments (BOP) support and program loans, of which many are also co-financed by other sources.

South cooperation, the assistance strategies of OPEC donors are likely to change in the 1980s. In view of the difficulty of forecasting future events, only general trends and orientations can be discerned. In this context, however, it is nearly certain that a more balanced and mutually beneficial pattern of cooperation will eventually replace lopsided relationships between OPEC donors and their beneficiaries.

The areas with great potential for expanded cooperation include trade, technical cooperation — preferably in an institutionalized frame — and co-financing with commercial sources and direct investment. The Fund has already started action in these areas. It has always been keen to identify and implement activities which offer remedies for pressing development problems, and which would have a mutually beneficial impact on all groups of LDCs. Thus the promotion of economic cooperation among developing countries is part of the Fund's core policies.

Trade. Trade relationships between OPEC countries and other developing countries have witnessed significant growth since 1973. The full potential for expanded trade cooperation between LDCs is nevertheless far from being exploited. Institutional and legal mechanisms including export credit arrangements, insurance and re-insurance schemes, *inter alia*, are required to facilitate greater exchanges among developing countries.

The Fund took an innovative initiative in the area of food assistance by promoting trade under a preferential arrangement.[3] It extended a grant of US$25 million for the period 1981-2 to the International Emergency Food Reserve (IEFR) which is jointly administered by the World Food Program (WFP) and the Food and Agricultural Organization of the United Nations (FAO).

The Fund's financial assistance was used for the purchase of foodstuffs from food-exporting developing countries which agreed to offer concessional terms. It was also used to cover the transportation costs of these commodities as well as those of food donated to WFP by developing countries. LDCs eligible for food aid financed by the Fund's grant were those food deficit nations with a per capita income in 1979 of less than US$500.

At the Fund's initiative, Argentina offered concessional selling terms: a price rebate of 10% on the cif value of food purchased from

---

3. The OPEC Fund for International Development, *Annual Report 1981*, Vienna, p. 24.

that country under the Fund's grant. It also expressed its willingness to enter into the same arrangements for the use of the Fund's BOP assistance for the purchase of foodstuffs from Argentina. Other food-exporting developing countries expressed their willingness to cooperate with WFP, and offered concessional terms for purchases under the Fund's grant.

Technical Cooperation and Institution-building. In this field the Fund was instrumental, in early 1983, in making the innovative initiatives mentioned previously, that contributed to the establishment of two international institutes in important, but not sufficiently supported areas, for LDCs. The African Center for Fertilizer Development's (ACFD) main objectives are to promote improved techniques of fertilizer production, to support research on the role of fertilizers in improving agricultural output, to establish responsible links with national, regional and international centers also concerned with fertilizer use and management, and to foster training. The Fund hosted the meeting which launched ACFD, participated in the preparation of its basic documents and in the initial arrangements for its management by the International Fertilizer Development Center (IFDC), and provided a grant of US$500,000 to finance its first program. The Fund also approved the use of US$3 million in local counterpart funds for the construction of ACFD's headquarters.

The second initiative related to the establishment of the International Development Law Institute (IDLI),[4] as an international non-governmental organization. Its main objectives are to improve the use of legal resources in the development process, to improve the negotiating capability of LDCs in the fields of development assistance, trade and foreign investments, to increase the efficiency of project implementation and to promote simplification and harmonization of rules and procedures related to external finance. In order to achieve its stated objectives, IDLI will have a program with three components: practical training (in financing agency regulations, business transactions and their legal aspects); technical assistance on law-related development problems; and documentation services.

The need for an institute for training and research on the legal aspects of external development finance had long been recognized.[5]

4. *OPEC Bulletin*, Vol. XIV, No. 3, Vienna, April 1983, pp. 84 and 85.
5. For an early promotion of the establishment of a facility for this purpose, see Ibrahim Shihata, 'Role of Law in Economic Development', *Egyptian Review of International Law*, Vol. 25 (1969), p. 119.

The Fund provided a grant of US$200,000 to support IDLI by providing scholarships for developing country lawyers to attend its first training program.

Cooperation with Commercial Sources. The OPEC Fund — with the objective of examining possibilities for greater cooperation aimed at increasing the size and volume of transfers to LDCs — took the occasion of hosting the sixth annual meeting of OPEC/Arab Funds with OECD/DAC members in mid-1983, to invite major commercial banks, both from Arab and Western countries, to attend. The agenda focused on co-financing among donor agencies and commercial sources of finance, and took into consideration the changed international situation of the early 1980s. Through this initiative, the Fund launched a challenge in difficult times, both for the North and the South, by discussing the possibilities of cooperation among all sources of finance to the LDCs. There is plenty of scope for developing countries to implement co-financing arrangements involving concessional and non-concessional sources. The Fund's intention was not only to spearhead a forum for discussion, but to support a corresponding strategy at operational level.

II NEW BUSINESS PARTNERSHIPS IN THE 1980s: CO-FINANCING WITH COMMERCIAL SOURCES OF FUNDS

The idea of combining concessional and commercial funds for developing countries is not completely new. It has already been tried successfully in several cases. The innovation now lies in introducing new forms of cooperation between concessional and non-concessional finance, and involving new types of partners: Arab and Islamic international banks, and, on a large scale, the smaller Western commercial banks. Making this innovation operational will be a major task.

The World Bank has recognized this, and has already accumulated experience in this area. Furthermore, it has spearheaded a trial program. Other financial institutions concerned with development in the LDCs are now called upon to design their own styles of new approaches and partnerships, and to follow up with concrete action.

IBRD's co-financing with private sources has grown in volume from US$85 million in fiscal year 1974 to US$3,300 million in fiscal year 1982; or from roughly US$200 million per annum in the mid-1970s to US$1.7 billion per annum in the early 1980s.[6] IBRD has accumulated the greatest experience in co-financing with commercial sources by number of projects, variety of partners, and modalities. The underlying philosophy is (similarly to co-financing with other donor agencies) to play a catalytic role in arranging financing with different sources of funds for LDCs, but also to introduce elements of competitiveness and increased efficiency in the use of funds by introducing commercial partners.

Under the impetus of its new management, IBRD's cooperation with commercial banks in providing development finance will be expanded in scope and scale.[7] IBRD has been studying new measures and modalities within which commercial banks could increase their activities without increasing their risks. Another aim is to increase the advantage of co-financing euro-credits for LDCs, in particular through longer maturities on which IBRD's participation could concentrate.

The main feature of IBRD's trial program of new instruments for co-financing with commercial banks is the participation of IBRD in the commercial loan itself. This can take place in two ways: instruments in which IBRD takes a direct stake in the later maturities of a commercial loan; and instruments in which IBRD offers a guarantee accepting a contingent obligation. In all cases IBRD would take up to 25% of the credit involved. The trial program provides an exposure to IBRD in the amount of US$500 million for a period of two years.

In a recent speech, the World Bank's President, A.W. Clausen[8] advocated lending and investing by commercial banks in LDCs as 'normal, healthy and necessary'. He stated explicitly that enhanced debt management, as well as stepped-up development finance could be achieved through more efficient cooperation between commercial lenders, aid agencies and governments.

The IFC, a World Bank affiliate, operates in a different style. Its purpose is to encourage productive private enterprises in LDCs. The uniqueness of its experience in co-financing is related to its mandate. It is the major international institution which can provide development finance in the form of equity participation as well as long-term

6. A.W. Clausen, *The World Bank and International Commercial Banks, Partners for Development*, International Monetary Conference, Vancouver, May 1982, p. 12 (published by the World Bank).
7. Ibid., p. 13.
8. A.W. Clausen, Address delivered to the Harvard Center for International Affairs, February 1983.

loans. Such financing is not given to governments, or under govern-
mental guarantees, but directly to the entity in charge of the project.
As an essential element of the World Bank group, IFC was described
as an umbrella 'which protects not only when the sun is shining'.[9] In
addition to its developmental impact, IFC makes profits, too. It does
not, however, distribute dividends and is not looked on by its shareholders as an investment outlet for their funds. Contributions to IFC
are made in much the same way as the contributions to the IBRD
itself, with the resulting constraints on their expansion.

At present, IFC is set for operational expansion. Its future activities will not only take place in the newly industrialized countries
(NICs), but also in the poorest regions. There, private enterprise has a
major role to play in supporting and accelerating development. IFC
intends to expand its activities in sub-Saharan Africa and thus
mobilize additional funds and expertise for this region from its
investment partners.

These stepped-up activities of IFC are of particular importance, in
view of the fact that bilateral direct foreign investment flows to LDCs
have decreased over the past decades. During the 1950s, such flows
grew at a little over 6% p.a. in real terms, and only at about 4% in the
1960s. After a peak of investment activities from 1970 to 1973, they
declined again in real terms, partly due to the financial independence
of some LDCs (mainly OPEC members) and due also to the general
international economic situation and changing attitudes towards
complex political, economic, social and cultural issues connected
with foreign investment and ownership.

At present, there is a general scarcity of risk capital, both for
developed and developing countries, much to the detriment of the
latter. Foreign direct investment, however, will continue to make a
significant contribution to development — over and beyond the
financing of LDCs' deficits — in helping to develop new primary
product sources, and in the transfer of technology and of marketing
skills.

With the objective of facilitating investment flows into LDCs, the
IBRD is investigating the possibility of creating a multilateral investment insurance agency.[10] Such a mechanism could assist in mobilizing additional investment capital for LDCs by meeting private

9. Hans Pollan, 'International Finance Corporation' in *UNIDO Symposium
ueber Finanzierung von Industrieprojekten in Entwicklungslaendern*, Vienna 1982,
p. 37.
    10. IBRD, Multilateral Investment Insurance Agency, R82-225, July 14, 1982.

investors' needs for reasonable security against certain non-commercial risks. This would facilitate closer cooperation between donor agencies and commercial banks in co-financing and participation in investment projects. Private investment in LDCs is a most effective agent for promoting economic development. A multilateral investment insurance agency would supplement the efforts of governments and the private sector, particularly in attracting foreign investors from different sources. Combining equity capital providers from various sources could give a new impetus for joint ventures in LDCs. By analogy with co-financing with commercial sources of funds, such an approach could change risk-perceptions, both for capital providers and recipients.

Among regional development finance institutions, the Inter-American Development Bank (IDB) has the greatest experience in co-financing with commercial sources of funds. Its complementary financing schemes are designed not only to increase its lending capacity, but also to reduce the risk in credit operations, thus improving the financial terms and conditions offered to borrowers by commercial sources. The key elements in gaining this advantage were: complete and objective evaluation of the merits of the project in question by IDB; and IDB's prestige in the international financial markets and banking community.

IDB recently initiated a new scheme, its 'additional external resources programme' to attract not only commercial loan finance, but equity as well. IDB sees the following advantages in providing venture capital in addition to loan finance: to improve the leverage of the project's capital structure and to provide access to this type of capital for small- and medium-scale private investors. Like other regional development banks, IDB feels that mechanisms for channelling venture capital to LDCs are not yet on a scale commensurate with demand.

The Asian Development Bank (ADB) is also investigating the possibility of establishing an equity participation program. In a workshop held in early 1982, particular attention was paid to the needs and aspirations of potential borrowers, and the need for a new scheme different from that of the IFC was stressed. Such a scheme, it was suggested, should not diminish ADB's loan-financing activities, but generate additionality rather than shift the flow of funds. It should focus on large enterprises, while also serving small private investors, preferably in industry. The scheme might assist temporarily sick projects, but not support wrong investment decisions. It should include private development finance institutions and consider the eligibility of commercial banks.

In addition to these specific recommendations, the workshop confirmed that demand for risk capital existed, indeed on a considerably larger scale than had been expected. It indicated possible ways in which risk capital, including capital from OPEC/Arab countries, could be channelled into development finance.

Also some of the Arab aid agencies provide equity capital, e.g. the Islamic Development Bank, the Abu Dhabi Fund, the Kuwait Fund and the Iraqi Fund for External Development. Among them, the most important institution for this type of operation has been the Islamic Development Bank. IsDB's total equity participation since the start of its operations amounts to over US$180 million. As a rule, IsDB's direct investment is limited to a maximum of one-third of total equity. This one-third should not be less than IsD 2 million or more than IsD 20 million for one project. In order to assist in financing smaller projects, IsDB has extended lines of equity to national financial institutions in its member countries; so far, 12 lines of equity, amounting to US$76 million.

The provision of equity by Arab funds may establish working relations with other investment companies, thus opening a new direction for cooperating generally with commercial sources of funds. Although the Arab funds have been very active in co-financing among aid agencies, they have yet to play a catalytic role in mobilizing additional funds from commercial souces, e.g. Arab commercial banks and investment companies. There is great scope for expansion, at a time when Arab international banks are interested in direct involvement in and with LDCs.

Given that ODA flows seem to be dominated at present by a stagnant or downward trend, and that the scope and extent of commercial bank lending is under debate, new action is needed to meet the increasing financial needs of the LDCs. If it is to be seriously pursued, such action has to bring benefits to all the parties concerned. Current economic problems provide the rationale, the context, and the challenge for this new concept of business partnerships in developing countries.

History shows that successful development of a country or even a whole region — for example the American Northwest in the nineteenth century or parts of Southeast Asia in the twentieth century — has been a viable economic proposition. Such experience indicates that even in the poorest countries, commercial opportunities may well exist, many of which have remained unidentified and neglected, as development-oriented schemes have not been linked systematically with profit-seeking.[11]

Co-financing with commercial sources is coming of age in a period of transition when the international financial system is undergoing revolutionary structural changes. During the last decade, OPEC countries have become important suppliers of funds to the international capital markets, and developing countries have become major borrowers. Intermediation has taken place mainly through Western international banks.

When co-financing with commercial sources was suggested as a useful mechanism for transferring capital from rich to poor countries, it was hoped that this would result in an additional flow of funds to the latter. It appears, however, that additionality has had a limited scope, partly because co-financing focused on middle-income countries which already had access to capital markets. Until recently, only the largest and primarily US international banks have been attracted to the concept of co-financing. Additional flows could be channelled to LDCs, if other institutions with less international experience and presence were to get involved in the process, and if the process itself assumed new dimensions where the risks and benefits were better ascertained.

A change in the competitive landscape in international banking and the arrival of newcomers may have a positive impact on co-financing. For the newly engaged private banks, this mechanism can provide a valuable service by opening new avenues of cooperation and providing exposure to a larger array of new customers. In this context, new and more diversified modalities and mechanisms could be beneficial.

The Rise of Arab and Islamic Banking

With the advent of the 1980s, the international financial situation is changing some of its parameters. Annual petrocapital surplus is fluctuating and dwindling, on the one side. On the other, the Arab banking system and Islamic financial institutions directly and

11. Cf. Ibrahim Shihata, *African-Arab Economic Partnership in Development. A Proposal for a New Multilateral Agency*, Bellogio, February 1982 (restricted distribution).

indirectly linked to the emergence of petrocapital — are gaining international consolidation. Within the concept of South-South financial cooperation, both categories of institutions cannot ignore the mechanism of co-financing. On the contrary, they could win impact and leverage through its use, albeit by different modalities of cooperation, reflecting the differences among them in history, mandate and concept of development finance.

With a few exceptions, mainly in Egypt, national Arab banks were established gradually after the Second World War. The turning point in Arab banking, however, was the first increase in oil price in the early 1970s. A phenomenal expansion then took place at the institutional as well as the operational levels. Thus, at the beginning of the 1980s, Arab banks had established their international networks in all traditional financial centres, as well as in the emerging ones, in the Caribbean, in Hong Kong and Singapore, and last but not least, in Bahrain, the regional Arab center with an international vocation.

After one decade of rapid expansion, three generations of Arab banks can be distinguished, all of which are operating, at least partly, in developing countries.

1.   The first generation are the national Arab banks, the initial backbone of the Arab banking system. The emergence of petrocapital increased their number and size. Some institutions underwent nationalization and mergers, depending on the prevailing economic situation in the country concerned. A sophisticated, exclusively national banking system was developed in Kuwait. The Kingdom of Saudi Arabia 'Saudisized' the banking sector from the mid-1970s onwards, imposing 60% national ownership on all pre-existing foreign institutions. The UAE and Bahrain developed banking sectors in which national and foreign banks operate side by side.

2.   Arab-Occidental consortium banks are the second evolutionary step of Arab banking. This concept of association is based upon maximizing the advantages of joint action of groups with different resources and experience and minimizing risks and costs. The consortium formula offered Arab banks access to international banking experience, sophisticated finance and banking technology. In addition, it provided an entry into new geographic areas and thus opened the possibility of participation in the international intermediation of petrocapital, at least to a certain extent. Western banks hoped to gain through this formula access to huge amounts of petrocapital and Arab markets at favourable conditions. To mention

one example, Arlabank International,[12] originally headquartered in Lima, but since February 1983 located in Manama, has a special position as a joint banking venture between Arab and other Third World shareholders from Latin America. It forms a financial bridge between the Arab region and Latin America and promotes South-South cooperation.

3. Inter-Arab joint ventures are the third generation of Arab banks. Along with some large national banks of the Gulf, they are likely to determine the impact of Arab banking at the international level in the 1980s. The most important inter-Arab joint venture in this field, in terms of capital resources, the Arab Banking Corporation, was established in Bahrain, in 1980. It combines shareholders from Kuwait, Libya and the UAE with an authorized capital of US$1 billion.[13]

In addition to inter-Arab commercial banks, inter-Arab investment corporations have been established as prominent examples of inter-Arab joint ventures.[14] Often they are associations between oil-rich and oil-importing Arab countries as equal partners and are located in the latter. The League of Arab States and OAPEC sponsored the creation of these institutions in several cases. Inter-Arab investment corporations often finance specific sectors, such as: petroleum (the Arab Petroleum Investment Company and the Arab Petroleum Services Company); maritime transport (Egypt); livestock development (Sudan and Somalia); real estate and tourism (Egypt, Tunisia, Morocco, Sudan and Syria). Since the early 1980s, Tunisia has attracted many Gulf countries and Algeria to establish joint multi-purpose and specialized (industry, agriculture) investment corporations in its territory.

Besides the 'conventional' Arab banks, a number of financial institutions of a rather different type has been established, basically in the Middle East; these are the Islamic banks and investment companies. Arab and Islamic banks have one thing in common, they stem from the same cultural background. Otherwise the underlying

12. Arlabank (Lima) became a wholly owned subsidiary of Arlabank International, effective 22 February 1983, and its former shareholders became the shareholders of the new bank.
13. Other important multilateral Arab banks include the Arab African International Bank and the Arab International Bank, both located in Cairo, as well as the Gulf International Bank, Manama.
14. Ibrahim Shihata, *The Other Face of OPEC*, Longman, 1982, Chapter 11, Inter-Arab equity joint ventures, pp. 141-69.

economic concepts and operating philosophy are quite different. Islamic financial institutions are not restricted to the Arab world, they do not receive petrocapital directly from their respective Governments as a general rule, and they do not follow Western banking principles. Their geographic area of operations is the member countries of the Islamic Conference, as well as countries where Muslim minorities live. Their shareholders represent basically Muslim private and institutional interests. Islamic banks attempt to operate according to the principles of Islamic law (Shariah). They assume interest-free banking based on profit- and loss-sharing schemes. The revival of Islamic economic values is said to date back to the 1950s and even before. Thus, the proliferation of Islamic banks in the mid-1970s coincided with the emergence of petrocapital and was not necessarily caused by it.[15]

At present, there are about twenty Islamic banks and investment companies in operation. They have attracted large amounts of savings from Muslim populations, mostly money which would otherwise have been held outside the banking circuit. Within a short space of time, Islamic banks generated handsome profits for their shareholders and investor clients. Not a single Islamic bank has failed or closed down so far.

At the international level, the Dar Al-Maal Al-Islami[16] (DMI — Islamic Finance House), promotes Islamic banking by establishing Islamic banks, investment and solidarity (insurance) companies in Muslim and other developing countries. The objectives of this private umbrella organization, an international Islamic holding, are to undertake all financial operations required today in the framework of the principles and precepts of Islamic law; to invest funds — within an

15. The idea of Islamic banking and the first practical experience pre-date the oil wealth of the Middle East. Theoretical discussions on interest-free banking had already begun in the 1940s in Pakistan. Islamic agricultural savings banks operated for a few years during the mid-1960s in Egypt. The first commercial Islamic banks, however, were established in the second half of the 1970s, whilst international Islamic investment companies and holdings appeared only in the 1980s. At present, new Islamic banks are in the process of establishment in Muslim countries in sub-Saharan Africa and South-East Asia. A process of Islamization of the entire banking system was introduced in Pakistan in 1979 and is planned for the Sudan. No concrete information is available on Islamic banking in Iran; the Iranian system aims allegedly even at avoiding any profits, and operates only on the basis of service fees in order to cover operating costs.

16. DMI was established in the Bahamas, in 1981, with operational headquarters in Geneva. It aims, like the Arab Banking Corporation, at a total capitalization of US$1 billion.

Islamic context — to generate 'licit' profits and to promote and consolidate cooperation generally between Muslim countries.

Even if the present OPEC current account surplus is negligible, the placement and administration of OPEC's cumulative financial assets — estimated at about US$400 billion at the end of 1982 — still remain to be dealt with. This stock is basically held in Western international banks. Traditional Arab banks and investment companies, both national and multilateral, are increasingly taking over part of this business. They are being called upon to play a role in the shift from placing financial assets short-term to long-term productive outlets. This is bringing about a certain reorientation from the North towards the South. However, this geographic shift of possible petrocapital flows being considered, for obvious reasons, as a sound business proposition and not as additional assistance flows.

Risk and Benefit Considerations in New Forms of Co-financing

The record of co-financing with commercial sources of funds over recent years indicates that present practice has only limited potential. Thus far, only 1% of commercial lending to developing countries has been associated with World Bank projects.[17] The main reasons for the limited use of present co-financing schemes are two: the terms of the commercial loans to LDCs and the 'security or protection blanket' sought by international banks operating in the Third World. In view of the differing conditions in capital markets and differing credit ratings of borrowers, a larger variety of instruments is also required. These new instruments should associate commmercial and investment banks more closely with aid agencies.

Although the increased use of commercial credits in development finance appears to be the formula for the 1980s, a caveat should be noted. This approach also has negative aspects. Developing countries sometimes have taken advantage of market offers without regard to their repayment capacities. Western banks sometimes have appeared to pursue growth of their assets without regard to the quality of such assets, or the end use of funds.

Without questioning the benefits of stepped-up commercial

17. A.W. Clausen, *The World Bank and International Commercial Banks, Partners for Development*, International Monetary Conference, Vancouver, May 1982, p. 12 (published by the World Bank).

financing in principle, LDCs[18] have voiced concern about increasing co-financing for development finance substantially and rapidly. The main questions are:

(i)   whether private flows offer a real alternative to increasing ODA;

(ii)   whether cross-default clauses do not create rigidities detrimental to developing countries;

(iii)   whether the new mechanisms generate additionality, and not merely a shift of funds from other sources, and into other sectors.

The argument continues that excessive reliance on private capital for development finance — at a time when interest rates are only slightly declining from historic peaks — could impair the growth and development of all developing countries. It is obvious that in the design of new instruments these and other arguments have to be taken into consideration. New instruments have to be clearly attractive for each of the three parties involved: the borrower, the commercial bank and the donor agency. In order to obtain additional advantages from the relationship, each partner must play a role and offer something to the others. Risks and costs have to be weighed against the benefits expected.[19] The role of the donor agency is particularly relevant as the honest intermediary whose ultimate objectives rest in serving the interests of the recipient country.

For *developing countries*, the potential advantages are that the large international banks already engaged in the Third World will remain active in this field if not lend larger amounts and that newcomers may be encouraged to join in. Furthermore, loan maturities could be extended. In order to obtain these likely benefits, LDCs have to face higher total project costs than would have obtained if adequate concessional financing had been available.

In each potential case of co-financing with commercial sources, the developing country has to gauge whether the benefits expected will outweigh the risks and costs. Market conditions will influence such decisions.

For *commercial banks*, new instruments of co-financing will provide additional protection, while enabling them to get a fair return on their investments. The donor agencies may be prepared to defend

18. Group of 77, Research Paper on Co-financing, in preparation for UNCTAD VI, 1983.
19. Cf. IBRD, 'Co-financing with Commercial Banks', November 23, 1982.

the financial package of a project in its entirety. This security blanket against country risk is additional to the protection inherent in financing a well conceived and appraised project of high economic priority.

In exchange for these advantages, commercial banks will have to show some flexibility in their traditional terms and conditions. The extension of maturities — compared with purely commercial transactions — appears to be the most important prerequisite. Furthermore, international banks will be expected to move into new countries and new sectors. An offer by a commercial bank to join in a financial package will have to bring clear benefits to the developing country, if that bank is to obtain the advantage of a donor agency's umbrella.

The interest to *donor agencies* from a wider range of co-financing instruments, in addition to the general increase of external finance, is the assurance that commercial credits can be mobilized in a wider variety of circumstances. Furthermore, these commercial flows can be obtained at terms more attuned to the repayment and development capacities of the recipient countries. Given that concessional sources will not suffice to meet even the most urgent investment needs, donor agencies will welcome new sources, which will permit them to diversify their assistance activities, sectorally and geographically.

A potential risk for donor agencies when joining commercial transactions is the question of whether they can defend successfully their preferred creditor status and privileged position in the financial community. A closer operational association between donor agencies and commercial institutions might damage the developmental image of the former and make it more difficult for them to obtain further capital increases from their respective governments. This could occur, although such an attitude would be in contradiction to the stated purpose of donor agencies of assisting borrowers in mobilizing commercial sources of funds. Provided that development criteria influencing the distribution of lending by sector and project were not adversely affected by new instruments, this risk should remain manageable.

New instruments for co-financing with commercial sources — along the lines proposed by the World Bank — have to balance, measure and test risks, costs and likely benefits for the three groups involved on a case-by-case basis. The market will be the arbiter of success or failure of new schemes. This fact appears to be a built-in safety component.

Increasing Transfers to LDCs

The number of projects where co-financing is not only feasible, but mandatory due to scarcity of development finance, tends only to increase. The proposed strategy of increasing commercial flows to developing countries should not detract from the need for larger concessional flows, particularly for LLDCs, and for social and infra-structural projects which cannot attract commercial funds. In the absence of innovative schemes, the bulk of international risk capital will flow only to developed and middle-income countries, both in the forms of loan finance and direct investment. In order to obtain stepped-up transfer of resources to developing nations on a competitive business basis, a more encouraging framework has to be developed. Such a framework could also generate investment opportunities in the poorest countries.

The recommendations of the Task Force on Non-Concessional Flows[20] provide useful guidelines on practical ways of channelling loan finance to the Third World. They include measures such as strengthening the capacity of multilateral development finance institutions to borrow from the international capital markets, and giving higher priority to co-financing with commercial sources. This would include the design of more market-oriented techniques, such as the A/B loan, in which the A loan is provided by the donor agency and the B loan is intended to attract commercial sources. The administrative and managerial practices of co-financing should also be improved, thus ensuring more timely and comprehensive information on potential projects suitable for co-financing.

Although neither the mandates nor the objectives of aid agencies and commercial banks are identical, joint and mutually-supporting actions between different sources of external finance in LDCs could be beneficial and rewarding for all parties concerned. Thus donor agencies could be instrumental in increasing non-concessional flows to developing countries in several ways.[21]

20. World Bank, Final Report to the Development Committee of the Task Force on Non-Concessional Flows, May 1982.

21. Cf. Ibrahim Shihata, 'The Role of Donor Agencies in Non-concessional Transfers to LDCs', *OPEC Review*, Vol. VI, No. 3.

1. The donor agency as a financial intermediary

Intermediation between financial markets and LDCs is possible only for agencies which can borrow from the market. Some agencies with great potential in this field have not yet played this role, mainly due to the availability of funds through other means, e.g. their own resources (Kuwait Fund), or loans from member governments (IMF). Intermediation is likely, however, to be more prominent in future as direct access to capital markets becomes more difficult for LDCs.

2. The donor agency as a co-lender with commercial sources

To facilitate mixed financing by donor agencies and commercial banks, projects could be structured in such a way as to accommodate more easily both types of funding (e.g. by isolating the infrastructure components from the cash-generating components of the project). Compared with private banks, the agencies are in the privileged position of having greater access to reliable information on the borrowers, capacity for project appraisal, acceptability by recipient governments, etc. They could use such advantages more systematically in attracting greater volumes of non-concessional funds in the co-financing of projects.

3. The donor agency as a catalyst in foreign direct investment

By providing equity participation and loans for projects appraised by it, the donor agency can, directly or through the intermediation of local development institutions, play an important catalytic role in stimulating additional risk capital from private sources.

4. The donor agency as an adviser and source of technical assistance

The expertise of donor agencies should be made available to interested LDCs in putting together financial packages attractive to foreign investors. They can help recipient governments in obtaining information on foreign sources of finance, in revising investment codes and improving investment climates, in tapping foreign markets and in building local markets by improving the adequacy and efficiency of local institutions, instruments and legislation.

5. The donor agency as an investor in LDCs' financial papers

Donor agencies are called upon to invest part of their liquid assets on bonds and other financial instruments issued by developing countries and their institutions, in addition to the bonds issued by or in developed countries. Through such purchases, donor agencies will help create a secondary market for the LDCs papers, thus paving the way for a greater marketability of such instruments in financial markets.[22]

6.   *The donor agency as a promoter of investment institutions*
Donor agencies can take the lead in sponsoring the establishment of institutions to finance new real investments, to implement such investments or to provide them with insurance against non-commercial risks. The World Bank's initiative in the creation of IFC, the Kuwait Fund's initiative in the creation of the Inter-Arab Investment Guarantee Corporation and the Arab Fund's initiative in the creation of the Arab Authority for Agricultural Investment and Development (AAAID) are all cases in point.

New initiatives could include the creation of the multilateral insurance guarantee scheme (against non-commercial risks) presently being considered by the World Bank, along with the creation of new multilateral investment corporations that would aim at making profits through direct investments in developing countries for clear developmental purposes. For instance, the World Bank's proposed energy affiliate could be established in the form of a multi-lateral energy investment corporation owned by governments (which may sell part of their shares to local concerns) that would aim at making profits from its overall activities (but not necessarily from each project) and at distributing dividends to its shareholders.[23]

7.   *The donor agency as guarantor of commercial loans*
The provision of a full guarantee coverage by donor agencies for commercial loans against the risk of default has been one of the functions most sought after by commercial banks. A full guarantee

22. This role, already practised by such agencies as the OPEC Fund and IFAD in the management of their portfolios, has not been favoured by the other donor agencies on the grounds that investment decisions should not be coloured by assistance considerations. It may be noted, however, that LDCs' bonds usually have a higher return and have not been the subject of default. If this practice is generalized, the danger of restricted marketability will also be reduced.

23. The first author has made a proposal to this effect for the creation of an international investment corporation for the development of Africa, an idea which could be further pursued on regional or sectoral lines. The assumption here is that investment opportunities abound in LDCs, even in the poorest, but quite often the conversion of such opportunities into actual investments requires investment concerns behind them which are large enough to be trusted and to be secure, yet whose interests go beyond the typical profit maximization goal of the Western multinationals. Under the circumstances, multilateral donor agencies may be the most suitable sponsors for the promotion of such initiatives (cf. footnote 11).

coverage, however, would not be likely to result in making available additional resources to the borrower, who would probably be better off borrowing the same amount directly from the guarantor agency.

In addition, this type of guarantee could lead to a distortion of market forces as it may encourage countries to overborrow and banks to favour borrowers benefitting from such guarantees. It might thus be preferable to leave to the commercial banks themselves the task of providing insurance coverage or safety nets in the case of default.

The catalytic functions of donor agencies described above are important, because at present obviously donors cannot meet all the external financial needs of developing countries. They are called upon to assist LDCs actively in receiving additional funds from other sources, the terms of which should however be compatible with the developmental goals and potential of the recipients. However, the strategy should not be limited to increasing non-concessional transfers as such. It should also strengthen the credit-worthiness of developing countries and their capacity to attract new funds on a competitive basis. This would improve the financial positions of developing countries and thus make them less dependent on the occasional vagaries of concessional flows.

The role of international commercial banks in this context should be complementary to that of donor agencies. During the 1970s, international Western banks contributed as a group in a decisive way to the economic dynamism of middle-income countries. In the 1980s, cooperation between all types of commercial banks and donor agencies ought to become closer, both in scope and coverage of operations. More institutions have to be attracted and new modalities developed, in order not to limit possible dynamism to restricted poles of development, such as the NICs and OPEC countries. Joint action should help most, if not all, developing countries.

International commercial banks, both Western and Arab, could find interesting and rewarding outlets in developing countries. The potential success of such a new orientation will depend on a number of factors, many of which relate to the policies and investment environment of the recipient countries themselves. The trend to recovery in industrialized countries will improve the export potential of developing countries. This, coupled with greater discipline in their economic management will improve their credit rating and repayment capacity. It is to be noted again, however, that the increase in commercial bank lending it not an objective in itself. In fact, without improving the general economic situation of LDCs, such an increase could further jeopardize the financial positions of these countries and of the institutions which provide financial support to them.

A closer, operational relationship between international banks and donor agencies would provide for the former information, insight and economic analysis of potential clients, as well as realistic risk assessments. Exchange of views, information and experience on debt, development aid, trade and other critical performance indicators between the two categories of fund providers, could lead to joint and mutually beneficial actions.

In order to enhance their potential role in developing countries, international commercial banks have also to take active steps. By granting longer maturities, they could strengthen the viability of capital-intensive projects, which may be more sensitive to cash flows than to the cost of borrowing as such.

This approach raises the issue of the short-term nature of the bulk of deposits in international banks. According to sound banking principles, short-term capital should not serve for long-term uses. Although this argument holds true for a single institution, it is not valid for a whole banking system. For the latter, collective action of commercial banks — in cooperation with central banks — could assist in protecting international banks against the risk. Efforts should concentrate on creating more favourable market conditions, and banking techniques that make long-term deposits more attactive and secure investment propositions to the potential sources of such deposits.

International banks could consider certain types of projects which are particularly suitable for co-financing, e.g. 'green-field' commercial investments which also require infrastructural support.[24] The financial package for such a project could be divided into commercial and concessional components depending on the type of finance required. The overall return on the total capital employed would be such as to attract investors on the merit of the project which receives partial financing on concessional terms.

International commercial banks could also initiate project finance for developing countries on their own. Over the last years, several of these banks had reaped the bulk of their profits in overseas operations. Therefore, it can be expected that they will maintain their outward-looking policy while developing new safeguards against the

24. Ibrahim Shihata, *The Other Face of OPEC*, Longman, 1982, pp. 70-3.

increasingly perceived risks. They could focus their lending on self-liquidating projects where potential risks of repayment may be less than in the case of general purpose loans. Tying the repayment to project earnings would provide further security, in addition to government guarantee of the loan.

Venture capital operations could be another new area of expansion for international banks. This field is relatively untested, as far as the Third World is concerned. Demand for venture capital is abundant. It is likely that donor agencies as well as host governments would support such operations directly or indirectly.

Islamic banks, which have proven in the last few years increased capacity in fund mobilization, are now looking for outlets for profitable schemes in the countries where they are located. They could be promising partners for this new activity.

Combining concessional and commercial sources in new cooperative schemes is not an easy task. It requires a continuous search for formulae to satisfy the requirements of the recipients without adding new risks to the providers of funds. Such formulae should contribute to finding solutions to the serious and potentially critical situation of development finance in Third World countries.

At present commercial banks share with aid agencies the role of constructing an international financial bridge between surplus and deficit regions. In so far as both succeed in mobilizing additional capital for productive purposes and additional asset creation, all economic groups will eventually benefit.

7 THE OPEC FUND AND THE NORTH-SOUTH DIALOGUE — SOME PERSONAL REFLECTIONS

Dr Ibrahim˙ F.I. Shihata

What I am concerned with in this chapter is the whole gamut of continuing discussions between the rich, developed countries of the West, generally referred to as the North, and the poor developing countries of Africa, Asia and Latin America, usually known as the South. In terms of people rather than states, this brings forth the relationships between a population of approximately 1,200 million partaking in 1980 of a gross national product of US$ 9,360 billion — or US$ 7,800 per capita — and a population of 3,200 million sharing in the same year, a gross national product of less than US$ 2,000 billion — or US$ 620 per capita.

The last figure would be much lower if the relatively higher-income countries — above US$ 1,000 per capita — among the developing nations were excluded, as it would leave an aggregate gross national product in 1980 of only US$ 780 billion for a population of more than 2.5 billion — about US$ 310 per capita.

This great disparity in wealth is even more drastically shown by the marginal share of the South in the world's economic activities. Even after including China, the South, with 73% of world population, accounted in 1978 for about 18% only of total world gross domestic product, 24% of world trade and investment, 7% of world industry, and 1% of world research.

The year 1974 witnessed the beginning of formal world-wide discussions on the need for structural changes in the world economic order. Developing countries took the initiative in starting these discussions. They were moved by their awareness that the world economic recession and the monetary disorders which began to loom in the early seventies were likely to have their most devastating effects on their own economies. They also saw in the sudden success of the oil-exporting developing countries in improving the terms of their trade, and in the unique position of these latter countries in controlling the developed world's import requirements of a most vital commodity, important leverages that could be deployed to negotiate a new package with the North involving other economic and financial issues.

The developed countries for their part, were mainly concerned with their own deteriorating economic performance. From the outset they showed little interest in an overall review of global issues with the developing countries as a group. They seemed to react seriously only when specific issues were to be discussed in ways and in fora that promised tangible benefits to them, rather than general political 'declarations', or ambitious 'plans of action'. In particular, they refused to accept fundamental changes in a world order which had been devised mainly by them, and had been, on the whole, working to their benefit.

The issues that divided the 'have' countries of the North from the 'have not' countries of the South, covered a wide range. They were adequately spelled out in the resolution on development and international cooperation adopted by the United Nations General Assembly's Seventh Special Session in September, 1975.

That resolution invited all countries to join in the search for solutions to world problems, pointing out in particular the following areas:

international trade;
transfer of real resources to developing countries;
international monetary reforms;
science and technology;
industrialization;
food and agriculture;
cooperation among developing nations; and
restructuring the economic and social sectors of the UN system.[1]

The Paris Conference

In 1975-77 the North-South dialogue made the headlines for a while when the Conference on International Economic Cooperation, which brought together eight industrial countries and nineteen developing countries, was held in Paris.

1. The urgent need to create a 'new international economic order' (NIEO) had been expressed by the UN at an earlier date. On May 1, 1974, the Sixth Special Session of the UN General Assembly adopted resolutions on the 'declaration of the establishment of a NIEO' and the 'program of action' to establish it, in order to 'correct inequalities and redress injustices, and make it possible to eliminate the widening gap between developed and developing countries'.

A few comments on the Paris conference may help in placing the parley between the North and the South in its proper perspective. Although the conference did not signal the beginning or the end of the North-South dialogue, it had nonetheless the merit of constituting a forum where the problems, though by no means solved, were thoroughly examined and well articulated. It helped focus world attention on the long-standing particular problems of development aid, primary commodities' exports, external debt, and more generally on the increasing gap between the North and the South.

The nineteen developing countries attended with the optimistic expectation of implementing the challenging recommendations of the UN Seventh Special Session. To their chagrin, the conference did not proceed to the goals conceived for a broad and fair program leading to the much-talked of new international economic order (NIEO). The rich countries did not offer any support for structural changes in the international economic system of the type envisaged by the South. Their commitments, as perceived by the developing countries, were mostly concerned with minor concessions on international trade and aid. Specifically, their positive response was limited to the following modest areas:

(1) With respect to the issue of financial and development assistance to the South, the industrial nations agreed to contribute one billion dollars in a special action program, on highly concessional terms, to help the urgent needs of the low-income countries 'facing general problems of transfer of resources'. Of this amount, US$ 385 million was later entrusted by the European Economic Community to the International Development Association for use in future project and program assistance to be disbursed over a number of years. Canada, Sweden and Switzerland later cancelled some debts of the least developed countries. The developed North also concurred, albeit without specific commitments, with the necessity of increasing official development assistance in real terms. Part of this assistance was to be assigned to the expansion of food production in developing countries, but the only specific agreement was to set a minimum target of 10 million tons of grains per annum for food aid, a target which remains unfulfilled to this date.

(2) In the area of trade, agreed arrangements were expressed in general, if not vague, terms, including points such as:

*furthering cooperation in primary commodities' marketing and distribution;
*assisting developing countries in their attempts to diversify domestic production and exports;
*working out measures in order to cope with the problem of synthetic goods, so as to ease their impact on natural products;
*establishing a generalized system of preferences more favourable to the developing countries; and
*giving special and advantageous treatment to the developing nations in multilateral trade negotiations.[2]

One important commitment which later lost much of its original comprehensive content was agreed upon in principle by the industrialized countries: to establish the Common Fund to finance buffer stocks for some primary commodities of export interest to the South, as discussed below.

(3) Finally, in the field of energy, no more than a restatement of the obvious was made, spelling out:

*the importance of energy availability and supply;
*recognition of the depletable nature of oil and gas, and the necessity for a gradual shift from an 'oil-based energy mix to more permanent and renewable sources of energy';
*the significance of conservation and increased efficiency of energy use; and
*the need to develop all forms of energy.

At the conclusion of the Paris conference, it was not surprising therefore, to see the developing countries express their regret at having most of the proposals for structural changes, and some other suggestions dealing with crucial questions, discarded by the North. As to the latter, its expression of regret mainly centered on the lack of agreement on issues related to energy 'cooperation'.

Collective Monologue

Ironically, the lengthy discussions of these North-South issues have

2. The Tokyo round trade package signed in Geneva on April 12, 1979, has so far (April 1983) been accepted by only eleven of the developing country participants in the multilateral trade negotiations, the rest finding it short of meeting their minimum demands.

generally been characterized by lack of real dialogue. They have been more in the vein of what is known in child psychology as collective monologue,[3] where each participant speaks only of his own worries, assuming that the matter must be uppermost in the minds of his inter-locutors.

Following the Paris conference, negotiations between the industrial and developing countries scattered among several fora. The issue of commodities was left to UNCTAD; compensatory financing to the joint IMF/IBRD Development Committee; the matter of external debt to both UNCTAD and the joint IMF/IBRD Development Committee; development and balance of payments assistance to the IBRD and IMF; and the question of access by the developing nations to the industrial markets to the General Agreement on Tariffs and Trade (GATT). Conscious of the negative effects of this multitude of fora and of their relative weakness in the councils of many of such fora, developing countries were soon to call for 'global negotiations' where all relevant issues could be discussed under UN auspices. Agreement was again reached in principle on the importance of this global approach but no other agreement has followed since.

In all the assemblies, and on most important issues, the developed countries reacted generally in a negative way to the developing countries' demands.[4] Whenever their response was positive, it came late, offering at times too little. At the root of this failure lay the seemingly incompatible differences between the North and the

3. Shihata, I., 'The OPEC Fund and the North-South Dialogue', *Third World Quarterly*, vol. 1, no. 4, October, 1979. Republished as chapter 6 in *The Other Face of OPEC*.
4. The specific demands put forward by the developing countries related in particular to the following:
* adoption of UNCTAD's Integrated Program for Commodities;
* energy conservation, development and finance;
* protection of the purchasing power of export earnings and assets;
* debt relief and debt reorganization;
* adoption by the developed countries of the 0.7% ODA target;
* access to the capital markets of the developed world;
* infrastructural development;
* full implementation of the Lima Declaration and Plan of Action (aim: for developing countries to increase their share of world industrial production to at least 25% by the year 2000);
* increased food production in developing countries, food security and food aid;
* transfer of technology through private foreign investments; and
* international financial and monetary reforms (i.e. increases in IMF and IBRD resources, new allocation of Special Drawing Rights, greater access by developing countries to these resources, and a greater role for them in the decision-making process).

South, who saw the world through different lenses: the developing nations calling for fundamental and structural changes in North-South comparative advantage in production and exchange, and the developed countries favouring only marginal adjustment. A broad consensus on principles and objectives among the nations of the North and South remained therefore a remote target.

The rhetoric which accompanied the South's demands for fundamental change seemed also to have contributed, inadvertently, to the North's lack of enthusiasm for a process which was, from the latter's point of view, untimely at best. In addition, the process as presented seemed to have required, unrealistically, great concern for long-term considerations, from politicians deeply involved in immediate problems that had little promise of quick solutions.

The resolutions of the Special Sessions of the UN General Assembly (1974; 1979); the prolonged debate in the Paris conference (1975-77): the detailed recommendations of the IMF Group of 24 (especially in 1979) and of the Brandt Commission (1980); the reports of the IMF/IBRD Development Committee and its 'task forces'; as well as the short exchanges of views at the Cancun Summit (1981); all fell short of producing any of the major changes which optimistic visionaries of the early seventies projected as pillars of the projected NIEO.

The debate continues, notwithstanding, without clear signs that future discussions will be different from previous ones. The fora are to be basically the same, most noticeably 'global negotiations' in the UN General Assembly and in UNCTAD VI, scheduled for June, 1983. Diagnosis of the problems, and the remedies proposed for solving them, do not seem to have altered either.

In fact, nothing substantial has happened to advance the process towards significant constructive results. Meanwhile, the world's economic situation has all but worsened for North and South alike. This raises important questions as to the real obstacles which stand in the way of successful negotiations in this most important field, and the elements which should be maintained in the form and substance of this complex process in order to make it yield workable compromises.

If a fruitless repeat performance is to be pre-empted, substantial efforts are therefore required to improve the process, change attitudes, and even modify the demands, all within a framework geared to reaching practical results. Above all, the time has come for participants in this process to look for acceptable answers to the basic economic problems which can be solved through joint measures, instead of wasting valuable efforts in drafting typical 'plans of action' which stand no chance of implementation.

TWO CASE STUDIES: IFAD AND THE COMMON FUND

In this attempt to consider the changes required, it may be useful to shed some light on two specific experiences where North-South negotiations yielded some concrete results, i.e. the negotiations which resulted in the agreements establishing the International Fund for Agricultural Development (IFAD) and the Common Fund for Commodities.

Each of these negotiations was held under different auspices, followed different procedures, and involved different issues. Each was concluded with a different degree of success. My involvement in both cases, especially in the negotiations for IFAD where I represented Kuwait and spoke on behalf of OPEC countries and, on occasion, of all developing countries, may be helpful in showing what I believe to be the elements of success in this complex process. This personal account may be of particular relevance in view of the fact that both cases are often cited as positive achievements of the North-South dialogue, without paying due attention to important contributing factors which may not be widely known.

IFAD

The idea of establishing an international fund to finance agricultural development in developing countries emanated from several sources, at a time when a new financial institution was the most commonly proposed remedy for an emerging international problem. The proposal took concrete form through reports prepared by the secretariat of the World Food Council in 1974 and 1975. It was suggested that this fund would be financed by the developed and OPEC groups of countries, more or less on an equal basis, each of these groups holding one-third of the total votes in the governing bodies of the new institution, while the rest of the developing countries, though under no obligation to contribute, would also enjoy one-third of the voting power.

The idea was presented as a new direction for financial cooperation. For the first time in an international financial institution, two-thirds of the votes would be given to developing countries, while at the same time leaving two-thirds of the votes in the hands of donor countries. The key element in this formula was obviously that OPEC members were both developing countries and major donors. A typical UN negotiating conference of interested countries was held in Rome in 1975 to discuss the proposal, after it had been supported in principle by the World Food Council and the UN General Assembly.

As the debate started, the major prospective donors of the North questioned the need for establishing a new fully-fledged institution to tackle a problem which could well be handled by the World Bank Group and regional development banks. They were tempted however, by the prospect of having a small group of developing countries, OPEC members, coming to share, on an equal basis, a burden traditionally considered to be basically that of the developed nations. Their main concern seemed to lie in ensuring, if such a fund were to be established at all, that it would have this 'promising' feature without emerging, however, as a fully-fledged development agency. In particular, they were against giving such an agency the power to appraise projects and administer loans on its own, thus duplicating the work of the other international financial institutions in which they played a major role.

OPEC countries, on the other hand, saw no reason for sharing such a financial burden on an equal basis with OECD nations, at a time when their combined GNP was only some 7% of the OECD countries. To them, the basic attraction of the proposal lay in the voting structure. OPEC countries argued that the division of votes among the developing nations (OPEC and non-OPEC) was an internal matter to be decided among themselves. Indeed, the OPEC countries maintained all along that they constituted an integral part of the Group of 77. They would accept the proposed distinction between the two categories within that group only for the purpose of helping to establish a new institution, and they would not accept creating any precedent for treating OPEC as a distinct category among developing nations. Representatives of OPEC countries concurred that IFAD should not build a large bureaucracy, but did not want to see it acting simply as a paying agent for pre-existing institutions.

Other developing countries expressed divergent views on the scope of activities of the new fund, the types of beneficiaries it could assist, and the terms and conditions of its loans, but were in agreement that their financial participation should remain optional and that the fund should have its own fully-fledged bureaucracy.

In my judgement, the debate would have reached no fruitful conclusions, but for the following important factors:

(1) Role of the OPEC Fund. OPEC countries, having by then established the OPEC Fund, declared, in May 1976, their readiness to contribute through that fund, US$ 400 million to the initial resources of IFAD, provided that developed countries would contribute US$ 600 million for the same purpose. By making this substantial pledge and by giving the OPEC Fund the responsibility of negotiating the details on their behalf, OPEC countries provided the credibility which previously had been lacking in the demands of the developing countries. They also provided the mechanism for a business-like approach. In response, the OECD countries began to bargain about the amounts to be contributed by each category, and to discuss the potential scope of IFAD's activities, taking its establishment, for the first time, as a foregone conclusion.

(2) Coordination of OPEC Countries' Positions. The position of the OPEC countries was coordinated by a single spokesman, a task which, as Director-General of the OPEC Fund, I undertook. The fact that they spoke with one voice in the negotiations, coupled with a financial pledge, ensured greater weight for OPEC countries' views both within the Group of 77 and *vis-à-vis* the OECD countries.

In the context of the Group of 77, representatives of OPEC countries, acting through their spokesman, put the view that negotiations on delicate details could not be conducted *en masse*, and that the Group had to choose three to six persons to discuss these issues with a small number from the OECD countries. They also proposed that representatives of the Group of 77 in this small forum should have a flexible mandate and should not assume, unrealistically, that the agreement to be reached ought to meet the demands of each single country in the Group. Such an assumption would necessarily preclude agreement.

(3) Effective cooperation in the Group of 77. A compromise was finally reached by the small 'contact group', in which:

the principle of parity in the contributions of OECD and OPEC was set aside (in the end OPEC countries pledged US$ 435.5

million, OECD countries US$ 557 million, and other countries, some US$ 30 million);

the proposed voting structure was kept intact; and

the new fund was to entrust, as a general rule but not in all cases, appraisal of projects to other international development agencies and to rely on such agencies for the administration of its loans, along with a host of other details.

The difficult task of getting the negotiated deal accepted by the whole Group of 77 then began. A few members of the Group questioned some aspects of the compromise, and the issue arose as to whether unanimous acceptance was required.

A few ardent speakers, who seemed at times more interested in restating doctrinaire attitudes than in the creation of the fund, presumably to please other audiences at home, spoke fervently against any compromise. Speaking in defence of the deal reached in the 'contact group', I argued that a package satisfying the requirements of every single member of the Group of 77 could not have been devised. To expect and to wait for such an unattainable package, would have meant postponing the establishment of IFAD *ad infinitum*. The issue was therefore whether to establish the institution within a framework that could be accepted by the bulk of its potential donors and recipients after comprehensive and exhausting discussions, or not have it at all.

Faced with such a difficult choice, the Group had to decide whether to continue acting in unanimity, which presumably had been its general practice, or to accept more effective procedures. A lengthy debate on this issue ended in agreement that consensus required only the approval of an overwhelming majority, and that the negotiated package had received such approval. This principle was subsequently followed by the drafting committee of the *Agreement Establishing IFAD* (chaired by myself) and by the 18-member Preparatory Committee (chaired by the representative of Saudi Arabia, Mr Abdul Mohsen Al Sudeary, who later became IFAD's first President) established after the signing of the agreement, to work out detailed guidelines and regulations while the procedures required for the agreement to enter into force were being followed by the parties to it.[5]

5. It is interesting to note that the principle of consensus as adopted in these

The South's Negotiating Stance. To sum up, the IFAD experience clearly demonstrated the importance for the South, in the context of negotiations on such an intricate matter as the establishment of a new multilateral development institution, of having:

(1) a technical secretariat to articulate proposals;
(2) a small forum to negotiate details;
(3) credible attitudes on the part of those who ask for a change in the status quo; and
(4) readiness of the group to depart, when necessary, from the principle of unanimity as a basis for decision-making.

The Common Fund

The need for 'an overall integrated program for commodities of export interest to developing countries' was expressed in the resolutions of the UN General Assembly's Sixth Special Session (1974). The adoption of such a program, along with its main proposed element, a common fund for financing buffer stocks and related measures, figured in practically all the agendas of negotiations on world economic reforms which took place throughout the rest of the decade. Establishment of the projected common fund became almost an article of faith for the South, and was repeatedly sought in the declarations of successive meetings of the Group of 77.

The UNCTAD secretariat provided the required 'doctrine' through its documents for UNCTAD IV in Nairobi (1976) where a resolution was adopted for the negotiation of a common fund under an 'integrated program for commodities'. Meanwhile, the non-aligned countries were working independently on the drafting of an agreement for the 'creation of a special fund for financing buffer stocks' to be established and financed exclusively by them. When the Non-Aligned Summit Conference of 1976 discussed that issue, it found comfort, however, in deciding to delay consideration of the proposal 'pending the outcome of negotiations on the UNCTAD common fund'.

Based only on the agreement in principle reached in Nairobi, in 1976, (no further agreement was reached in the preparatory meetings which followed), a UN plenipotentiary negotiating conference

---

negotiations still prevails in the practice of the Executive Board of IFAD, in spite of the voting system provided for in its constituent agreement.

was held in 1977 under UNCTAD's auspices, to negotiate and finalize the draft agreement establishing the common fund. Despite the rhetorical support for the principle, and the sound, albeit ambitious ideas initially expressed in the UNCTAD secretariat's documents (which envisaged the fund as a US$ 6 billion multi-commodity stocking agency that would intervene directly in commodity markets), it was obvious from the outset that the differences between the Group of 77 and the OECD countries were too wide to allow the conference to reach agreement. A modified version submitted by the secretariat envisaged a fund with initial resources of US$ 3 billion of which US$ 1 billion would represent the share-capital and US$ 2 billion would be mobilized through borrowing. A tripartite structure similar to that of IFAD was mentioned. As an illustration, reference was made to a capital contribution of 37.5% each by the importing and exporting groups of countries (of the commodities involved), leaving 25% of capital to be subscribed by OPEC members.

The OPEC countries, as an expression of solidarity with other developing nations, declared their full support for the common fund concept. They requested, in early 1977, the Director-General of the OPEC Fund to act as coordinator of their delegations to the negotiating conference. When I attended the conference in this capacity, I was merely an observer rather than a direct participant, as was the case in IFAD. Nevertheless, I suggested to the UNCTAD secretariat, who agreed, that first its proposals should be scrutinized from a technical point of view by an expert group. This group, composed mainly of bankers, would ascertain the most suitable financial structure required, especially in view of the proposed reliance of the common fund on financial markets. After an informal meeting, chaired by myself, and involving IMF experts, private bankers and UNCTAD staff, had been held in Washington DC in the fall of 1977, two bankers' meetings were held in Geneva which greatly helped the secretariat in reformulating its proposals and in preparing more realistic supporting documents.

As the UN conference resumed its work, the different groups were gradually able to crystallize their positions. Developing countries wanted the proposed fund to be a central source of finance endowed with its own share capital and with the power to borrow, in the magnitudes proposed by the secretariat.

The objectives of such a fund were to include the financing of international commodity stocks, as well as other measures for perishable and other commodities whose problems could not be solved easily by stocking but which experience pèrsistent price fluctuations. Financing such other measures was to include grants and soft loans to the poorest members. The Group of 77 further wanted this fund to finance national stocks coordinated through an international commodity arrangement or organization (ICO) and to facilitate the establishment of new ICOs of special interest to the developing countries.

The OECD countries, on the other hand, who were slow to produce specific proposals, suggested a fund based on a system of mutual assistance among existing ICOs through a pool arrangement, without creating a new international institution. Credits extended through such an arrangement were to be made to participating commodity organizations on a commercial basis, and for the sole purpose of financing buffer stocks.

Each organization would deposit in the pool, 75% of the resources required to stabilize the prices of the commodity concerned within the limits negotiated by the producer and consumer governments who were members of that organization. Against that, it would have a guaranteed drawing right of up to 100% of its maximum financial requirements. The fund would in this version have been a cooperative of participating ICOs, governments contributing only to the ICOs of which they were members. Deposits of ICOs with financial surpluses would then finance credits to other ICOs which made stock purchases. If drawings on the fund exceeded total deposits, additional resources could be obtained by borrowing from the market against warrants on commodity stocks held by the ICOs, and by loans from international financial institutions.

OECD countries further proposed that measures other than buffer stocking should be kept outside this arrangement as they felt they should be handled by existing facilities, such as the IMF and the World Bank. OECD countries were prepared, however, to consider a role for the fund in respect of the ICOs which supervise internationally coordinated but nationally-held stocks.

The difference in group positions continued and the attempts of the chairman of the conference in 1979 to narrow the range of such differences through specific proposals failed. There were wide differences among the OECD countries themselves in respect of the proposed fund, the Netherlands and the Scandinavian countries coming close to the position of the Group of 77. Conducting the negotiations always as confrontation among categories helped therefore to polarize attitudes, and delayed compromise. Countries on both sides which could have acted otherwise probably felt committed to a group position which was quite often more rigid than a large number of countries would have been prepared to accept.

The coordinated role of OPEC countries in these negotiations was expressed in particular in three successive statements which I was mandated to make before the UN conference. In March 1977, at the initial stage of deliberations, a clear position was announced in support of the concept 'as a mechanism for bringing about a fundamental improvement in the pattern and terms of trade of primary commodities'. Tribute was paid, however, to the importance of seeing this mechanism as mutually beneficial to both producers and consumers 'in what, if it is to succeed fully, must be a universal and global endeavour'. Thus, while indicating that the UNCTAD secretariat's proposals provided 'a sound basis for negotiation', serious alternatives were invited and were promised careful consideration 'in a constructive and business-like manner'.

OPEC member countries, which then accounted for less than 3.5% of the trade shares in the 18 relevant commodities, were not, however, to be treated as a distinct category in this context. The common fund was not envisaged as a mechanism for the transfer of resources from OPEC to other developing countries. OPEC countries would therefore participate 'in the same manner as other developing countries do' but were ready in addition to consider 'special arrangements to ease the burden (of participation) on the poorest countries' and to study the possibility of eventually extending loans to the fund 'as a sound investment of liquid assets'. While maintaining this low-key posture, the statement added a point which was then unpopular among some representatives of the Group of 77 but which, as I was later told by several leading delegates, had a considerable impact on enabling the conference to reach agreement in the end. It may therefore be worth quoting in full:

As the Common Fund is presently envisaged to act as a central lender to various international commodity organizations, its financial needs will depend, in the first instance, on the availability of commodity organizations with the power to borrow from an international agency. At present only two such organizations exist. Others may be created as time passes. If one is to look to the matter in a practical way, the Fund's financial resources should obviously be related to its operational needs, starting at a level commensurate with the requirements of the existing commodity organizations, while allowing for future increases as new potential borrowers from the Fund come into existence. If I am to insert a personal note in this context, experience tells me that the practical and modest approach to solving problems yields a greater measure of acceptability, especially if it is flexible enough to adapt itself to new situations as they come out. It is also useful to realize in drawing the final agreement that it is neither possible nor advisable to try from the outset to find a specific answer to every minute detail. The objective could well be realized by reaching, in due course, a basic agreement on the general rules which would allow the Fund to be established and to handle problems as they arise.[6]

The second intervention of the OPEC Fund came in November 1978, at a time when protracted negotiations showed no sign of real progress. The emphasis then was to try to accelerate the pace of negotiation by providing concrete elements of support. A short statement was made which clearly indicated that all OPEC members intended to participate in the common fund and to contribute to its resources 'according to the criteria to be agreed upon in the conference'. In addition, the OPEC Fund was prepared 'to consider providing financial support to the Least Developed Countries in order to enable them, if they so wish, to meet part of their contribution to a common fund acceptable to the international community, including in particular the developing countries'. Finally, the OPEC Fund would in due course provide additional support to finance measures other than stock-piling to the benefit of the poorer countries through a 'second window' of the proposed fund.

The third intervention came a year later, in October 1979, when the elements of agreement had started to emerge. Specific pledges had to be made to provide the required credibility and to alleviate fears regarding the financial stability of an institution whose callable capital consisted to a substantial extent of contributions of developing countries. The points made at this stage were as follows:

(1) OPEC countries would participate as original members. Apart from the equal share expected from each member, they were willing to cover, if need be, up to one third of the variable portion of the mandatory contributions to be assigned to developing countries. (The Group of 77 later decided on a

6. UNCTAD document, TD/IPC/CF/CONF/8, paragraph 28.

general formula for the distribution of this portion among themselves, based on the UN Scale of Assessment (2/3) and GNP (1/3) without assigning any pre-established share for OPEC countries.)

(2) The OPEC Fund was ready to pay the equal portion of the mandatory contributions of all the Least Developed Countries acting as their agent *vis-à-vis* the common fund. (Later on, the OPEC Fund decided to provide grants for 35 countries, including the 31 LLDCs, to meet all their contributions to the common fund's direct capital.)

(3) The OPEC Fund was prepared to make a voluntary contribution to the second window of the common fund (for financing measures other than stock-piling) in an amount which would make its total assistance for common fund purposes in the order of US$ 100 million.

The statement emphasized again the conviction that 'a well conceived and well managed common fund will be in the joint interest of the developed and developing countries alike'. The objectives of this last intervention were put in no ambiguous terms:

In making this announcement at this stage, the OPEC Fund aims, in particular, at accelerating the process of the negotiation of the agreement establishing the Common Fund by opening the door for the membership of a large number of countries, with a ready and solid source of finance backing them. It aims further at strengthening the financial position of the Common Fund in the capital market by meeting the largest part of the contributions of its financially least able members. Finally, it hopes to set an example for the other countries in a position to do so, to follow suit, both in announcing their voluntary contributions to the second window and in making available additional amounts to enable the Most Seriously Affected Countries, which are not among the Least Developed, to meet their mandatory contributions to the Common Fund. The OPEC Fund is indeed prepared to make its commitments to the Least Developed Countries as part of a larger pool, the contributors to which would include other donors and the beneficiaries of which would, accordingly, be a larger number of developing countries.[7]

7. UNCTAD document, TD/ICP/CF/CONF/20, paragraph 69-74.

The coordinated approach followed by the OPEC countries in the negotiations on the establishment of the Common Fund for Commodities was one of the several important factors which finally led to agreement on a final text in 1980.[8] The decision of the UNCTAD secretariat to deal with the issue as a business matter of banking and finance and not necessarily as an attempt to introduce a drastic change in the structure of world trade, though belated, was also an important factor. The process could perhaps have been shorter, however, i) if rhetoric had been reduced to a minimum, ii) if original demands had been formulated more realistically, after consultation from the outset with the banking community, iii) if group positions on each detail had been avoided, iv) if specialists had been participating (most delegates consisted of diplomats, members of the permanent missions to the UN in Geneva) and, v) if greater emphasis had been placed on the mutual benefits which were likely to accrue to both sides from improving the terms of trade of developing countries. In hindsight, it is also believed that a more successful outcome would have been achieved, if the concentration of the UNCTAD secretariat and the South's delegates on the creation of the Common Fund had distracted less from the equally if not more important task of creating the ICOs required for the common Fund to function properly.

8. The *Agreement Establishing the Common Fund for Commodities* envisages a new institution which will finance, through its first window, stocking activities for the beneficiary ICOs, and through its second window, other measures of commodity development. Its 'directly contributed capital' (dcc) will consist of US$ 470 million (if its membership includes 150 countries, as optimistically envisaged). Each member will pay an equal share of US$ 1 million. The remaining US$ 320 million will be contributed as follows: 10% by the Group of 77; 68% by OECD countries; 17% by socialist countries; and 5% by China. At least US$ 70 million of the dcc is expected to be allocated to the second window in addition to US$ 280 million of voluntary contributions. Member countries of the beneficiary ICOs are also expected to issue guarantees to the Fund in the form of callable guarantee capital, to be called upon in case of default by the respective ICO *vis-à-vis* the fund. In addition, each ICO associated with the fund will deposit one third of its maximum financial requirement (mfr) with the Fund, will assign all its stock warrants to the fund and will use it as its only banker for its buffer stock operations. In time of need, each ICO will be entitled to withdraw its deposit and the remainder of its mfr from the fund. The ICO and its members, through their callable guarantee capital, will be responsible for repaying the Fund. In addition, the Fund will have the power to borrow from the market and from international financial institutions on the strength of its own capital, the callable guarantee capital of the members of associated ICOs, and the stock warrants assigned to the Fund by those ICOs. 47% of the voting power will be assigned to developing countries, 42% to OECD countries, 8% to socialist countries and 3% to China. See *Agreement Establishing the Common Fund for Commodities*, UNCTAD, TD/IPC/CF/CONF/24 (July 29, 1980).

PRE-REQUISITES OF A SUCCESSFUL DIALOGUE

Without underestimating the central importance of the often missing political will of the developed countries to accept significant changes in the status quo,[9] other conditions are also required from the developing countries and may themselves facilitate the emergence of such a will where it is lacking. The examples cited above were meant to point out the relevance for the countries of the South of adopting workable approaches and following effective procedures in their negotiations with their Northern counterparts. Emphasizing the importance of such procedural prerequisites should not, however, undermine the equally if not more important substantive requirements. Both form and substance are at any rate quite interrelated in this complex process.

Resolute Domestic Action

As I have elaborated elsewhere on a number of occasions[10], the South's demands for a new international economic order will be void of moral justification, and therefore of credibility, in the absence of new domestic economic orders which better reflect its policy makers' concern for development issues, within a framework of a just distribution of gains in their societies. The prevalent patterns of consumption in many developing countries, especially among the ruling elites who invariably set the example to others, cannot be reconciled readily with the frequently heard revolutionary demands for international (meaning external) reforms. The scarce resources of many developing countries are far from being properly managed at a time when the proper allocation and management of resources seems to be the most decisive factor in the development process.

The assumption that the North has built its prosperity on the

9. The 'lack of political will' should not be over-emphasized either. As Emile Van Lennep, the Secretary General of OECD, stated in a recent address 'there is at the highest political level (in the North) a clear recognition that in what has become a highly interdependent world economy there is a strong common interest in maintaining and accelerating economic progress in developing countries', Press/A (82) 51 at p. 1 (25 Oct 1982). The problem for the North seems to lie more in finding ways whereby such progress could be achieved in the South without adversely affecting the North, a typical dilemma in a 'rich-poor relationship'.

10. See, e.g., *The Other Face of OPEC*, pp. 20-39; 94.

exploitation of the South and should therefore pay for the latter's 'right to development' is, regardless of any judgement on its historical accuracy, simply inadequate to provide a sound basis for a productive dialogue. Without unduly exaggerating their strength, developing countries should not assume that their salvation is dependent on actions to be taken by the North. By making such an assumption, they would in fact be depriving themselves of their legitimate right and obligation to develop, and subordinating their economic future to the good will of others, who do not always have the interest or the means to deliver.

Instead, developing countries are best advised to realize that development must start at home, as has always been the case. Their basic demand should therefore center around the creation of an international environment in which serious development efforts on their part are not hindered by formidable external factors, such as those prevailing at present. Such a formulation of the South's demands combines the quest for changes in the international order with prior acceptance by the South's decision-makers of new resolute domestic policies, with all the sacrifices they necessarily entail.

The changes required in the domestic policies of developing countries are most clearly manifest in two areas which remain generally unaffected despite all the on-going debates on possible reforms. Surprisingly, these two areas have, for various but unacceptable reasons, been excluded from most discussions on economic changes. Their present dimensions make it impossible, however, to ignore them in any serious discussion. These areas are the questions of unprecedented population growth and massive increase in armaments expenditures.

Population

Growth of population threatens the future, and in several cases the present, economic life in most developing countries. Yet serious action is either lacking or falls short of producing significant results. Recent studies indicate that developing countries, China included, which accounted in 1980 for 3.3 billion of the world's population of 4.4 billion (i.e. 75%) will account, in the year 2000, for some 4.8 billion of a total population of some 6 billion (i.e. 80%). The crude birth rate and the gross reproduction rate in the South are more than double those in the North — see Table 8. The South lacks the physical and institutional means to meet the requirements of such a fast-growing population. In large parts of the developing world, food

Table 8: Population Statistics

	Crude birth rate %	Crude death rate %	Life expectancy years	Gross reproduction rate %
Developed countries (North America, Europe, USSR, Australasia)	1.58	0.96	72.5	0.98
Developing countries	3.14	1.10	57.0	2.04

Source: UNFPA, *World Population Wall Chart*, 1982.

production is not growing, or is growing at a slower rate than population.[11]

The resulting constraints have immediate effects on the balance of payments of many food-importing developing countries, and almost inevitably lead to severe distortions in other sectors. In particular, education and employment policies are badly affected, with overall negative implications on the development prospects of the countries concerned. It is striking that a problem with that dimension is still taken lightly in most densely populated countries in deference to local considerations which are all but ignored by the same decision makers when it comes to issues of lesser importance to the future generations of these countries.

Armaments

The other area of concern is the spending on armaments in developing countries. Much has been said about the wasteful and menacing arms expenditures in the world which, as the Brandt Commission lucidly explained, dwarf any spending on development while making mankind poorer not safer.[12] It is also generally realized that

11. This is particularly true in Africa. For details see IBRD's *World Development Report 1982*, p. 42 and *Accelerated Development in Sub-Saharan Africa — An Agenda for Action*. According to these sources, agricultural output per capita in Africa grew at 0.2% a year during the 1960s but then fell by 1.4% a year in the 1970s. According to FAO, however, 'the annual rate of decrease in average per capita food production during the 1960s (0.7%) actually worsened during the 1970s (1.6%)'. FAO/OAU, *Famine in Africa: Situation, Cause, Prevention, Control*, 1982.

12. The Independent Commission on Development Issues, *North-South, An Agenda for Survival*, p. 117, 1980.

savings in arms spending in the North could represent the most promising prospect for massive increases in official development assistance to the South. Acccording to the Brandt Commission, 'the cost of a ten year program to provide for essential food and health needs in developing countries is less than half of one year's military spending'.

Yet, instead of providing examples of restraint in this area, developing countries have been spending a greater proportion of their GDPs on their armed forces than the developed countries, with the added burden that most of their arms are imported and are paid for in hard currencies. Worse still, the rate of growth in military expenditures in recent years has been higher in the South than in the North. In 1981, Third World countries, excluding China, were reported to have spent US$ 83 billion on arms, almost double the amount spent in 1971.[13] In most cases, this great growth in spending on armaments was not in response to greater defence needs as much as to the intensive marketing campaigns of the arms exporters, coupled with the importers' illusion that greater quantities of arms bring greater security and stability.

The fact remains that the Third World as a whole spends on weapons much more than it spends on education and health combined.[14] In several cases expenditure on arms is more than double the spending on economic development, which results in lower growth rates and almost always in greater chances of armed conflict.

It may not be realistic, however, to expect any single developing country to reduce arms spending unilaterally while its neighbours continue the arms race. This is indeed an area where national action has to follow collective arrangements, at least on the sub-regional level. Taking such action assumes mutual conviction among neighbouring countries in the peaceful settlement of disputes. This conviction, which seemed strong in the post-World-War-II years, has been increasingly weakened as military aggression went unpunished in a number of cases.

Developing countries have to realize, however, that excessive spending on arms cannot provide a solution for their problems. If there are winners in this race, they are likely to be those who export the arms to them. Developing countries should therefore practise

13. See, Stockholm International Peace Research Institute, *World Armament and Disarmament Year Book*, 1981.
14. Sivard, R.L., 'World Military and Social Expenditure', *South*, no. 21, July 1982, London.

greater restraint in the face of attempts by outside powers to mani-
pulate political differences among them, in order to promote their
own short-term interests at the expense of the parties to the disputes.
It is distressing to see some developing countries facing such manipu-
lation at times with complete predisposition.

Intra-South Cooperation

In addition to the action each developing country is called upon to
take within its borders, a vast realm is open for joint action by these
countries in the fields of economic and technical cooperation. Several
conferences have already been held on this matter, most notably in
Buenos Aires (1979), Caracas (1980) and New Delhi (1981), and
several UN agencies have already established new bureaucracies to
handle the subject.

Actual cooperation remains modest, however, outside the impressive area of financial assistance provided by OPEC member
countries. Most of the new initiatives proposed at present have also
assumed in one way or another, a pattern of 'cooperation' where a
few OPEC countries who are in surplus, continue to subsidize the
others. This simplistic approach cannot lead to practical conclusions,
especially as most OPEC countries are experiencing increasing
financial difficulties. More balanced patterns of cooperation
resulting in mutual benefits are needed now more than ever. The
following areas could be of particular promise in this respect although
they are by no means exhaustive.

Direct investments

The transfer of resources among developing countries for the
creation of new real investments is still limited. In many cases it is
effected through outside intermediaries. A number of bilateral and
multilateral investment corporations have been established mainly
between Arab/OPEC sources and other developing countries.
National investment companies in the Gulf area are slowly increasing
their activities in developing countries. The Islamic Development
Bank has given clear preference in its activities to equity participation, and the Kuwait Fund has been authorized to go into direct
investments in addition to its lending activities. More recently, the
Arab countries that are members of the Gulf Cooperation Council
have set up a joint investment authority which is expected to con-

centrate on external investments.

These are all welcome developments. They should gradually open the door for an increase in the real wealth of the South, converting the paper claims held with Western banks into new productive investments. They should also result in large-scale commercially viable enterprises capable of benefitting from a more fair cooperation with the transnational corporations of the North. But this trend should be encouraged to grow faster.

Potential host countries should take conscious measures to improve investment climates in their territories and to accelerate international efforts for the establishment of the multilateral investment guarantee scheme presently being considered by the World Bank. The relatively industrialized developing countries in particular should take a leading role in this trend as they stand to gain most from it. They should provide funds as well as managerial and technical skills for the formation of new investment companies and joint ventures, which will eventually result in increased demand for their goods and services. It is a great mistake to think of this field as one where the initiative may be taken only by the Arab/OPEC countries who are in surplus, or to consider it a continuation of the aid phenomenon, which is lopsided by definition.

Investment opportunities abound in the Third World, and some of them require joint action. All developing countries are in principle qualified to participate in such action, once they perceive it as a business endeavour where each participant should have a fair return. In fact, joint investment corporations established by developing countries (including the countries in which the corporations operate) are likely to have a much greater sense of security than other typical foreign investors.

Consider the case of India. This is a country which has indeed a very low per capita income. But it is also one of the few major industrial powers and is rich in managerial skills and technology. It also has huge financial assets, low per capita income notwithstanding. India certainly has the capacity to sponsor|the formation of joint ventures in many fields, where concerns from other developing countries could join for investment on a commercial basis, inside and outside India. As I had the occasion to explain to Indian officials years ago, the volume of funds that can be generated in this way will exceed by far the amounts India may be able to receive on concessional terms from other (i.e. OPEC) developing countries. It is gratifying to see this trend starting to bear fruit.

Trade

The exports of developing countries witnessed, in the seventies, an unprecedented expansion in volume and value. Most of this expansion centered, however, on two areas: exports to the DAC countries of the OECD, which moved from a low of US$ 47.7 billion in 1970, to US$ 424 billion in 1980 (or from US$ 31.8 billion to US$ 171.3 billion if fuel is excluded)[15] and trade between the OPEC and non-OPEC developing countries, which has increased on average by some 40% a year since 1974.[16] Outside these areas, the increase in trade transactions among developing countries has not been impressive.

Agreements reached on trade liberalization in several sub-regions have also faced serious obstacles, in most cases in the form of non-tariff barriers, exceptions and the like. Here again the scope for new initiatives is wide open. A serious implementation of the already existing agreements on economic unity, economic integration, customs unions and trade liberalization would itself result in significant changes. Experience shows, however, an obvious gap between written agreements and reality. In some regions, countries bound by agreements of this type do not even maintain diplomatic relations. The relatively industrialized developing countries could again take a lead in this area, by advocating systems of preferences among developing countries in favour of the poorer among them. Such arrangements would put these countries in a better position when they ask for similar preferences from the developed countries.

The OPEC Fund is at present, through its *Procurement guidelines*, granting certain preferences, upon the request of the borrowing country, for goods and services procured under its loans and produced in developing countries. The Arab Fund has similar arrangements for procurement from Arab countries; IFAD has a developing countries' preference clause in its constituent agreement and procurement guidelines. It remains to be seen, however, whether such policies will lead to practical changes. The assumption is that the borrowing country will be authorized to procure from a source in another developing country even if that source is more expensive up to a certain limit ($7^1/_2$% in the case of the OPEC Fund). Will the borrowing countries be prepared to make such sacrifices for the sake

15. OECD, *Trade Statistics*, 1982, DAC (82) 20, Table IV-I.
16. GATT, *Report on Prospects for International Trade*, 1979.

of greater inter-South trade and cooperation? And what are the semi-industrialized developing countries prepared to do in return?

Another preference clause introduced in the *Procurement guidelines* of the OPEC Fund stands a greater chance of application. Competitive bidding for goods and services, according to this clause, may be limited to a certain developing country or countries, if they agree to co-finance the project involved on concessional terms acceptable to the Fund. Both the Fund and the borrower have, in this case, to be satisfied with the technical ability of the firms among which bidding is to be limited. This clause has already been applied in the implementation of a coal survey project in Mozambique which Brazil agreed to co-finance with the Fund. It has also been applied to the OPEC Fund's grant to the World Food Program (WFP) designed to finance food imports from the developing countries which agree to sell foodstuffs to the WFP on concessional terms. Argentina, Burma and Zimbabwe have already cooperated in the implementation of this scheme.[17]

Technical Cooperation

An oil exploration project financed by the OPEC Fund is being implemented in Tanzania at present. The drilling contractor is Sonatrach of Algeria and the reviewing consultants are the inter-governmental Arab Engineering Company.[18] This is a rare example of technical cooperation in an exclusively inter-South context maintained through the conscious efforts of the OPEC Fund. Another example is the Mozambique coal project referred to above where the technical work is being carried out by Brazilian concerns.

The governments of developing countries should look for similar areas of cooperation where the experience of consultants and contractors of other developing countries may be of relevance to their needs. It would be counter-productive, however, if this is taken to mean discrimination among consultants on account of their nationalities regardless of their technical capacities. It means only that where a country is likely to benefit more from the relevant expertise of another developing country, it should make an effort towards securing that expertise. Some developing countries have successfully developed technologies which can be used readily in the similar

17. For details see the annual reports of the OPEC Fund for International Development for 1981 and 1982.
18. For details see the OPEC Fund for International Development, *Annual Report 1982*.

conditions of other developing regions. The contribution China can make in this particular field should be of great relevance.

Labour

The magnitude of the movements of labour among developing countries in recent years is indeed impressive, especially between certain Asian and Middle Eastern countries and the Arab countries of the Gulf.[19] The annual volume of workers' remittances from six Arab countries only, is already estimated in two-digit figures of billions of US dollars. This important phenomenon remains, however, largely unregulated. The financial benefits to the workers' home countries have a high social cost in both the home and the host countries, as a recent study commissioned by the OPEC Fund has proven.[20] It is time therefore that the countries concerned take the required steps to maximize the benefits and minimize the harm for both sides, as well as for the workers themselves.

Conclusion

Throughout this chapter I have concentrated on what the South ought to be doing in a relationship which can succeed only if the two sides actively cooperate. This is not to suggest that the contribution the South is called upon to make in this process is necessarily more important than the action required from the North. The emphasis is only the result of my conviction that the South cannot aspire to a successful dialogue if its countries look only for concessions from the North while introducing no changes in their own attitudes.

In a world faced with increasing strains on the economies of both the North and the South, developing countries must prove their credibility through their own serious actions. To assume that their salvation must be brought about by the North is to impart to the latter an ability which is obviously beyond its present means. It also deprives the South of its legitimate right and duty, to develop itself. What is required in the first instance is the serious resolve of the South to improve its own lot, and the action that must follow that resolve. The North should be called upon to cooperate in the creation of an

19. See World Bank, *Report on Labour Migration and Manpower in the Middle East and North Africa*, 1981.
20. Center for Arab Unity Studies, *Manpower Movement Among Arab Countries, Problems, Effects and Policies* (in Arabic), 1982.

international environment in which developing countries which adopt such serious policies can readily achieve the positive results of their efforts, without being hindered by insurmountable external factors.

The present world recession has demonstrated beyond doubt that the pace of growth in the South depends to a great extent on the degree of the North's prosperity. The immediate task facing both at present is to put the world economic recovery into motion. In doing so, they are well advised not to lose sight of the real causes of the present situation, which resulted mainly from actions the North took, or failed to take in time, and was only exacerbated by certain attitudes in the South. The development of the South has become progressively relevant to the prosperity of the North. International division of labour, international trade and international finance must therefore be gradually adapted to these new realities, or risk further disorders, to the detriment of all.

Further acrimony and confrontation between North and South are likely to result in greater losses to both. What should be pursued therefore are the mutual gains that will accrue from world recovery based on the development of the South and the revival of the North. It does not matter much if such a process is called a new world economic order, or simply a progressive integration of the South into a system of global interdependence to which the present order, or lack or order, will be well adapted.

ANNEX 1: THE OPEC FUND'S LOANS AND GRANTS, 1976—APRIL, 1983, BY REGION

For a list of acronyms, see p. 282. In each case, the institution that is administering the Fund's loan is printed in bold type in the list of co-financiers.

AFRICA

1 Angola

Project Loan

Lobito Route Rehabilitation Project — Benguela Railway.
- *Loan of US$3 million*; interest-free; 20-year maturity, including a 5-year grace period; January 14, 1980
- Co-financiers: **BADEA**, Governments of Belgium, the Netherlands and Sweden, and UNDP
- Executing agency: Companhia Caminho de Ferro de Benguela (CCFB)
- Total cost: US$18.2 million

The project is to rehabilitate part of the Benguela railway line which originates in the Angolan port of Lobito and extends though Zambia's copper belt to the region of Shaba in Zaire. The project's objectives are to provide CCFB with sufficient motive power, rolling stock, spare parts, track material, and technical assistance to restore the line's capacity.

2 Benin

Project Loans

Godomey-Bohicon-Abomey Highway.
- *Loan of US$1.6 million*; interest-free; 20-year maturity, including a 5-year grace period; January 10,1978
- Co-financiers: IDA and **KFAED**
- Executing agency: Directorate of Roads and Bridges (DRB)
- Total cost: US$21.3 million

This project involves the rehabilitation of 107km of the Godomey-Bohicon-Abomey Highway, the resurfacing of about 195km of bituminous roads and 450km of laterite roads, the strengthening of the ongoing routine maintenance programme, as well as technical assistance to the Directorate of Roads and Bridges. The project is expected to improve significantly the movement of goods and people in the country.

Line of Credit to Banque Beninoise pour le Developpement (BBD).
- *Loan of US$4.5 million*; interest-free; 20-year maturity, including a 5-year grace period; December 14, 1979
- Co-financier: **IDA**

BBD, a development finance bank established for the purpose of assisting economic

..... social development projects, will use the proceeds of the line of credit to provide financing for projects totally owned by Benin nationals, at least one fifth of the funds going to artisans.

Second Highway Project.
- *Loan of US$6.0 million*; interest-free; 20-year maturity, including a 5-year period; July 15, 1981
- Co-financier: **IDA**
- Executing agency: Directorates of Roads and Bridges (DRB)
- Total cost: US$19.5 million

The project is designed to continue the strengthening of the DRB begun under the Godomey-Bohicon-Abomey Highway Project, and to introduce road safety measures and rehabilitate 54km of paved main roads and 500km of gravel roads. The Benin road system is essential to the domestic economy and handles traffic of neighboring countries as well. The project will benefit the estimated 400,000 road users, by reducing their vehicle operating costs and improving safety. Significant benefits are also expected from strengthening DRB institutionally.

Atacora Province Rural Development Project.
- *Loan of US$4.0 million*; interest-free; 20-year maturity, including a 5-year grace period;
- Co-financier: IFAD (**IDA**)[1]
- Executing agency: Centre d'action Regional pour le Developpement Rural (CARDER)-Atacora
- Total cost: US$14.9 million

The project is the first province-wide, coordinated effort to develop the Atacora Province in northwestern Benin. Its main objectives are: i) to increase the incomes of about 30,000 rural families through increased crop and livestock production; ii) to improve the standard of living of the region's population through improved water supply and management; and iii) to strengthen CARDER-Atacora, the local institution responsible for coordinating and executing rural development activities.

The main benefits are increased production of maize, groundnuts, rice and sorghum. This would benefit about 28,000 farm families (210,000 people), increasing their net annual income by between 30% and 54% to between US$388 and US$746 depending on the zone of the province. Families with an annual income of between US$29 and US$111 per year would realize annual incomes of between US$83 and US$194 as a result of participation in the project.

Apart from its quantifiable benefits, the project would have a considerable impact on the structure and operations of CARDER-Atacora. With the technical assistance provided under the project, the institution would be able to manage future rural development projects. In addition, it would be able to apply better financial control, input supply management, monitoring, and evaluation over these projects.

---

1. Although not a co-financier of the project, IDA is administering IFAD's loan and the Fund's loan.

South Benin Fuelwood Development Project.
- Loan of US$2.5 million; interest-free; 17-year maturity, including 5-year grace period;
- Co-financiers: **AfDF**, WFP
- Executing agency: Direction des Eaux, Forets et Chasse (MFEEP)
- Total cost: US$17.16 million

The project aims at alleviating the acute shortage of energy for domestic uses through the expansion of the fuelwood on offer on the South Benin market. Furthermore, the project will contribute to the development or improvement of basic infrastructure in the region, such as roads, buildings, housing, community centers, etc. It consists of the plantation of 5,900 ha of fuelwood mainly in South Benin, 3,500 ha of which will be Government-owned and 2,400 privately owned. For the Government-owned plantations, the project will include land clearance, soil preparation, planting and maintenance. As for the privately-owned plantations, it will provide the technical assistance required, establish 8 nurseries with transportation means, and distribute the food provided by the World Food Program destined for plantation owners. The plants will be provided free of charge and credits will be granted to the cooperatives and production units.

Apart from the salaries earned, the project is expected to directly benefit 400 families participating in the Government-controlled plantations, increasing their annual revenue from the present 96,000 FCFA level to FCFA 225,000 by the production of maize and other subsistence crops in the prepared areas. The private/rural plantations will benefit 4,000 individual producers, whose revenues will increase from the present FCFA 166,200 to an estimated level of FCFA 256,850. Further, it is estimated that the project, which will stretch across the whole of South Benin, will provide an example for the development of fuelwood in the region, and hopefully, will trigger the development of further such plantations greatly needed by the country.

Balance of Payments Support Loans.
- *Loan of US$2.0 million*; interest-free; 25-year maturity, including a 5-year grace period; March 2, 1977
- Utilization: Purchase of insecticides
- *Loan of US$4.5 million*; interest-free; 10-year maturity, including a 3-year grace period; July 14, 1980
- Utilization: Not yet determined

Local Counterpart Funds

Line of Credit to Banque Beninoise pour le Developpement (BBD).
- Allocation: US$2.0 million equivalent; August 1, 1978
- For project description see above.

3 Botswana

Project Loans

Mahalapye-Serule Road.
- Loan of US$1.0 million; interest-free; 20-year maturity, including a 5-year grace period; October 7, 1977
- Co-financier: **IBRD**

● Executing agency: Directorate of Roads and Bridges
● Total cost: US$28.0 million

The Mahalapye-Serule Road is part of the North-South artery which links Botswana with Zambia in the north, South Africa in the south and Zimbabwe in the east.

The project, considered by the Government as vital to the Botswana economy, will replace an existing earth road, vulnerable to rain, by a main structure built to all-weather standards through flat terrain. Traffic interruptions during heavy rains would be avoided; road user and maintenance costs are expected to be significantly reduced.

The project also involves the provision of (a) technical assisance by consultants in the preparation of a feeder roads programme, to be part of a larger rural development project; (b) a road maintenance study undertaken by IBRD in its Third Road Project in Botswana; and (c) provision of equipment and construction of classrooms and office space in the Roads Department Training School, which is expected to increase significantly its capacity to train operators.

Gaborone International Airport Project.
● *Loan of US$3.0 million*; 4% interest; 20-year maturity, including a 5-year grace period; May 21, 1982
● Co-financiers: **AfDB**, KFW, KFAED, BADEA, SF
● Executing agency: Ministry of Works and Communications
● Total cost: US$55.43 million

The objective of the project is to increase air transportation facilities by the construction of a modern international airport in the capital city capable of handling both long and medium-range jet aircraft and occasional wide-bodied jets.

Balance of Payments Support Loans
● *Loan of US$2.0 million*; interest-free; 15-year maturity, including a 5-year grace period; November 26, 1979
● Utilization: vaccine, agriculture
● *Loan of US$1.0 million*; 4% annual interest rate; 10-year maturity, including a 3-year grace period; July 29, 1980
● Utilization: not yet determined

Local Counterpart Funds

Foot and Mouth Disease Vaccine.
● Allocation: US$2.0 million equivalent; August 22, 1980

The project envisages the establishment of a temporary laboratory to test and produce 2 million doses of foot and mouth vaccine, and subsequently, a permanent laboratory to manufacture over 15 million doses per year. The latter amount is sufficient to eradicate the disease in Botswana and will allow for the export of the surplus vaccine to neighboring countries

Gaborone International Airport Project.
● Allocation: US$1.0 million equivalent; May 21, 1982
For project description, see above

Common Fund

A grant in the amount of US$1.02 million was extended on May 21, 1982 to Botswana to cover its mandatory subscription of shares of directly contributed capital of the Common Fund for Commodities.

4 Burundi

Project Loans

East-Mpanda Rural Development.
- • Loan of US$2.0 million; interest-free; 20-year maturity, including a 5-year grace period; January 15, 1980
    - • Co-financiers: **AfDB**, IFAD, EDF and World Food Program
    - • Executing agency: Société Régionale de Développement de l'Imbo (SRDI)
    - • Total cost: US$42.5 million

The project comprises the development of 6,000 ha of land in the Ruzizi Valley, of which 2,400 ha will be irrigated; the resettling of families in the region from the over-populated nearby hills; and assistance to the families already established in the project area. The latter component will include well drilling and the construction of schools, dispensaries, warehouses and supply stores.

Bujumbura Storm Water Drainage.
- • Loan of US$3.0 million; interest-free; 20-year maturity, including a 5-year grace period; November 12, 1980
- • Co-financiers: **BADEA** and AfDB
- • Executing agency: Régie de Distribution d'Eau et d'Electricité
- • Total cost: US$14.0 million

The project consists of the rehabilitation of the Bujumbura storm water drainage system, including the construction of rainwater collectors throughout the city. The project will prevent flooding, and thereby protect public and private property, and reduce the high incidence of bacterial diseases and malaria.

Mosso Sugar.
- • Loan of US$7.0 million; interest-free; 20-year maturity, including a 5-year grace period; October 8, 1981
- • Co-financiers: ADF, **BADEA** and AfDB
- • Executing agency: Société Sucrière du Mosso
- • Total cost: US$70.6 million

The project involves the cultivation and processing of sugar cane to produce 16,000 tons of commercial white sugar per year. It comprises the establishment of a drainage and irrigation system for the 1,925 ha area to be cultivated with sugar cane, the construction of a sugar refining factory with a nominal capacity of 1,000 tons per day and the building of a township for the agro-industrial complex. Energy for the factory will be supplied through the combustion of waste sugar cane, which will produce enough energy to meet most of the power needs of the factory, irrigation pumps and domestic energy consumption in the township. In addition to meeting almost all of Burundi's sugar needs through the 1980s, the project will also provide employment and attract people to a sparsely populated, under-cultivated area of the country.

Balance of Payments Support Loans
- *Loan of US$1.7 million*; interest-free; 25-year maturity, including a 5-year grace period; February 4, 1977
- Utilization: equipment
- *Loan of US$4.5 million*; interest-free; 15-year maturity, including a 5-year grace period; July 16, 1979
- Utilization: equipment, food

Local Counterpart Funds

Bujumbura-Mutambara Road Project.
- Allocation: US$1.7 million equivalent; July 11, 1978

A 75km track linking Bujumbura, Burundi's capital city, with Mutambara in the south of the country, will be paved. The road will have a paved width of 6 meters. The project also includes the construction of 20 bridges. The project will facilitate the transport of goods and passengers through the southern area of the country, thereby stimulating agricultural development in that area.

Coffee Improvement Project.
- Allocation: US$1.11 million equivalent; February 8, 1980

The chief benefits of this project are the increased production of coffee and improved processing. Over a 5-year period this project will support the development of small-holder coffee and other food crop production in Ngozi Province through the distribution of farm inputs and the strengthening of extension services.

Second Highway Project.
- Allocation: US$2.67 million equivalent; February 8, 1980

The purpose of the project is to enhance and modernize road transportation within the country through the reconstruction of the main 65km Bujumbura-Cibitoke-Rugombo Road to two-lane bituminous standard. The project comprises the replacement of obsolete bridges and the paving of steeply-graded road sections.

Water Extension Project.
- Allocation: US$255,000 equivalent; June 9, 1980

The project's objective is to modernize and extend the water supply facilities in Bujumbura in order to meet the increasing demand for water in the city. It consists of laying 155,390 meters of piping and is designed to complement a project financed by IDA.

Bujumbura Storm Water Drainage Project.
- Allocation: US$465,000 equivalent; November 12, 1980

For project description see above.

Common Fund

A grant in the amount of US$1.0 million was extended on October 30, 1981 to Burundi to cover its mandatory subscription of shares of directly contributed capital of the Common Fund for Commodities.

5 Cameroon

Project Loan

Line of Credit to Banque Camerounaise de Developpement (BCD).
- Loan of US$4.5 million; interest-free; 20-year maturity, including a 5-year grace period; August 28, 1979
- Co-financiers: AfDB and **IBRD**

The loan proceeds are to be on-lent by the Government of Cameroon to the BCD, a national semi-public institution, and the country's main development finance agency.

The BCD's principal aim is to assist, financially and technically, in the implementation of projects in all sectors to promote Cameroon's economic and social development.

For that purpose, it participates, inter alia, in the financing of small and medium-scale enterprises and handicrafts.

Balance of Payments Support Loan

- *Loan of US$4.95 million*; interest-free; 25-year maturity; including a 5-year grace period; February 4, 1977
- Utilization: fungicide for cocoa plants

6 Cape Verde

Project Loan

Telecommunications Project.
- Loan of US$1.50 million; interest-free; 20-year maturity, including a 5-year grace period; May 21, 1982
- Co-financiers: AfDB, Iraqi Fund, Government of Brazil (Loan to be administered by OPEC Fund directly)
- Executing agency: Direction Nationals des Postes et Télécommunications
- Total cost: US$12.5 million

The objective of the project is to upgrade the existing telecommunications system to respond to the increasing demands of the country and to accommodate particularly the number of economic projects presently being undertaken. It is intended to reinforce communications between the administrative and economic centers and the rest of the islands comprising the nation, as well as the rest of the world.

Balance of Payments Support Loans

- *Loan of US$1.55 million*; interest-free; 25-year maturity including a 5-year grace period; January 10, 1977
- Utilization: electrical equipment
- *Loan of US$1.0 million*; interest-free; 15-year maturity, including a 5-year grace period; July 28, 1978
- Utilization: foodstuff
- *Loan of US$1.0 million*; interest-free; 15-year maturity, including a 5-year grace period; July 11, 1979
- Utilization: foodstuff
- *Loan of US$1.5 million*; interest-free; 10-year maturity, including a 3-year grace period; April 21, 1980

- Utilization: foodstuff
- *Loan of US$1.0 million*; interest-free; 10-year maturity, including a 3-year grace period; May 27, 1981
- Utilization: foodstuff

Local Counterpart Funds

1977/78 Emergency Program.
- Allocation: US$1.55 million equivalent; March 29, 1978

This emergency program was prompted by the negative effects of the prolonged drought which has been plaguing Cape Verde. The purpose of the program is to increase areas under agricultural development by developing the country's hydro-agricultural and transport infrastructure. The program is labor-intensive providing significant employment and therefore providing a source of income to the rural population.

'Bolacha' and Pasta Factory.
- Allocation: US$1.0 million equivalent; January 10, 1980

The objective of the project, whose implementation is supervised by the United Nations Industrial Development Organization, is to build a modern industrial unit for the production of 'Bolacha' (biscuit) and pasta to meet domestic demand and allow for exports.

Telecommunications Project.
- Allocation: US$1.0 million; May 21, 1982

For project description see above.

Common Fund

A grant in the amount of US$1.0 million was extended on March 1, 1982 to Cape Verde to cover its mandatory subscription of shares of directly contributed capital of the Common Fund for Commodities.

7 Central African Republic

Project Loan

Road Rehabilitation Project.
- Loan of US$5.1 million; interest-free; 20-year maturity, including a 5-year grace period; July 28, 1982
- Co-financiers: **KFAED**, IDA, AfDB, Central African Development Bank and Fonds d'Aide et de Cooperation of France
- Executing agency: Ministry of Transport and Civil Aviation
- Total cost: US$48.1 million.

The major objective of the project is to rehabilitate the most important segment of the country's road network, a key element in the economic rehabilitation of the Central African Republic. The project will also help strengthen the institutional framework necessary to ensure the maintenance of the road network, largely by national personnel, once rehabilitation has taken place.

Balance of Payments Support Loan

- *Loan of US$1.75 million*; interest-free; 25-year maturity, including a 5-year grace period; December 23, 1976
- Utilization: crude oil and educational materials

Local Counterpart Funds

Education Project.
- Allocation: US$0.7 million equivalent; December 23, 1977

This project is designed to support Government's efforts to improve educational facilities and to develop a long-term plan for the education sector. The project will strengthen the country's existing institutions in the education sector as well as assist in alleviating the country's manpower shortages and dependence on expatriate personnel. The Fund's contribution will meet the Government's total share of project financing.

Common Fund

A grant in the amount of US$1.3 million was extended on October 31, 1981 to the Central African Republic to cover its mandatory subscription of shares of directly contributed capital of the Common Fund for Commodities.

8 Chad

Project Loan

Mamdi Polder Irrigation
- Loan of US$2.45 million; interest-free; 20-year maturity, including a 5-year grace period; October 2, 1978
- Co-financiers: **IsDB** and BADEA
- Executing agency: Société de Développement du Lac (SODELAC)
- Total cost: US$18.65 million

This irrigation project involves the reclamation of a polder in the archipelago of the Lake Chad area, the construction of the necessary irrigation and drainage networks and the preparation of the polder for cultivation. The project provides for levelling and terracing and calls for the organization of the polder in small units to be distributed to farmers. The establishment of services including training facilities is part of the project.

Balance of Payments Support Loan

- Loan of US$2.4 million; interest-free; 25-year maturity, including a 5-year grace period; February 3, 1977
- Utilization: fertilizer

Local Counterpart Funds

Mamdi Polder Project.
- Allocation: US$2.4 million equivalent

The utilization of these local counterpart funds will complement the Fund's foreign exchange participation in the project.

9 Comoros

Project Loans

Road Improvement and Maintenance.
- Loan of US$1.0 million; interest-free; 20-year maturity, including a 5-year grace period; July 28, 1978
- co-financiers: AfDB and **IDA**
- Executing agency: National Center for Planning, Finance and Methods (NCPFM)
- Total cost: US$11.68 million

The project involves the expansion of the main road network, a three-year road improvement and maintenance programme, the preparation of a subsequent highway project, as well as technical assistance. A further objective of the project is to improve the institutional framework for the development of the road sector. The road construction element, which accounts for 50% of the estimated costs, will benefit one of the country's most densely populated and undeveloped areas. The new road system will facilitate the implementation of an integrated rural development programme planned for the near future.

Mutsamudu Port Project.
- Loan of US$2.0 million; interest-free; 20-year maturity, including a 5-year grace period
- Co-financiers: AfDB, KFAED, BADEA, **IsDB**, ADF
- Executing agency: Ministry of Equipment and Environment
- Total cost: US$45.8 million

The project aims at expanding the existing facilities at Mutsamudu on the island of Anjouan, and building a deep-water port capable of berthing large ships.

Balance of Payments Support Loan
- *Loan of US$0.5 million;* interest-free; 20-year maturity, including a 5-year grace period; May 16, 1977
- Utilization: cement, oil, foodstuff
- *Loan of US$0.5 million;* interest-free; 15-year maturity, including a 5-year grace period; July 28, 1978
- Utilization: foodstuff
- *Loan of US$1.0 million;* interest-free; 10-year maturity, including a 3-year grace period; March 17, 1980
- Utilization: oil

Common Fund

A grant in the amount of US$1.0 million was extended on February 23, 1982 to Comoros to cover its mandatory subscription of shares of directly contributed capital of the Common Fund for Commodities.

10 Congo

Project Loan

Chemin de Fer Congo-Ocean (CFCO) Railway Realignment.
- Loan of US$8.0 million; 4% interest; 20-year maturity, including 4-year grace period; October 24, 1980
- Co-financiers: **KFAED**, SF, IDA, EDF
- Executing agency: Agence Trans-congolaise des Communications (ATC)
- Total cost: US$357.2 million

The project consists of (a) the completion of the realignment of the CFCO Railway, including earthworks, bridges and tunnels in Bilinga and Loubomo; track and ballast; signaling and telecommunications equipment; (b) the procurement of machinery; and (c) consulting services for supervision and assistance to ATC.

Balance of Payments Support Loan

- *Loan of US$4.0 million*; 4% interest; 15-year maturity, including a 5-year grace period; November 17, 1978
- Utilization: equipment, foodstuff

Local Counterpart Funds

Second Education Project.
- Allocation: US$4.0 million equivalent; November 17, 1978

The local counterpart funds which will be generated under the above BOP support loan to the Congo will be set aside to finance the Government's contribution to the Second Education Project. The project is designed to expand and improve primary teacher training, to locally prepare and produce educational materials, to train technical instructors and reinforce the Government's educational planning capability. The project will introduce substantial qualitative improvements in the country's educational system.

11 Djibouti

Project Loan

Boulaos Power Extension Project.
- Loan of US$2.5 million; interest-free; 20-year maturity, including a 5-year grace period; July 15, 1982
- Co-financiers: KFAED, AFESD, **IsDB** and Caisse Centrale de Cooperation Economique of France
- Total cost: US$47.5 million

The project's objective is to expand the existing Boulaos Power station by adding two units of 15 megawatts diesel generators and the required transformer and transmission facilities. The added facilities will be connected to the electricity distribution system of the City of Djibouti. The project will help meet demand for electricity in the medium term.

Balance of Payments Support Loans

- *Loan of US$1.5 million*; interest-free; 10-year maturity, including a 3-year grace period; June 14, 1980

- Utilization: not yet determined
- *Loan of US$1.0 million*; interest-free; 10-year maturity, including a 3-year grace period; July 20, 1981
- Utilization: not yet determined

12 Egypt

Project Loan

Line of Credit to the Development Industrial Bank (DIB).

- Loan of US$8.75 million; interest-free; 20-year maturity, including a 5-year grace period; December 15, 1977
- Co-financier: **IBRD**

One of the purposes of the DIB, established in Egypt in 1975, is to provide finance to cooperatives, artisans and small-scale industries. The DIB has also a broader vocation: 'to promote and finance productive industrial enterprises mainly in the private sector'. Its establishment relates to Egypt's efforts to mobilize private savings for industrial development.

The loan — to be on-lent by the Government of Egypt to the DIB — aims at allowing the Bank to use its increased financial resources to extend medium and long-term credit to small industrial enterprises on semi-commercial terms. Interest earned on these credit operations will be rechanneled for purposes of technical assistance, training and marketing assistance for handicrafts and small-scale industries.

Balance of Payments Support Loan

- *Loan of US$14.45 million*; interest-free; 25-year maturity, including a 5-year grace period; January 10, 1977
- Utilization: purchase of capital goods, spare parts, foodstuff, raw material for agricultural and industrial sectors.

Local Counterpart Funds

Talkha II Fertilizer Project.

- Allocation: US$14.45 million equivalent; October 21, 1977

The project consists of a single stream 396,000 tons per year ammonia plant, two identical urea plants with a combined capacity of 570,000 tons per year, and a facility for manufacturing the required polythene bags. The town of Talkha, some 135km north of Cairo, is situated close to the newly developed gas field of Abu Mahdi which will supply the main input for the production of fertilizers. The site has good rail and road connections sufficient to handle the distribution of fertilizers within the 100km radius in which most of the product will be utilized.

13 Equatorial Guinea

Balance of Payments Support Loans

- *Loan of US$0.5 million*; interest-free; 25-year maturity, including a 5-year grace period; May 16, 1977
- Utilization: importation of agricultural development products, sulphate, etc.
- *Loan of US$1.0 million*; interest-free; 15-year maturity, including a 5-year grace

period; November 22, 1979
- Partial utilization: importation of oil
- *Loan of US$1.0 million*; interest-free; 10-year maturity, including a 3-year grace period; September 21, 1981
- Utilization: not yet determined

14 Ethiopia

Balance of Payments Support Loan

- *Loan of US$4.8 million*; interest-free; 25-year maturity, including a 5-year grace period; February 3, 1977
- Utilization: purchase of sorghum-maize

Local Counterpart Funds

Second Minimum Package Program.
- Allocation: US$4.8 million equivalent; February 6, 1979

The Minimum Package Program is an agricultural development scheme which aims at increasing cereal yields through the provision of extension services, supply of farm inputs and credit, construction of low-cost rural roads, and training facilities for farmers. The program is designed to reach 1.1 million farmers, particularly poor farmers, in 12 of the country's 14 regions.

Common Fund

A grant in the amount of US$1.12 million was extended on November 12, 1981 to Ethiopia to cover its mandatory subscription of shares of directly contributed capital of the Common Fund for Commodities.

15 The Gambia

Balance of Payments Support Loans

- *Loan of US$1.65 million*; interest-free; 25-year maturity including a 5-year grace period; January 10, 1977
- Utilization: Yundum Airport
- *Loan of US$2.0 million*; interest-free; 15-year maturity, including a 5-year grace period; July 27, 1978
- Utilization: capital goods
- *Loan of US$1.0 million*; interest-free; 15-year maturity, including a 5-year grace period; July 16, 1979
- Utilization: foodstuff
- *Loan of US$1.5 million*; interest-free; 10-year maturity, including a 3-year grace period; April 25, 1980
- Utilization: imports of electricity generators and spare parts
- *Loan of US$1.5 million*; interest-free; 10-year maturity, including a 3-year grace period; April 14, 1981
- Partial Utilization: foodstuff

- *Loan of US$1.5 million*; interest-free; 10-year maturity, including a 3-year grace period; March 12, 1982.
- Utilization: not yet determined

Local Counterpart Funds

Yundum Airport Phase II.
- Allocation: US$1.65 million equivalent; October 20, 1977

The strengthening and lengthening of the existing runway and apron at Yundum Airport, and the renewal of lighting and provision of navigational aids are the main components of this project. The Gambia possesses few productive resources beyond the production and export of groundnuts. However, its natural beauty and clement weather from October-April make the essential ingredients for a profitable and expanding tourism sector. The present inadequate runway hinders the development of tourism, but the successful completion of the project will remove this constraint resulting in increased foreign exchange earnings, increased aircraft landing fees and passenger service charges accruing to the Government.

Yundum Airport Phase III.
- Allocation: US$3.0 million equivalent; April 26, 1979 and October 24, 1979

As seen above, the Fund has approved, for use in Phase II of the Yundum Project, the allocation of US$1.65 million equivalent in local counterpart funds generated under a balance of payments support loan extended in 1977. Phase III of the project consists of: extension of runway to 3,600 meters and parking apron to 6 aircraft stands; consultancy services, and additional navigation aids, firefighting and safety equipment. The project will benefit the country through increased tourism and consequently larger foreign exchange earnings.

Common Fund

A grant in the amount of US$1.03 million was extended on December 21, 1981 to the Gambia to cover its mandatory subscription of shares of directly contributed capital of the Common Fund for Commodities.

16 Ghana

Project Loans

Kpong Hydropower Project.
- Loan of US$3.7 million; interest-free; 20-year maturity, including a 4-year grace period; May 18, 1979
- Co-financiers: IBRD, SF, CIDA, **KFAED**, BADEA
- Executing agency: Volta River Authority (VRA)
- Total cost: US$243.3 million

The project constitutes the second phase in the planned development of the Volta River's hydro-power potential. Hydroelectric power is an important element in the overall development of Ghana and the country's efforts to diversify the economy, and also represents an alternative to imported oil for power generation. The Kpong project, which is the least-cost hydro-power project that can be implemented at this time, will be able to meet demand growth for power in the 1980s.

Line of Credit to the National Investment Bank of Ghana (NIB).
- Loan of US$1.5 million; interest-free; 20-year maturity, including a 5-year grace period; February 18, 1980
- Co-financiers: **IDA** and EEC Special Action Fund

The loan proceeds will be on-lent by the Government of Ghana to the NIB, a publicly-owned development finance institution which provides debt capital to private and public enterprises. NIB is the main agency in the country for medium and long-term financing to the manufacturing sector. The line of credit will help promote Ghanaian-owned small-scale manufacturing enterprises, with special emphasis on export-oriented schemes.

Volta River Authority Systems Improvement Package Project.
- Loan of US$6.0 million; interest-free; 20-year maturity, including a 5-year grace period; July 18, 1980
- Co-financier: **IBRD**
- Executing agency: Volta River Authority (VRA)

The project is to rehabilitate some facilities of the VRA power system, which supplies electricity to the Electricity Corporation of Ghana, the smelter of the Volta Aluminium Company at Tema, several mining industries, the Akosombo township, and the Communauté Electrique de Bénin which in turn supplies electricity to Togo and Benin. The project comprises the importation of power line carrier communication equipment, a spare step-up transformer and other equipment to avoid the frequent and costly system collapses of the VRA grid. The Fund's loan covers all the financing requirements of the rehabilitation scheme.

Balance of Payments Support Loan
- *Loan of US$7.8 million*; interest-free; 25-year maturity, including a 5-year grace period; February 3, 1977
- Utilization: equipment

Local Counterpart Funds

Kpong Resettlement Project.
- Allocation: US$2.08 million equivalent; August 11, 1977

The project involves the resettlement of about 4,600 persons to make land available for the proposed Kpong Hydroelectric Project. Project works include the construction of a new township with all necessary infrastructural facilities. Compensation arrangements for the loss of commercial farming to farmers on land previously occupied are also provided for. The project is expected to substantially improve the standard of living of the population concerned by providing facilities and medical care hitherto unavailable.

Twifo Oil Palm Project.
- Allocation: US$4.09 million equivalent; August 11, 1977

The project involves the development of an agro-industrial complex for the production and mining of oil palm fruits in the Twifo Mampon area of Central Ghana. The project is expected to employ 1,200 people.

Bui Hydroelectric Feasibility Study.
 • Allocation: US$1.63 million equivalent; August 11, 1977
The project involves the preparation of a feasibility study and detailed engineering drawings for the Bui Hydroelectric Power Station.

17 Guinea

Project Loan

Industrial Rehabilitation and Promotion Project.
 • Loan of US$11.0 million; interest-free; 20-year maturity, including a 5-year grace period; January 12, 1982
 • Co-financier: **IDA**
 • Executing agency: Ministry of Industry
 • Total cost: US$23.2 million
The project's objective is to rehabilitate five state-owned industrial enterprises and to promote privately owned industrial enterprises, in line with the Government's industrial strategy geared at achieving an annual growth rate of 10% in industrial output by 1990.

Balance of Payments Support Loans
 • *Loan of US$2.35 million*; interest-free; 25-year maturity, including a 5-year grace period; December 23, 1977
 • Utilization: purchase of foodstuff
 • *Loan of US$4.5 million*; interest-free; 15-year maturity, including a 5-year grace period; July 28, 1978
 • Utilization: foodstuff, cement
 • *Loan of US$2.0 million*; interest-free; 15-year maturity, including a 5-year grace period; August 28, 1978
 • Utilization: crude oil and foodstuff
 • *Loan of US$2.0 million*; interest-free; 10-year maturity, including a 3-year grace period; July 29, 1982
 • Utilization: not yet determined

Local Counterpart Funds

Clinker Project.
 • Allocation: US$1.5 million equivalent; July 4, 1978
The project will establish a clinker grinding plant at Conakry with an annual capacity of 250,000 metric tons. The plant will meet the country's increasing demand for clinker. The project will assist the Government in its goal of achieving self-sufficiency in cement production and correcting the prevailing consumption balance between urban and rural areas. The allocation will meet all the local financing requirements of the project.

Siguiri Rural Development Project
 • Allocation: US$6.35 million equivalent; February 11, 1981
The local counterpart funds will go towards a project to initiate development in the Siguiri Region on the left bank of the Niger River. It comprises the renovation of the irrigation system on 6,820 hectares of land, rehabilitation of the existing feeder road

network; and the provision of credit, extension and health services as well as technical assistance and training of the farmers.

Common Fund

A grant in the amount of US$1.07 million was extended on March 25, 1982 to Guinea to cover its mandatory subscription of shares of directly contributed capital of the Common Fund for Commodities.

18 Guinea-Bissau

Balance of Payments Support Loans

- *Loan of US$1.65 million*; interest-free; 25-year maturity, including a 5-year grace period; January 10, 1977
- Utilization: purchase of foodstuff and other essential consumer goods (rice, sugar and petrol)
- *Loan of US$1.0 million*; interest-free; 15-year maturity, including a 5-year grace period; July 28, 1978
- Utilization: foodstuff, spare parts, gas oil
- *Loan of US$1.0 million*; interest-free; 15-year maturity, including a 5-year grace period; July 16, 1979
- Utilization: foodstuff, spare parts, gas oil, butane
- *Loan of US$2.0 million*; interest-free; 10-year maturity, including a 3-year grace period; April 21, 1980
- Utilization: oil
- *Loan of US$1.5 million*; interest-free; 10-year maturity, including a 3-year grace period; May 27, 1981
- Utilization: oil
- *Loan of US$1.5 million*; interest-free; 10-year maturity, including a 3-year grace period; October 12, 1982
- Utilization: not yet determined

Local Counterpart Funds

Cumere Factory.

- Allocation: US$2.65 million equivalent; November 11, 1977 and February 15, 1980

The factory to be established will process groundnuts and paddy in order to produce and market locally, and abroad, crude and refined groundnut oil, protein groundnut meal, animal feed, decorticated rice and soap. The project is expected to increase the foreign exchange earnings of the country and to make products hitherto imported available for the local market.

Various Sectors.

- Allocation: US$1.0 million equivalent; April 21, 1980

Funds to be used in the financing of UNDP-assisted projects:
- — Rice seeds — selection and production;
- — Professional training;
- — Feasibility studies for development of Corubal River Basin;

— Water supply; and
— Development planning assistance.

Self-construction Project in Antulla.
● Allocation: US$358,800 equivalent; January 29, 1981
The project aims at reducing the housing shortage in Antulla by constructing 24 housing units with the assistance of the inhabitants themselves and using local materials.

Housing Project for Expatriate Technical Assistance Staff.
● Allocation: US$328,400 equivalent; January 29, 1981
The project is the extension of a larger housing scheme and entails the construction of 12 apartments to accommodate expatriate technical assistance staff.

Seminars for Professors.
● Allocation: US$233,600 equivalent; January 29, 1981
The primary objective of the project is to improve the techniques of educators and improve the planning and organization of educational programs. The project consists of seven seminars in which a total of 3,000 educators will participate.

Community Development Project.
● Allocation: US$96,700 equivalent; January 29, 1981
The project involves expansion of primary health care activities in the regions of Cacheu and Tombali. Teams of social workers will train basic health workers and midwives; the construction of village pharmacies will be started, general hygienic conditions improved, and adequate medical stock maintained.

Reclaiming of Land for Rice Cultivation.
● Allocation: US$222,400 equivalent; January 29, 1981
The objective of the project is to increase rice production through both the use of mangrove land and the rehabilitation of land currently under cultivation. The mangrove land is to be reclaimed through the construction of dikes, and the remaining land through the establishment of improved drainage systems.

Rural Extension Pilot Project in Bachil.
● Allocation: US$313,500 equivalent; January 29, 1981
The primary objective of the project is to promote the socio-economic development of the region through the establishment of cooperatives and the reconstruction of rural communities. It includes reclaiming 300 ha of land for rice cultivation, extension of agricultural credit, construction of 10km of road and the provision of technical assistance to farmers.

Project for the Development of the Department of Soils of Guinea-Bissau.
● Allociation: US$307,300 equivalent; January 29, 1981
The project is aimed at extending adequate services towards achieving self-sufficiency in food. It will help provide institutional support to the Department of Hydraulic Agriculture in its task of assessing optimal areas for the cultivation of specific crops.

Contingencies for above Projects.
- Allocation: US$13,600 equivalent; January 29, 1981

Common Fund

A grant in the amount of US$1.0 million was extended on December 21, 1981 to Guinea-Bissau to cover its mandatory subscription of shares of directly contributed capital of the Common Fund for Commodities.

19 Ivory Coast

Project Loan

Soubre Hydroelectric Project.
- Loan of US$20.0 million; 6% interest rates; 20-year maturity including a 5-year grace period;
- Co-financiers: IBRD, KFAED, EIB, AfDB, CDC, CCCE, **BADEA**, and others
- Executing agency: Energie Electrique de la Cote d'Ivoire (EECI)
- Total cost: US$630.67 million

The objectives of the project are twofold: first, to increase the power generating output of EECI by about 1,600 GWh to meet an estimated increased demand for electricity after 1986 and reduce fuel consumption in thermal generating plants; and second, to enhance EECI's managerial, technical and financial capacity and increase its efficiency. It consists of: a) the Soubre Power Station; b) the associated transmission; c) the related engineering and consulting services; d) the provision of heavy machine tools for EECI's maintenance workshops; e) studies of the country's energy resources and needs and National Energy Plan; and f) the on-the-job training and fellowships for future professors at the High School of Electricity.

The proposed Soubre Hydroelectrical Project appears to be the least cost solution, as compared to a number of other alternative hydro projects. It is thus expected to be the most effective means of meeting the Ivory Coast's rising electricity needs.

20 Kenya

Project Loans

Nairobi Water Supply Project.
- Loan of US$3.0 million; interest-free; 20-year maturity, including a 5-year grace period; December 15, 1977
- Co-financiers: **IBRD** and SF
- Executing agency: Water and Sewerage Department (WSD)
- Total cost: US$27 million

The project is the third stage of a program designed to meet Nairobi's water supply requirements until 1988. The project would effect a net increase of 23 million imperial gallons per day to the supply of treated water delivered to Nairobi.

The works include construction of an intake structure on the Chania River, some modifications to the existing Sasumua Dam, a water treatment plant, a 36km transmission main, the complete network of distribution reservoirs, pumping stations, trunk and distribution mains.

Tea Factories Project.
- Loan of US$5.3 million; interest-free; 20-year maturity, including a 5-year grace period; December 19, 1978
- Co-financier: **IBRD**
- Executing agency: Kenya Tea Development Authority (KTDA)
- Total cost: US$36.0 million

The OPEC Fund loan has financed three tea processing factories with a view to benefitting both income and employment in Kenya, since the factories will eventually employ 2,000 persons.

Line of Credit to the Kenya Commercial Bank Group.
- Loan of US$3.0 million; interest-free; 20-year maturity, including a 5-year grace period; November 30, 1981
- Co-financier: **IFC**

The Government of Kenya will on-lend the proceeds of this line of credit to the Kenya Commercial Bank Group, the largest commercial bank in the country and wholly owned by the Government. Half of the proceeds will be extended as sub-loans to small farmers and rural businesses and the rest to small and medium-sized urban businesses. The line of credit has been designed in close consultation with the Government of Kenya, to assist beneficiaries who would otherwise not have access to institutionalized credit.

Bura Irrigation and Settlement Project.
- Loan of US$12.0 million; interest-free; 20-year maturity, including a 5-year grace period; July 15, 1982
- Co-financiers: **IBRD**, IDA, KFAED, EDF, the Governments of Kenya, the Netherlands and the WFP
- Executing agency: National Irrigation Board (NIB)
- Total cost: US$215.7 million

The overall objective of the project is to develop over a period of five and a half years about 6,700 irrigated hectares on the West Bank of the Lower Tana River and settle on smallholdings about 5,150 landless and poor families selected from all parts of Kenya. The necessary infrastructure would be provided to support a population expected to reach 65,000 by 1985. The farms will contribute to Kenya's foreign exchange earnings as well as produce food crops for subsistence. The project will also help develop, through technical assistance and training, Kenya's capacity to manage future major irrigation projects. The components of the project to be financed by the OPEC Fund include: i) a cotton ginnery and ii) agricultural machinery and equipment.

Program Loan

Restructuring Program.
- Loan of US$4.0 million; interest-free; 15-year maturity, including a 5-year grace period; April 21, 1980
- Co-financiers: **IDA** and EEC Special Action Fund

The loan proceeds are to be used for the importation of raw materials, intermediate goods, spare parts and capital goods for the agricultural sector. These imports are in support of the Government's comprehensive economic program designed to stabilize the Kenyan economy and make it less vulnerable to external economic forces.

Balance of Payments Support Loan
- *Loan of US$5.0 million*; interest-free; 25-year maturity, including a 5-year grace period; January 12, 1977
- Utilization: purchase of spare parts for railways

Local Counterpart Funds

Nzoia Sugar Project.
- Allocation: US$2.5 million equivalent; August 10, 1977

The Nzoia Sugar Project, implemented in Western Kenya, in an area known as the sugar belt, is part of the Kenyan Government's efforts to attain self-sufficiency in sugar and to have a surplus for export by 1985. The factory to be established will eventually produce 2,000 tons of sugar per day with sugar cane supplied from a 10,000 ha plantation. The successful completion of the project will result in an annual foreign exchange saving of US$16-19 million. When in full scale operation, the complex will employ 2,750 workers, a particularly important benefit considering the high unemployment factor in the region.

Nairobi Water Supply Project.
- Allocation: US$2.5 million equivalent; December 15, 1977

For project description see above.

The International Center of Insect Physiology and Ecology (ICIPE).
- Allocation: US$1.5 million equivalent; April 20, 1980

Partial financing of the local cost expenditures of ICIPE's Capital Development Project for Agricultural Pest Research Facilities. The project comprises the construction of a laboratory complex, farmhouse and animal unit, maintenance complex, clinic, school and ancillary buildings at the Mbita Point Field Station on the shores of Lake Victoria.

Phase I of the Mbita Point Capital Development Project.
- Allocation: US$0.5 million equivalent; November 19, 1982

Partial financing of the Mbita Point Project (ICIPE). The components to be financed comprise laboratories, administration and maintenance complexes, and ancillary facilities.

21 Lesotho

Project Loan

Maseru International Airport Project.
- Loan of US$3.0 million; interest-free; 20-year maturity, including a 5-year grace period; August 28, 1979
- Co-financiers: **KFAED**, SF, ADB
- Executing agency: Ministry of Works
- Total cost: US$43.95 million

The project will provide Lesotho with a direct link to the outside world and enable the country to have immediate access to international markets, in particular to other African countries, thus giving impetus to trade and tourism. It will also contribute to the expansion of the Lesotho National Airline and create job opportunities.

Balance of Payments Support Loans

- *Loans of US$1.9 million*; interest-free; 25-year maturity, including a 5-year grace period; January 20, 1977
- Utilization: purchase of grain dryers
- *Loan of US$1.5 million*; interest-free; 10-year maturity, including a 3-year grace period; July 18, 1980
- Partial utilization: transport aircraft
- *Loan of US$2.5 million*; interest-free; 10-year maturity, including a 3-year grace period; July 15, 1981
- Utilization: not yet determined

Local Counterpart Funds

Maseru International Airport Project.
- Allocation: US$1.9 million equivalent; July 3, 1980

For project description see above.

Common Fund

A grant in the amount of US$1.0 million was extended on December 7, 1981 to Lesotho to cover its mandatory subscription of shares of directly contributed capital of the Common Fund for Commodities.

22 Liberia

Project Loans

Tubman Bridge and Bomi Hills Road Project.
- Loan of US$3.0 million; 4% interest; 20-year maturity, including a 4-year grace period; December 19, 1978
- Co-financiers: **SF**, AfDB
- Executing agency: Ministry of Public Works (MPW)
- Total cost: US$24.0 million

The project consists of the construction of a two-lane bitumen standard road 64km long and a new bridge on Saint Paul River, 266.4m long and 14m wide. Provisions for consultancy services are also made.

The benefits of this project would accrue to an area representing 30% of Liberia and inhabited by more than half a million people. This area is rich in forestry resources, agriculture and iron ore.

Bushrod Power Expansion Project.
- Loan of US$5.0 million; 4% interest; 20-year maturity; including a 4-year grace period; October 24, 1980
- Co-financier: **IBRD**
- Executing agency: Liberia Electricity Corporation
- Total cost: US$39.4 million

The project consists of the expansion of the existing Bushrod power station located 8km north of Monrovia. It will help meet the increased demand for power from both industrial and low-income users.

Iron Ore Rehabilitation Project.
- Loan of US$8.3 million; interest-free; 14-year maturity, including a 5-year grace period; January 12, 1982
- Co-financiers: **IBRD**, AfDB and Government of Netherlands
- Executing agency: The National Iron Ore Company (NIOC)
- Total cost: US$51.1 million

The basic objectives of the project are to increase both mining operations and iron ore output, reduce operating costs, and improve infrastructure (bridge and railroad).

23 Madagascar

Project Loans

Andekaleka Hydroelectric Power Project.
- Loan of US$6.5 million; interest-free; 20-year maturity, including a 5-year grace period; May 18, 1979
- Co-financiers: **KFAED**, IDA, CIDA, BADEA, SF
- Executing agency: Madagascar Electricity and Water Corporation (JIRAMA)
- Total cost: US$160 million

The project will be the largest plant in the country, practically doubling the existing capacity in the interconnected system around Antananarivo. It will permit substantial fuel savings, and also provide for the strengthening of JIRAMA, particularly in the areas of planning and staff development.

Tsimiroro Heavy Oil Exploration Project.
- Loan of US$5.0 million; interest-free; 20-year maturity, including a 5-year grace period
- Co-financier: **IDA**
- Executing agency: Office Militaire National pour les Industries Strategiques (OMNIS)
- Total cost: US$19.0 million

The project aims at establishing the economic feasibility of exploiting the already proven Tsimiroro heavy oil accumulation and the Bemolanga tar sands, and gathering data on the petrophysical characteristics of the reservoir, with the intention of attracting private sector interest in subsequent pilot projects and eventual commercial production.

It includes: i) exploration of the Tsimiroro heavy oil deposit; ii) an engineering study for a future pilot plant at Tsimiroro; iii) a related study of the feasibility of upgrading the heavy oil; iv) a process comparison study for the selection of an appropriate extraction process for the Bemolanga tar sands; and v) training of professionals from OMNIS, Madagascar's national oil company.

Balance of Payments Support Loans.
- *Loan of US$3.1 million*; interest-free; 25-year maturity, including a 5-year grace period; January 10, 1977
- Utilization: foodstuff
- *Loan of US$5.0 million*; interest-free; 10-year maturity, including a 3-year grace period; June 12, 1980

- Utilization: imports of rice flour
- *Loan of US$10.0 million*; interest-free; 10-year maturity, including a 3-year grace period; May 29, 1981
- Utilization: imports of foodstuff
- *Loan of US$10.0 million*; interest-free; 10-year maturity, including a 3-year grace period; April 7, 1982
- Partial utilization: imports of foodstuffs

Local Counterpart Funds

Edible Oil Refinery at Tamatave.
- Allocation: US$3.1 million equivalent; November 17, 1978

The project is intended to meet domestic needs for edible oil and includes civil works and equipment for a refinery, decanting and other pre-bottling operations of palm oil. The project is expected to fully meet domestic demand for palm oil by 1986 and substitute domestically refined products for those presently imported.

24 Malawi

Project Loan

Kasungu-Jenda Road.
- Loan of US$1.8 million; interest-free; 20-year maturity, including a 3-year grace period; December 15, 1977
- Co-financier: **IDA**
- Executing agency: Ministry of Roads and Supplies
- Total cost: US$13.55 million

The Kasungu-Jenda Road Project, which primarily involves the construction of about 53 miles of two-lane bituminous surface road, is part of a regional development strategy for the northern half of Malawi, particularly the Mzimba area, where several rural development projects are being initiated. Benefits will mainly accrue to a population estimated at about 80,000 in areas around Mzimba. Road users will also benefit from reduced vehicle operating and maintenance costs, travelling time and elimination of losses incurred when the existing road becomes impassable during the rainy season.

Common Fund

A grant in the amount of US$1.4 million was extended on October 14, 1981 to Malawi to cover its mandatory subscription of shares of directly contributed capital of the Common Fund for Commodities.

25 Mali

Project Loans

Sevare-Gao Road Project.
- Loan of US$7.0 million; interest-free; 20-year maturity, including a 5-year grace period; July 27, 1979
- Co-financiers: **IsDB**, BADEA, KFW
- Executing agency: Direction Nationale de l'Infrastructure des Transports (DNIT), Ministry of Transport and Public Works

• Total cost: US$78.7 million

The Sevare-Gao Road is part of the Malian section of the Trans-Saharan Highway which will ultimately give sea-access to the land-locked countries of Mali and Niger through Algeria in the north and Nigeria in the south. The project will help open up the Fifth (Mopti) and the Seventh (Gao) Regions of Mali by linking their two capitals. It will promote their integration with the rest of the country, by inducing traffic and stimulating economic activities.

Biomass Power Scheme Project.
- Loan of US$6.45 million; interest-free; 20-year maturity, including a 5-year grace period; July 20, 1981
- Co-financier: **IDA**
- Executing agency: Electricité du Mali (EDM)
- Total cost: US$33.83 million

The project represents the first part of a two-phase project designed to rehabilitate EDM, the parastatal water supply and power utility, and to extend the services of this utility agency. The project, which is centered around a core of technical assistance to redress EDM's current operational problems, will permit better use of Mali's renewable energy resources by extending the service area and coverage of the Selingue hydroelectrical power scheme now being commissioned, and by the use of agricultural residues for power production in a biomass plant to be built at Mopti/Sevare. Besides providing for urgent works on Bamako's water supply system, the project will also cover project preparation works for the second phase of EDM's program.

Balance of Payments Support Loans
- *Loan of US$3.55 million*; interest-free; 25-year maturity, including a 5-year grace period; January 10, 1977
- Utilization: purchase of bags for agricultural products
- *Loan of US$3.5 million*; interest-free; 15-year maturity, including a 5-year grace period; July 28, 1978
- Utilization: imports of rice
- *Loan of US$6.0 million*; interest-free; 10-year maturity, including a 3-year grace period; July 4, 1980
- Utilization: imports of foodstuff and agricultural products
- *Loan of US$10.0 million*; interest-free; 10-year maturity, including a 3-year grace period; April 9, 1981
- Utilization: imports of foodstuff and material
- *Loan of US$5.0 million*; interest-free; 10-year maturity, including a 3-year grace period; April 7, 1982
- Partial utilization: foodstuff, material

Local Counterpart Funds

Sevare-Gao Road Project.
- Allocation: US$7.05 million equivalent; July 4, 1980

For project description see above.

Common Fund

A grant in the amount of US$1.04 million was extended on July 20, 1981 to Mali to cover its mandatory subscription of shares of directly contributed capital of the Common Fund for Commodities.

26 Mauritania

Project Loan

Guelb Iron Ore.
- Loan of US$5.0 million; interest-free; 20-year maturity, including a 5-year grace period; November 3, 1978
- Co-financiers: ADF, AfDB, AF, Arab Mining Company, CCCE, EIB, IBRD, **KFAED**, SF, IsDB
- Total cost: US$510 million

The Guelb Iron Ore Project is expected to produce initially 6 million tons of enriched iron ore. The production and exportation of iron ore is vital to the economy of Mauritania which depends on this commodity for 80% of its foreign exchange revenues. The Fund loan will contribute to the financing of equipment needed for the first implementation stage of the project, as well as for the construction of housing units required at the start of the works.

Balance of Payments Support Loans

- *Loan of US$1.6 million*; interest-free; 25-year maturity, including a 5-year grace period; January 8, 1977
- Utilization: purchase of rice
- *Loan of US$5.5 million*; interest-free; 10-year maturity, including a 3-year grace period; April 24, 1980
- Utilization: foodstuff
- *Loan of US$8.0 million*; interest-free; 10-year maturity, including a 3-year grace period; May 27, 1981
- Partial utilization: foodstuff
- *Loan of US$10.0 million*; interest-free; 10-year maturity, including a 3-year grace period; October 12, 1982
- Utilization: not yet determined

27 Mauritius

Project Loan

Champagne Hydroelectric Project.
- Loan of US$2.0 million; 4% interest; 20-year maturity, including a 5-year grace period; March 16, 1981
- Co-financiers: **KFAED**, BADEA, CCE and EIB
- Executing agency: Central Electricity Board (CEB)
- Total cost: US$49.96 million

The project is designed to increase the total installed generating capacity of the country. It comprises the construction of a dam and hydroelectric power station and ancillary facilities on the east coast of the island. The project will reduce the country's dependence on imported energy and will help meet the peak load requirements of the

Mauritius electricity system, thus eliminating power cuts and their associated disruptions.

Balance of Payments Support Loan

- *Loan of US$2.0 million*; 4% interest; 10-year maturity, including a 3-year grace period; January 14, 1980
- Utilization: imports of foodstuff

28 Morocco

Project Loans

Sidi Cheho Al-Massira Hydro Project.

- Loan of US$3.0 million; interest-free; 19-year maturity, including a 4-year grace period; October 6, 1977
- Co-financier: **IBRD**
- Executing agency: Office National de l'Electricité (ONE)
- Total cost: US$167 million

This loan for the partial financing of the Side Cheho Al-Massira Hydroelectric Project will assist in the rational development of water resources in the Oum-er-R'bia Basin and help meet the growing demand for electric power, as well as for water for irrigation, industrial and domestic uses. The project involves the construction of a concrete buttress-type dam at Sidi Cheho on the Oum-er-R'bia River, construction of a 120 MW power station, including an adjacent 225 kV substation and ancillary works as well as construction of 200km of 225 kV transmission lines. The project will also provide potable water to the Atlantic coastal zone, meeting expected demand until the year 2000, and will produce irrigation water for 17,000 ha. of land.

Line of Credit to Banque Nationale pour le Developpement Economique (BNDE).

- Loan of US$2.0 million; 4% interest; 20-year maturity, including a 5-year grace period; December 28, 1978
- Co-financier: **IBRD**

BNDE will use the loan proceeds to extend credit for the foreign exchange costs of viable small scale projects submitted by Moroccan investors.

Tamzaourt Dam Project.

- Loan of US$5.0 million; 4% interest; 20-year maturity, including a 5-year grace period; July 10, 1979
- Co-financier: **KFAED**
- Executing agencies: Department of Water Engineering, and Department of Roads (Ministry of Supplies and National Welfare); Souss Office for Agricultural Investment
- Total cost: US$172.3 million

The project is aimed at allocating rationally, and increasing the use of, available water resources in the Souss Valley near the city of Agadir (Southern Morocco). Thus, it will help improve agricultural production, which has been limited by a water shortage. Non-agricultural benefits will also be derived, such as the supply of water to Agadir for domestic and industrial uses. More generally, the project will be instrumental in enhancing the development prospects of the area through higher productivity in agriculture, higher incomes, and greater commercial activity.

Second Line of Credit to the BNDE.
- *Loan of US$15.0 million*; 2% interest; 20-year maturity, including a 5-year grace period; October 12, 1981
- Co-financier: **KFAED**

The line of credit proceeds are to be on-lent by the Government of Morocco to BNDE, which will in turn extend sub-loans to small manufacturing enterprises. The project is of particular importance to the Moroccan economy as it will enhance growth in the small manufacturing sector and will limit increase in imports, thus alleviating balance of payments constraints.

29 Mozambique

Project Loans

Mucanha Vuzi Coal Development Project.
- *Loan of US$2.3 million*; interest-free; 20-year maturity, including a 5-year grace period; January 12, 1982
- Co-financiers: Government of Brazil; Loan Administration is being undertaken directly by the OPEC Fund
- Executing agency: State Secretariat for Coal and Hydrocarbons

The project consists of preliminary studies to determine the technical, economic and financial feasibility of coal mining development in the Mucanha Vuzi region, in line with the country's objective of developing its coal industry and thus acquiring foreign exchange needed for Mozambique's economic development. The Government of Brazil, which participates in the financing of the studies, will also ensure the supply, through Brazilian enterprises, of the required technology and equipment. The project will help promote economic and technical cooperation between two developing countries, and is hoped to serve as an example to further South-South relations.

Tea Rehabilitation Project.
- *Loan of US$6.0 million*; interest-free; 20-year maturity, including a 5-year grace period
- Co-financier: **AfDB**
- Executing agency: National Tea Production Company (EMOCHA)
- Total cost: US$23.6 million

The project consists of rehabilitating the existing tea processing factories and building three new plants to improve the quality of the processed tea as a tool for export promotion.

Balance of Payments Support Loans
- *Loan of US$6.55 million*; interest-free; 25-year maturity, including a 5-year grace period; March 2, 1977
- Utilization: purchase of crude oil
- *Loan of US$5.0 million*; interest-free; 15-year maturity, including a 5-year grace period; May 21 1979
- Utilization: crude oil

- *Loan of US$3.5 million*; interest-free; 10-year maturity, including a 3-year grace period; July 21, 1980
- Utilization: crude oil

Local Counterpart Funds

Bridge over the Zambesi River.
- Allocation: US$11.55 million equivalent; July 31, 1978, November 26, 1979 and September 15, 1980

The construction of bridges spanning the Zambesi River to link the southern and northern parts of the country is fundamental to Mozambique's development. The allocation will help finance a bridge 2,400 meters in length which crosses the Zambesi River near Caia in the Sofala Province. The bridge will facilitate local transport and the movement of goods within the country.

Mucanha Vuzi Coal Development Project.
- Allocation: US$0.8 million equivalent; January 12, 1982

For project description see above.

30 Niger

Balance of Payments Support Loans

- *Loan of US$2.9 million*; interest-free; 25-year maturity, including a 5-year grace period; February 4, 1977
- Utilization: purchase of rice and cement
- *Loan of US$3.85 million*; interest-free; 15-year maturity, including a 5-year grace period; August 28, 1979
- Utilization: crude oil
- *Loan of US$4.0 million*; interest-free; 10-year maturity, including a 3-year grace period; April 21, 1980
- Utilization: imports of oil products
- *Loan of US$6.0 million*; interest-free; 10-year maturity, including a 3-year grace period; May 27, 1981
- Partial utilization: imports of foodstuff

Local Counterpart Funds

Zinder-Agadez Road Project.
- Allocation: US$1.7 million equivalent; May 13, 1980

The local counterpart funds are to be used in the partial financing of the engineering studies required for the Zinder-Agadez Road Project. The road is a 447km segment of the Trans-Saharan Highway Project, which will ultimately link Algeria, Niger, Mali and Nigeria. The Zinder-Agadez Road will reduce transportation costs, revitalize economic activity and improve communications in Central and Southern Niger.

Birni N'Konni Irrigation II.
- Allocation: US$4.45 million equivalent; June 2, 1982

The project consists of the implementation of the second phase of the Birni N'Konni Irrigation Scheme. It aims at building an irrigation system in the area and at applying selected cropping patterns to enhance production of large quantities of cereals destined for local consumption.

Rural Hydraulic Program.
• Allocation: US$1.591 million equivalent; June 22, 1982
The objective of the program is to bore 67 wells in the regions of Dosso, Tahoua and Maradi with a view to securing water supply for an estimated 30,000 people. The program seeks to alleviate the effects of drought by providing sufficient water all year round.

Livestock Project.
• Allocation: US$0.25 million equivalent; June 22, 1982
The project is part of an overall rural development and livestock program. It covers feedstock production and aims at financing the provision of grains to be further processed into animal feed and distributed in the needy areas of the country.

Agadez Water Supply Project.
• Allocation: US$1.136 million equivalent; June 22, 1982
The project's objective is to supply water to the suburbs of Agadez, where small industries and a hospital are being established. It falls within a national water supply program aiming at securing a daily provision of 40 liters of water per inhabitant in urban centers, and 25 liters per inhabitant in rural areas.

Water Bore-Drilling and Geotechnical Studies.
• Allocation: US$1.203 million equivalent; November 4, 1982
The project aims at undertaking water bore-drilling and geotechnical survery in order to assess water resources for use in the construction of the Zinder-Agadez Road.

Ploughing of Irrigated Land.
• Allocation: US$0.5 million equivalent; November 4, 1982
The project is part of a national rural development program. It includes the ploughing of 5,000 ha of land for the production of millet, sorghum and paddy.

Zinder-Agadez Road Project.
• Allocation: US$1.232 million; November 29, 1982
Additional studies required for the Zinder-Agadez Road Project. The road is a 447km long segment of the Trans-Sahara Highway Project, which will ultimately link Algeria, Niger, Mali and Nigeria.

Common Fund

A grant in the amount of US$1.02 million was extended on March 17, 1982 to Niger to cover its mandatory subscription of shares of directly contributed capital of the Common Fund for Commodities.

31 Rwanda

Project Loan

Mukungwa Hydroelectric Project.
- Loan of US$2.35 million; interest-free; 20-year maturity, including a 5-year grace period; December 15, 1977
- Co-financier: **BADEA**
- Executing agency: Ministry of Public Works and Equipment
- Total cost: US$34.46 million

Rwanda is experiencing shortage of power. The Mukungwa Hydroelectric Project will develop a domestic source of primary energy to meet the country's power supply needs until early 1980s.

Balance of Payments Support Loans

- *Loan of US$1.7 million*; interest-free; 25-year maturity, including a 5-year grace period; February 3, 1977
- Utilization: purchase of salt, rice, condensed milk, oil, matches, garden hoes, jute sacks.
- *Loan of US$4.5 million*; interest-free; 15-year maturity, including a 5-year grace period; August 28, 1979
- Utilization: foodstuff, steel
- *Loan of US$3.0 million*; interest-free; 10-year maturity, including a 3-year grace period; September 5, 1980
- Utilization: foodstuff, steel and oil

Local Counterpart Funds

Mukungwa Hydroelectric Project.
- Allocation: US$0.46 million equivalent; December 15, 1977

For project description see above.

Common Fund

A grant in the amount of US$1.04 million was extended on November 16, 1981 to Rwanda to cover its mandatory subscription of shares of directly contributed capital of the Common Fund for Commodities.

32 Sao Tome & Principe

Balance of Payments Support Loans

- *Loan of US$0.35 million*; interest-free; 25-year maturity, including a 5-year grace period; May 16, 1977
- Utilization: foodstuff
- *Loan of US$1.0 million*; interest-free; 10-year maturity, including a 3-year grace period; July 20, 1981
- Partial utilization: foodstuff

33 Senegal

Project Loans

Sotexka Textile Project.
- Loan of US$5.0 million; 4% interest; 20-year maturity, including a 4-year grace period; October 24, 1980
- Co-financiers: **AfDB** and IsDB
- Executing agency: Société des Textiles de Kaolack (SOTEXKA)
- Total cost: US$53.3 million

The project consists of the setting up of an integrated textile complex with a projected yearly capacity of 8,820,000 ready-to-wear cotton and cotton/polyester clothes. The project includes site development, construction of production sheds, storage, servicing and administration blocks; procurement and installation of production equipment; and auxiliary equipment. The output is earmarked for export.

Chemical Industries Project.
- Loan of US$14.0 million; interest-free; 20-year maturity, including a 5-year grace period; July 20, 1981
- Co-financier: **BADEA**, AfDB, IBRD and EIB
- Executing agency: Industries Chimiques du Sénégal (ICS)
- Total cost: US$284 million

The project consists of the construction of a fertilizer complex, which comprises facilities for the production of sulphuric acid, phosphoric acid, and relevant chemical products for the production of different types of fertilizers. The project is designed to increase the value of the phosphates produced by Senegal by processing them into intermediate goods (phosphoric acid) and final products (fertilizers).

Balance of Payments Support Loans
- *Loan of US$3.4 million*; interest-free; 10-year maturity, including a 3-year grace period; February 3, 1977
- Utilization: foodstuff
- *Loan of US$4.0 million*; interest-free; 15-year maturity, including a 5-year grace period; December 19, 1978
- Utilization: foodstuff
- *Loan of US$4.5 million*; 4% interest; 10-year maturity, including a 3-year grace period; July 21, 1980
- Utilization: foodstuff
- *Loan of US$10.0 million*; interest-free; 10-year maturity, including a 3-year grace period; April 7, 1982
- Utilization: not yet determined

Local Counterpart Funds

Feasibility Studies for the Agricultural Development of the Soungrougrou Valley.
- Allocation; US$1.0 million equivalent; July 31, 1978

The studies would develop a master plan for the agricultural development of the Soungrougrou Valley. The studies include a survey of water availability and recommendations for its optimal use for agricultural production, an analysis of all physical characteristics of the Soungrougrou Valley relevant to rice production and solutions to constraints in the area's agricultural development. The studies will also recommend measures to ensure that artisanal fishing activities in the area are maintained as well as to strengthen livestock development. The studies are expected to provide the basis for future agricultural projects. The allocation covers all the estimated cost requirements of the feasibility studies.

Societe Nationale des Forages (SONAFOR).
 • Allocation: US$2.05 million equivalent; April 2, 1979 and July 20, 1981
The local counterpart funds will help finance well-boring activities in Senegal for the benefit of the rural sector. The latter has been severely affected by the drought which has afflicted the country for several years.

Debi-Lampsar Irrigation Project.
 • Allocation: US$0.95 million equivalent; July 4, 1978
In order to reduce reliance on rainfed agriculture, the Government of Senegal is making large efforts to develop the country's irrigation potential. The project consists of construction of irrigation works on over 2,300 ha of land for eventual paddy and tomato cultivation, agricultural support services to 1,100 farmers, and technical support to the national agency responsible for development of the Senegal River delta and valley. The project will play a vital role in the present and future agricultural development of the Senegal River Basin.

'Hydraulique Pastorale'.
 • Allocation: US$1.0 million equivalent; March 31, 1980
The project is designed to stem the erosion of grazing areas which is caused by the southward spread of desert sands. To this end, wells have been drilled in the Fleuve and Longa regions where stock farms for animal breeding will be developed. Solar energy will be used to pump water from wells and to provide the energy required for animal incubators.

Agricultural Storage.
 • Allocation: US$2.4 million equivalent; November 29, 1979
The project, under the responsibility of a government agency, the Office National de Coopération et d'Assistance pour le Développement, involves the construction, throughout the country, of weatherproof cereal storage facilities with a total capacity of 130,000 tons. These facilities are expected to reduce cereal losses, of which 30% are due to rodent activity, decrease transport costs, and improve health standards.

Demba Ba Solar Pumping Station.
 • Allocation: US$1.0 million equivalent; June 2, 1982
The project is part of an overall integrated livestock development program in Eastern Senegal. It consists of the installation of a pilot water pumping station running on solar energy and aims at providing water for the Demba Ba Community's livestock.

M'Bour and Louga Rural Development Project.
 • Allocation: US$1.5 million equivalent; June 2, 1982
The project has been determined as a priority project by the Government of Senegal in the context of its Development Plan and aims at (i) increasing food production; (ii) assessing and restructuring rural cooperatives; (iii) providing better working condi-

tions for the rural population; and (iv) improving health services in the M'Bour and Louga region.

Labgar Solar Pumping Station.
  • Allocation: US$1.0 million equivalent; November 4, 1982
The project is to provide the Labgar rural community with water pumps running on solar energy. Apart from its social and health benefits, the project is expected to promote subsistence agriculture, enabling the area to play a more effective role in Senegal's economy.

Rural Water Pumps Project.
  • Allocation: US$2.0 million equivalent; November 4, 1982
The project aims at supplying 100 diesel engine water pumps to rural areas of Senegal. It will help partially meet the demand for water and improve the living conditions in the concerned areas through a reliable and safe water supply.

34 Seychelles

Balance of Payments Support Loans
  • *Loan of US$0.3 million*; interest-free; 25-year maturity, including a 5-year grace period; May 16, 1977
  • Utilization: crude oil
  • *Loan of US$0.3 million*; 4% interest; 15-year maturity, including a 5-year grace period; July 27, 1978
  • Utilization: foodstuff
  • *Loan of US$0.2 million*; 4% interest; 15-year maturity, including a 5-year grace period; May 17, 1979
  • Utilization: foodstuff
  • *Loan of US$0.5 million*; 4% interest; 10-year maturity, including a 3-year grace period; April 21, 1980
  • Utilization: foodstuff
  • *Loan of US$1.0 million*; 6% interest; 10-year maturity, including a 3-year grace period; July 20, 1981
  • Utilization: foodstuff
  • *Loan of US$1.0 million*; 6% interest; 10-year maturity, including a 3-year grace period; April 7, 1982
  • Partial utilization: foodstuff

Local Counterpart Funds

National Housing Programme — I.
  • Allocation: US$0.15 million equivalent; November 23, 1977
The funds committed to this programme will be used for the purchase of 80 ha of land in the La Gogue district, some 4km from the capital city of Victoria for a proposed housing scheme of 100 units. This programme, which is intended to benefit the poorest segment of the population, involves three phases: the acquisition of land; the introduction of necessary infrastructural inputs and the establishment of a revolving interest-free mortgage funding facility. The programme is expected to improve health

and hygiene conditions and alleviate the social problems arising from families living in overcrowded and unhealthy surroundings.

National Housing Programme — II.
   • Allocation: US$0.15 million equivalent; July 24, 1978 and November 30, 1979
The National Housing Programme — II will provide properly planned housing sites with adequate water supply, sanitation and power supply on which families in the lower income groups can build homes with Government financial and technical assistance. The allocation will meet the total cost of purchasing a 50 ha site for this purpose.

Land Purchase by Government for Development Purposes.
   • Allocation: US$0.5 million; November 30, 1979
The project involves the purchase of 115 ha of land to be used for various development purposes:

   (1) Establishment of 3 state farms on Mahe and Praslin which will enable the country to reduce its dependence on food imports and also to boost its export crops;
   (2) Building and renovating educational facilities in Anse Royale, Glacis, Praslin, Amitie and Anse Etoile;
   (3) Installing an electricity generator and building housing units;
   (4) Establishing social centers, clinics and day care centers; and
   (5) Creating a new National Tourism and Hotel School.

Land Acquisition for Development Purposes.
   • Allocation: US$346,153 equivalent; November 3, 1980
The present 5-year Development Plan (1979-83) of the Seychelles gives top priority to self-owned housing. It also places emphasis on the improvement of educational opportunities. The local counterpart funds are to meet the cost of land purchases for the following purposes:

   the Bel Eau/Bel Air School;
   the National Youth Service School; and
   the Revolving Fund for Housing.

Extension of Anse Royale School.
   • Allocation: US$16,894 equivalent; July 20, 1981
The local counterpart funds will be used for the acquisition by the Government of 4 ha of land adjoining the existing school and would allow for the required extension of additional classrooms, a sports field, and day nursery facilities.

Land and Hangar for Aircraft.
   • Allocation: US$70,433 equivalent; July 20, 1981
The funds will be used by the Government to purchase a hangar and adjoining house and land to accommodate aircraft needed for the surveillance of territorial waters. The aircraft will help guard against unauthorized fishing and protect the community's economic interests.

Purchase of Land for a Community Center.
● Allocation: US$66,520 equivalent; July 20, 1981
The local counterpart funds will be used to purchase a plot of land, which will be used as the site of a community center. The center is part of a Government scheme to organize leisure and recreation centers for youth in each district of the country.

Inner Island Water Supply Project.
● Allocation: US$0.583 million equivalent; November 4, 1982
The project aims at improving the water supply of the islands of St. Anne, Cerf, Long, Moyenne and Round. The water supply system will allow for an increase in the volume of water and thus satisfy present and future demand.

35 Sierra Leone

Projects Loans

Third Power Project.
● Loan of US$1.6 million; interest-free; 20-year maturity, including a 4-year grace period; May 21, 1979
● Co-financiers: **IDA** and BADEA
● Executing agency: Sierra Leone Electricity Corporation (SLEC)
● Total cost: US$16.8 million
The project will involve: building urgently needed additional generating capacity, strengthening the distribution facilities, and preparing a study on the Bumbuna hydro-electric development. It will allow for a more reliable power supply in Sierra Leone, and will benefit the overall population, of which only 10%, at the present time has access to electricity. The project will consist of: installation of a 9.2 MW diesel-electric generating unit at the King Tom Power Plant, construction of the first stage of a 33 kV distribution facility in Freetown, installation of 2.3 MW diesel-electric generating units in 10 provincial centers, supply of data processing equipment, technical assistance, and consultants' services.

Highway Maintenance Program.
● Loan of US$7.0 million; interest-free; 20-year maturity, including a 5-year grace period; March 16, 1981
● Co-financier: **IDA**
● Executing agency: Ministry of Works (MOW)
● Total cost: US$27.2 million
The project is designed to improve the road maintenance operations of the MOW and comprises resealing of selected paved roads, rehabilitation of certain gravel roads, introduction of improved maintenance equipment, and a training component. In addition, it will assist in the reorganization of MOW's maintenance teams. By improving the road network, the project will remove serious transportation bottlenecks to achieving the Government objective of increased production of rice and cash crops.

Power Engineering and Technical Assistance Project.
● Loan of US$5.0 million; interest-free; 20-year maturity, including a 5-year grace period; May 28, 1982
● Co-financier: **IDA**

- Executing agnecy: Sierra Leone Electricity Corporation (SLEC)
- Total cost: US$11.0 million

The project aims at rehabilitating SLEC's existing electricity generating facilities and improving its management. It further intends to establish a new and independent authority to implement the major Bumbuna hydro power scheme and subsequently to absorb SLEC which will become its distribution branch. In addition, the project will provide for detailed engineering studies related to the Bumbuna Project.

Balance of Payments Support Loans.
- *Loans of US$2.05 million*; interest-free; 25-year maturity, including a 5-year grace period; February 4, 1977
- Utilization: spare parts, foodstuff
- *Loan of US$1.0 million*; interest-free; 10-year maturity, including a 3-year grace period; November 20, 1980
- Utilization: not yet determined

Local Counterpart Funds

Integrated Agricultural Development Project (Eastern Region).
- Allocation: US$0.267 million equivalent; August 11, 1977

The project includes the construction of 12 market centers in the Eastern Region and establishment of a farmer's finance company which would provide short, medium and long-term credit to farmers. This project will benefit some 14,000 farm families and will expand marketing activities in the region.

Integrated Agricultural Development Project (Northern Region).
- Allocation: US$0.267 million equivalent; August 11, 1977

The project involves the construction of 20 miles of new roads and the improvement of 280 miles of existing feeder roads. Additionally, 5 market centers, a farmers' training center, a seed multiplication farm and 100 village water wells will be built. This particular project will benefit some 21,000 families and expand marketing activities.

Gambia-Mattru Oil Palm Project.
- Allocation: US$0.267 million equivalent; August 11, 1977

The project involves the expansion of an existing plantation from 3,000 to 7,000 acres and the establishment of 3,500 acres of out-growers. An oil mill with a capacity of 15 tons of fresh fruit purchase per hour will also be constructed. This project will benefit some 1,500 farm families by improving farmer services, marketing activities and health facilities. It is expected to result in a US$19 million foreign exchange saving over a 25 year period.

Kailahun and Magburaka Water.
- Allocation: US$0.290 million equivalent; August 11, 1977

The project is intended to develop potable water supplies in the Kailahun and Magburaka districts of Sierra Leone. The civil works of this project have been seriously delayed due to lack of local funds: when completed, the project is expected to significantly increase the quantity of potable water available to the populace.

PCM and Children's Hospital.
- Allocation: US$0.133 million equivalent; August 11, 1977

The project involves the construction of a new wing of the Children's Hospital and the extension of the maternity wing of the PCM Hospital. The completion of this project has been delayed for some years because of inadequate domestic funds to pay contractors.

Kailahun Hospital.
• Allocation: US$0.178 million equivalent; August 11, 1977
This project involves completion of the second phase of the Kailahun Hospital. The civil works component of the project has been advancing at a slow rate for the past six years due to lack of domestic capital.

Lumley Health Center.
• Allocation: US$0.089 million equivalent; August 11, 1977
The project will expand buildings to house the Lumley Health Center, which has been selected as one of two centers for Fertility Advisory Services to receive technical and financial assistance from UNFPA. The project is expected to have significant long-term benefits for family welfare. It will assist in both the expansion of health services and family planning capabilities.

Rehabilitation of Primary School Premises.
• Allocation: US$0.200 million equivalent; August 11, 1977
The premises of many primary schools in the country are unsatisfactory as the buildings are often in need of urgent physical repair. This condition was further aggravated in 1975 by a storm disaster in the country which severely damaged buildings and for the repair of which no funds were available. These funds will therefore be used to reconstruct and repair existing school premises.

SLBS Mass Communication and Education Project.
• Allocation: US$0.357 million equivalent; August 11, 1977
This project is designed to modernize and expand the radio and TV broadcasting facilities of the country to reach a larger audience, particularly in the rural areas. The equipment has been purchased, but remains in storage because of the shortage of local funds to finance civil works necessary for the completion of the project. The funds provided for this project will allow work to resume. The project will allow the Government to educate a greater part of the population than otherwise possible. Programs in basic sciences and culture will be emphasized.

Common Fund

A grant in the amount of US$1.04 million was extended on January 27, 1982 to Sierra Leone to cover its mandatory subscription of the shares of directly contributed capital of the Common Fund for Commodities.

36 Somalia

Project Loans

Mogadishu Sewerage and Storm Water Drainage.
• Loan of US$2.66 million; interest-free; 20-year maturity, including a 5-year grace period; July 28, 1978

- Co-financiers: **AfDB**, IsDB
- Executing agency: Mogadishu Water Agency (MWA)
- Total cost: US$13.9 million

When completed the project will meet waste and storm water disposal requirements of Mogadishu up to the year 1985. It constitutes the first phase of a Master Development Plan for the capital city of Somalia. The project components are a sewerage system with all mains, pumping stations and treatment plants for waste water and include training, supervision services and maintenance equipment. There are tangible as well as many intangible benefits from this project, some of which are difficult to qualify. Of importance is the reduction in the current high rate of morbidity and mortality due to waterborne diseases.

Juba Sugar Project.
- Loan of US$5.5 million; interest-free; 20-year maturity, including a 4-year grace period; January 14, 1980
- Co-financiers: SF, **ADF** and Government of the United Arab Emirates
- Executing agency: Juba Sugar Project
- Total cost: US$185.0 million

The project, implemented on the West Bank of the Juba River, is designed to produce 70,000 metric tons per annum of mill white sugar by 1984. It includes the development of 8,195 ha of irrigated sugar cane and the construction of a sugar factory with the capacity to process 2,650 t/day of sugar cane, along with related facilities. The project's objective is to substitute for the substantial and growing imports of sugar as well as to produce an exportable surplus.

Balance of Payments Support Loans
- *Loan of US$2.05 million*; interest-free; 15-year maturity, including a 5-year grace period; January 12, 1977
- Utilization: edible oil, dates
- *Loan of US$5.0 million*; interest-free; 15-year maturity, including a 5-year grace period; July 16, 1979
- Utilization: crude oil
- *Loan of US$9.0 million*; interest-free; 10-year maturity, including a 3-year grace period; May 27, 1981
- Partial utilization: imports of oil
- *Loan of US$9.0 million*; interest-free; 10-year maturity, including a 3-year grace period; July 15, 1982
- Utilization: not yet determined

Local Counterpart Funds

Juba Sugar Project.
- Allocation: US$5.0 million equivalent

For project description see above.

Mogadishu Sewerage and Storm Water Drainage.
- Allocation: US$2.05 million equivalent

For project description see above.

Common Fund

A grant in the amount of US$1.02 million was extended on May 2, 1982 to Somalia to cover its mandatory subscription of the shares of directly contributed capital of the Common Fund for Commodities.

37 Sudan

Project Loans

Kassala-Haiya Road — I.
- Loan of US$3.25 million; interest-free; 20-year maturity, including a 5-year grace period; October 7, 1977
- Co-financier: **SF**
- Executing agency: Ministry of Public Works

The Kassala-Haiya Road project involves the construction of a road of 350 kilometres between these two towns and is a vital link in the Khartoum — Port Sudan Road, which connects the major production areas within Sudan with the country's port and centers of consumption. The road is expected to stimulate economic development and increase the production of agricultural produce in the areas through which it passes. Additional benefits include all-weather road surface, reduced vehicle maintenance costs and increased foreign exchange earnings.

Power II Project.
- Loan of US$9.5 million; interest-free; 20-year maturity, including a 5-year grace period; December 4, 1978
- Co-financier: **IDA**
- Executing agency: Public Electricity and Water Corporation
- Total cost: US$31.7 million

The project comprises the following elements: diesel generating units of 15 MW at Khartoum; a hydroelectric unit of 42 MW at Roseires; a diesel unit of 5 MW at Juba; extensions of transmission lines; and upgrading of the distribution system. This project will improve the reliability of power supply and the operation of the Roseires power station. Industry, which has been suffering from frequent interruptions in supply, will benefit significantly from this project.

Kassala-Haiya Road Project — II.
- Loan of US$7.7 million; interest-free; 20-year maturity, including a 5-year grace period; January 14, 1980
- Co-financiers: **SF** and SIDA
- Executing agency: Roads and Bridges Public Corporation
- Total cost: US$205.0 million

For project description see above.

Balance of Payments Support Loans
- *Loans of US$7.45 million;* interest-free; 10-year maturity, including a 3-year grace period; December 23, 1976
- Utilization: road building and water development, equipment and crude oil

- *Loan of US$12.0 million*; interest-free; 10-year maturity, including a 3-year grace period; April 17, 1981
- Partial utilization: oil
- *Loan of US$14.0 million*; interest-free; 10-year maturity, including a 3-year grace period; April 7, 1982
- Partial utilization: medical equipment

Local Counterpart Funds

Medani-Kosti Road Project.
- Allocation: US$3.2 million equivalent; January 19, 1978

The Medani-Kosti Road is an important link between areas of economic activity, the capital of Khartoum and the country's ports. This highway, 217km in length, will link the trade routes between the western and southern regions of the Sudan by connecting the production centers in the Wadi Medani to the port city of Kosti. The project is expected to stimulate economic development in the areas served by the highway.

Rahad Irrigation Project.
- Allocation: US$4.25 million equivalent; January 19, 1978

This project enables the irrigation of an area of some 300,000 feddans for the production of groundnuts and cotton on the east bank of the River Rahad. The project is expected to radically alter the socio-economic character of the project area. Traditional subsistence farming will be replaced by the introduction of modern farming techniques accompanied by the establishment of integrated village schemes with public schools, health services, etc.

Common Fund

A grant in the amount of US$1.36 million was extended on October 19, 1981 to the Sudan to cover its mandatory subscription of the shares of the directly contributed capital of the Common Fund for Commodities.

38 Tanzania

Project Loans

Mufindi Pulp and Paper.
- Loan of US$5.0 million; interest-free; 20-year maturity, including a 5-year grace period; December 19, 1978
- Co-financiers: IDA, **KFAED**, KFW, SIDA
- Executing agency: Mufindi Paper Mills Co.
- Total cost: US$248.2 million

The project is an integrated pulp and paper mill with initial capacity of 60,000 tons per annum. It will provide for logging roads and equipment, a chemical pulp mill with a bleach plant, a mechanical pulp mill, and the associated paper finishing facilities, power generation and supporting infrastructure as well as environmental safeguards. Planned annual output is 23,000 tons of printing and writing paper, 22,000 tons of kraft paper and 7,000 tons of newsprint, among other products.

Kidatu-Mufindi Power Transmission Project.
- Loan of US$5.0 million; interest-free; 20-year maturity, including a 4-year grace period; April 21, 1980
- Co-financiers: **AfDB**, NIB, CDC
- Executing agency: Tanzania Electric Supply Company Ltd. (TANESCO)
- Total cost: US$67.28 million

The project objective is to extend TANESCO's transmission grid system to supply electricity to the Mufindi pulp and paper mill. It will also meet present and future loads in the southwest region of the country, which includes the townships of Mufindi, Iringa and Kidatu.

Songo Songo Oil and Gas Exploration Project.
- Loan of US$12.0 million; interest-free; 20-year maturity, including a 5-year grace period; January 12, 1982
- Co-financiers: **IDA**, EIB
- Executing agency: Tanzania Petroleum Development Corporation (TPDC)

The project objective is to evaluate the hydrocarbon (oil and gas) potential of the Songo Songo field and to that end, three additional wells will be drilled in the area. The project will also include reservoir studies and a field development plan, technical assistance to TPDC in carrying out its drilling program, and training. The Fund loan to this project is the first to be extended for the financing of activities related to oil and gas exploration and assessment. Such activities will enable Tanzania to formulate a program for the development of the Songo Songo field and to attract the necessary assistance for its implementation.

Kimbiji Hydrocarbon Exploration Project.
- Loan of US$10.0 million; interest-free; 20-year maturity, including a 5-year grace period; July 15, 1982
- Financier: OPEC Fund (will also administer loan directly)
- Executing agency: Tanzania Petroleum Development Corporation (TPDC)
- Total cost: US$16.18 million

The Government of Tanzania will use the loan proceeds for the complementary financing of the Kimbiji Hydrocarbons Exploration Project. The project, which involves technical and financial cooperation between an OPEC member country (Algeria) and another developing country, constitutes part of Tanzania's overall program to appraise the hydrocarbon reserves of the Kimbiji region, a coastal area 38km southeast of Dar-es-Salaam. The program consists of three deep exploration wells, the first of which (Kimbiji East-1) was drilled in 1981-82 using a rig and personnel provided by SONATRACH, the Algerian State Oil Company and was financed by a US$10 million loan from the Algerian Government. The Fund's loan aims at assisting the Government of Tanzania in completing the program with the cooperation of SONATRACH.

Balance of Payments Support Loans
- *Loan of US$5.45 million*; interest-free; 10-year maturity, including a 3-year grace period; January 11, 1977
- Utilization: crude oil
- *Loan of US$5.0 million*: interest-free; 10-year maturity, including a 3-year grace period; January 22, 1980

• Utilization: foodstuff and oil
• *Loan of US$10.0 million*; interest-free; 10-year maturity, including a 3-year grace period; April 9, 1981
• Utilization: oil

Local Counterpart Funds

Mufindi Pulp and Paper Project.
• Allocation: US$5.45 million equivalent: December 19, 1978
For project description see above.

Songo Songo Oil and Gas Exploration Project.
• Allocation: US$5.0 million equivalent; January 12, 1982
For project description see above.

Common Fund

A grant in the amount of US$1.9 million was extended on December 22, 1981 to Tanzania to cover its mandatory subscription of the shares of directly contributed capital of the Common Fund for Commodities.

39 Togo

Project Loan

Lome-Notse-Tohoun Road Project.
• Loan of US$7.4 million; interest-free; 20-year maturity, including a 5-year grace period; July 28, 1981
• Co-financier: **IDA**
• Executing agency: Ministry of Public Works, Mines and Power (MPWMP)
• Total cost: US$31.2 million
The project is primarily designed to strengthen and enhance the activities and capacity of the MPWMP. It comprises a three-year training program for road maintenance personnel, pre-investment studies of the Notse-Tohoun Road, and technical assistance to the General Directorate of Transport. In addition, the loan will help acquire road maintenance equipment and spare parts, and will provide for pavement strengthening of certain road sections and improvement of selected east-west links to new agricultural areas.

Balance of Payments Support Loan

• *Loan of US$3.5 million*; interest-free; 15-year maturity, including a 5-year grace period; November 15, 1979
• Utilization: insecticides and motor fuel

40 Tunisia

Project Loans

Sidi Salem Multipurpose Project.
• Loan of US$6.0 million; 4% interest; 20-year maturity, including a 5-year grace period; October 5, 1978
• Co-financiers: **IBRD**, KFAED, EEC, Government of China, KfW
• Executing agency: Ministry of Public Works and Agriculture
• Total cost: US$385.8 million

The project comprises construction of the Sidi Salem Dam and generation and distribution of electric power. A main carrier canal will provide water for domestic and irrigation use to the areas of greater Tunis and Cap Bon. Irrrigation works and agricultural development will cover an area of 10,600 ha. The Sidi Salem is a rock fill dam with a storage reservoir of 550 million m³. The benefits of this multipurpose project are varied. The agricultural crop pattern will improve with greater water supplies for citrus fruit and vegetables. This produce has good export potential. Water and power are both in demand by industry, agriculture and the household sector.

Highway Maintenance Project.
- • Loan of US$6.0 million; 4% interest; 20-year maturity, including a 4-year grace period; October 24, 1980
- • Co-financier: **IBRD**
- • Executing agency: Direction des Ponts et Chaussées — Ministry of Public Works
- • Total cost: US$92.1 million

The project comprises the improvement of the Tunisian highway network through road rehabilitation, expanded and more efficient maintenance, highway department staff training and planning assistance, and the introduction of a program of traffic management and road safety.

41 Uganda

Project Loan

Line of Credit to the Development Bank of Uganda.
- • Loan of US$15.0 million; interest-free; 20-year maturity, including a 5-year grace period; July 16, 1982
- • Co-financiers: **IDA** and EIB

The main objective of the line of credit is to contribute to Uganda's Economic Recovery Program. The proceeds of this line of credit will be channeled through the Development Bank of Uganda and will help revive domestic production of essential commodities. Both public and private enterprises will be the target beneficiaries and emphasis will be placed on the rehabilitation or expansion of existing enterprises and promotion of projects which maximize use of local resources.

Program Loan

Rehabilitation Program.
- • Loan of US$5.0 million; interest-free; 15-year maturity, including a 5-year grace period; April 21, 1980
- • Co-financiers: **IDA** and EEC Special Action Fund

The loan proceeds will be used to finance essential imports to restore production of exportable cash crops and to initiate rehabilitation and improvement of other key productive sectors.

Balance of Payments Support Loan
- • *Loan of US$4.55 million*; interest-free; 10-year maturity, including a 3-year grace period; January 11, 1977
- • Utilization: public transport vehicles and spare parts

Common Fund

A grant in the amount of US$1.27 million was extended on June 28, 1982 to Uganda to cover its mandatory subscription of the shares of directly contributed capital of the Common Fund for Commodities.

42 Upper Volta

Project Loans

Banfora-Hounde Road Project.
- Loan of US$2.10 million; interest-free; 20-year maturity, including a 5-year grace period; December 15, 1977
- Co-financier: **IDA**
- Executing agency: Ministry of Public Works, Transport, Urban Development and Architecture
- Total cost: US$22.1 million

The loan is to finance part of the major trunk line linking the country's most important agricultural region with the capital and the economic center of Bobo Dioulasso. The Banfora-Bobo Dioulasso-Hounde road of over 183 kilometres will be reconstructed to paved standard and ancillary equipment will be provided. The project will result in reduced vehicle operating and maintenance costs as well as improved passenger and freight transport, particularly of agricultural products for exports.

Sakoince-Hounde Road Project.
- Loan of US$2.4 million; interest-free; 20-year maturity, including a 5-year grace period; November 16, 1978
- Co-financier: **AfDF**
- Executing agency: Ministry of Public Works
- Total cost: US$32.2 million

The Government of Upper Volta will use the proceeds of this loan for the partial financing of the construction of a paved road between Sakoince and Hounde in the center of Upper Volta. This would be the second Fund loan for the financing of the international route aiming at linking Ouagadougou with the port of Abidjan.

Balance of Payments Support Loans
- *Loan of US$2.25 million*; interest-free; 25-year maturity, including a 5-year grace period; January 11, 1977
- Utilization: foodstuff, spare parts for vehicles, industrial equipment
- *Loan of US$3.0 million*; interest-free; 15-year maturity, including a 5-year grace period; November 16, 1978
- Utilization: food, chemicals, equipment, spare parts
- *Loan of US$1.5 million*; interest-free; 15-year maturity, including a 5-year grace period; November 26, 1979
- Utilization: food, chemicals, equipment, spare parts
- *Loan of US$6.0 million*; interest-free; 10-year maturity, including a 3-year grace period; March 18, 1980
- Utilization: foodstuff, equipment

- *Loan of US$10.0 million*; interest-free; 10-year maturity, including a 3-year grace period; May 27, 1981
- Partial utilization: foodstuff
- *Loan of US$5.0 million*; interest-free; 10-year maturity, including a 3-year grace period; April 7, 1982
- Utilization: not yet determined

Local Counterpart Funds

Extension of the Green Belt Zone in Ouagadougou.
- Allocation: US$2.237 million equivalent; November 30, 1977

The program involves the implementation of a housing program and accompanying infrastructural services within the urban area of Ouagadougou. Some 36 ha of land have been purchased by the Government for this program to meet the urgent housing needs of the inhabitants of the area. The program involves two phases; the first requires the infrastructural development of the land and the second the construction of housing units. The funds which accrue to the Government from the sale of the plots and houses will be recycled in a special fund to finance similar future development programs. Apart from the program's obvious social benefits, it is expected to have a significant impact on the country's construction sector, as well as generate income to the Government.

Feasibility and Pre-financing Studies for the Kompienga Hydroelectric Project.
- Allocation: US$1.5 million; March 31, 1980

The Société Voltaique d'Electricité, responsible for the distribution of electricity in Upper Volta, has been entrusted with the task of surveying suitable sites for the development of the country's hydroelectric potential. Preliminary studies have already identified the Koulbi-Noumbiel and the Kompienga sites. The local counterpart funds are to be used in the financing of a feasibility study for a hydroelectric project at the latter site.

Teaching Hospital and Adjoining Medical School.
- Allocation: US$9.0 million equivalent; July 9, 1981

The Government of Upper Volta will apply the local counterpart funds to the construction of a teaching hospital with a 250 bed capacity and an adjoining medical school. The project includes the construction of a hospital as well as nursing and medical school. It further entails the provision of housing for resident employees, hospital equipment, and a water purification station.

Common Fund

A grant in the amount of US$1.02 million was extended on April 7, 1982 to Upper Volta to cover its mandatory subscription of shares of directly contributed capital of the Common Fund for Commodities.

43 Zaire

Project Loans

Line of Credit to Société Financière de Developpement (SOFIDE).
- Loan of US$5.0 million; interest-free; 20-year maturity, including a 5-year grace period; May 17, 1978

• Co-financiers: **IDA**, EIB, KFW

• Total cost: US$19.0 million

SOFIDE was established in 1970 to assist, both financially and technically, enterprises in all productive sectors of the economy. The line of credit is extended to ease the shortage of long-term development credit, a bottleneck which impedes investment activity and economic growth in Zaire. Most of the proceeds of this line of credit will reach small investors outside Kinshasa so alleviating acute regional and income disparities.

Railway Project.

• Loan of US$7.0 million; interest-free; 20-year maturity, including a 4-year grace period; August 28, 1979

• Co-financiers: **SF**, IDA, AfDB

• Executing agency: Société Nationale de Chemins de Fer Zairois (SNCZ)

• Total cost: US$150.2 million

The project covers the SNCZ's most urgent investment requirements for the period of its Investment Plan, 1979-82, and is part of its long range program for track rehabilitation and operational improvement. It will enable the SNCZ to make essential rehabilitation of line capacity to normal levels, increase fleet utilization, and improve availability and utilization of locomotives and rolling stock.

Shaba Power Rehabilitation Project.

• Loan of US$5.0 million; interest-free; 20-year maturity, including a 5-year grace period; October 30, 1981

• Co-financier: **IDA**

• Executing agency: Société Nationale D'Electricité (SNEL)

• Total cost: US$30.0 million

The main objective of the project is to rehabilitate the generating stations and the existing transmission and distribution system in the Shaba region in order to prevent failure of the supply of energy to the vital mining industry. Technical assistance will also be provided to the staff of the SNEL which is responsible for the generation and transmission of electricity throughout Zaire.

44 Zambia

Project Loan

Third Railway Project.

• Loan of US$4.5 million; 4% interest; 20-year maturity, including a 5-year grace period; August 28, 1979

• Co-financiers: **IBRD**, CIDA

• Executing agency: Zambia Railways (ZR)

• Total cost: US$194.6 million

The project is based on an investment plan (1979-83) prepared by ZR and is aimed at avoiding a deterioration in the ZR's operations and a reduction in its transport capacity. It will help modernize the rolling stock fleet of the railway company and increase its utilization and effective capacity to handle the expected growth in traffic through 1986. This project consists of the renewal of 112km of track; improvement of the telecommunications system; purchase of locomotives and wagons and provision of spare parts; improvement of maintenance and handling facilities; provision of advisory services at senior and middle management levels, as well as training facilities.

Project Loan

Line of Credit to the Development Bank of Zambia.
- Loan of US$15.0 million; 1% interest; 20-year maturity, including a 5-year grace period; July 13, 1982
- Co-financiers: **BADEA**, AfDB and IBRD

The main objective of the line of credit is to assist in the development of the industrial, agro-industrial and agricultural sectors of Zambia. It will help provide resources for the expansion or rehabilitation of existing enterprises and the promotion of activities that contribute significantly to: increasing production and employment opportunities, using local raw materials, and procuring and saving foreign exchange. Special attention will be given in the extension of credit to small-scale enterprises.

45 Zimbabwe

Program Loan

Manufacturing Rehabilitation Imports Program.
- Loan of US$10.0 million; interest-free; 15-year maturity, including a 5-year grace period; October 29, 1981
- Co-financier: **IBRD**
- Total cost: US$75.0 million

The proceeds of the loan will assist Zimbabwe in removing bottlenecks and rehabilitating the manufacturing sector. The main benefits of the proposed imports program will be utilization of capacity which otherwise would be idle, increased production of manufactured goods, and larger exports. The increased supply of manufactured goods will also help meet domestic demand. The imports program is expected to generate about 8,600 additional jobs.

ASIA

1 Afghanistan

Project Loan

Helmand Valley Road Project.
- Loan of US$3.55 million; interest-free, 20-year maturity, including a 4-year grace period; December 14, 1979
- Co-financier: **ADB**
- Executing agency: Ministry of Public Works
- Total cost: US$26.6 million

The project involves the construction of a two-lane secondary road (150km) and four feeder roads which will connect it to points located in the Upper Helmand Valley, a region with a significant agricultural potential. The roads will serve to accelerate the region's economic development.

Balance of Payments Support Loan

- *Loan of US$3.75 million*; interest-free, 15-year maturity, including a 5-year grace period
- Utilization: foodstuffs

Local Counterpart Funds

Cotton Textile Mill at Kandahar.
- Allocation: US$3.75 million equivalent; August 11, 1977
- Total cost: US$41.7 million

The designed yearly production capacity of this textile plant is 40 million meters of cotton cloth, 1,000 tons of cotton yarn and 10 million meters of grey cloth.

The project is expected to have a financial rate of return of 35%. The foreign exchange saving is estimated at US$290.0 million. Employment will be provided for some 4,000 persons.

2 Bangladesh

Project Loans

Dacca International Airport at Kurmitola.
- Loan of US$3.5 million; 20-year maturity, including a 5-year grace period; October 6, 1977
- Co-financiers: Government of France and **IsDB**
- Executing agency: Department of Civil Aviation and Airports Development Agency
- Total cost: US$73.8 million

Bangladesh is one of the developing countries with the lowest per capita income. It is one of the most populated, and it has only recently acquired independent statehood. The needs for productive investments, infrastructure and institution-building are urgent and immense.

The airport is essential to the country as it represents its main gateway by air with the rest of the world.

This project is one of the many examples of three-way co-operation between a host developing country, a government of an industrialized country providing finance and technical services (France) and OPEC member countries acting through their collective aid facility (The OPEC Fund) as well as other aid institutions (IsDB).

Greater Khulna Power Distribution Project.
- Loan of US$8.5 million; interest free; 20-year maturity, including a 5-year grace period; August 28, 1979
- Co-financier: **IDA**
- Executing agency: Bangladesh Power Development Board (BPDB)
- Total cost: US$43.6 million

The project's objectives are to rehabilitate, strengthen and expand the power distribution systems in the urban areas of the Khulna District; to provide training facilities and teachers for a training center in Khulna run by the BPDB; and to contribute to a major institution-building effort by strengthening BPDB's planning capability and improving its financial situation.

Ashuganj Fertilizer Project.
- Loan of US$10.0 million; interest free; 20-year maturity, including a 5-year grace period; December 14, 1979
- Co-financiers: **IDA**, ADB, USAID, KfW, the Governments of Iran, the United Kingdom, and Switzerland; and others
- Executing agency: Ashuganj Fertilizer and Chemical Company (AFCC)
- Total cost: US$452.7 million

The project consists of the design and construction of an ammonia/urea fertilizer plant with a capacity of about 1,600 tons per day of urea and 925 tons per day of ammonia at Ashuganj, about 100km north-east of the capital city of Dacca. Construction of supporting facilities and the provision of advisors and training services are also included in the project. With the plant coming on-stream, self-sufficiency in urea fertilizer production will be attained in Bangladesh.

East-West Electrical Interconnection Project.
- Loan of US$10.0 million; interest free; 20-year maturity, including a 5-year grace period; May 17, 1980
- Co-financiers: **KFAED**, IsDB, and Abu Dhabi Fund
- Executing agency: Bangladesh Power Development Board (BPDB)
- Total cost: US$92.8 million

The project is designed to connect the country's eastern and western electrical grids to reduce the western zone's dependence on oil imports for electricity by installation of a 94.4-mile long 230 kV transmission line from the Tounji Station in the eastern zone across the Jamouna River to the Ashourdi Station in the west. Apart from the foreign exchange savings, the interconnection will also promote efficient usage of electricity, as the excess generating capacity of the east will be used to meet electricity shortfalls in the west.

Bakhrabad-Chittagong Gas Project.
- Loan of US$21.0 million; interest-free; 20-year maturity, including a 5-year grace period; October 24, 1980
- Co-financiers: **IDA** and Government of Japan
- Executing agency: Bakhrabad Gas System Ltd.
- Total cost: US$157.0 million

The project comprises a gas well drilling program and the construction of gas gathering and conditioning facilities, a transmission pipeline and a distribution system. The project will reduce oil imports and will help meet the growing fuel demand for both industrial and domestic purposes.

Ashuganj Thermal Power Project.
- Loan of US$30.0 million; interest free; 20-year maturity, including a 5-year grace period; July 15, 1982
- Co-financiers: **KFAED**, IDA, ADB, and KfW
- Executing agency: Bangladesh Power Development Board (BPDB)
- Total cost: US$328.4 million

The project involves the extension of the Ashuganj steam power plant which is located on the left bank of the Meghna River, about 70km northeast of Dacca. Two gas-fired units of 150 megawatts each will be added to the plant's current equipment, including boilers and ancillary electrical and mechanical equipment. The project also includes the installation of 230 kV double circuit 48km transmission line and a simulator to train the staff of BPDB.

Program Loan

Importation of Rock and Phosphate and Finished Fertilizers.
- Loan of US$7.0 million; interest free; 20-year maturity, including a 5-year grace period; December 19, 1978
- Loan administrator: IDA

Fertilizers are perhaps the major critical input for the economy of this agricultural country. Returns from increased use of fertilizers in Bangladesh are high. The Bangladesh Import Program, partially financed by IDA, will alleviate the current fertilizer shortage for agricultural development and assist the country's fertilizer industries.

Balance of Payments Support Loans

- *Loan of US$13.9 million*; interest free; 15-year maturity, including a 5-year grace period; January 20, 1977
- Utilization: crude oil
- *Loan of US$25.0 million*; interest free; 10-year maturity, including a 3-year grace period; July 20, 1981
- Utilization: cement, fertilizer

Local Counterpart Funds

Fertilizer Industry.
- Allocation: US$7.0 million equivalent; November 29, 1979

The proceeds from the Government domestic sales under the fertilizer and rock phosphate imports program will be used to meet local cost requirements of the fertilizer industry in Bangladesh.

Ashuganj Thermal Power Project.
- Allocation: US$10.0 million equivalent; December 16, 1982

For project description see above.

Thana Health Complex Phase I & II.
- Allocation: US$13.9 million equivalent; March 29, 1978 (Phase I)
- Allocation: US$6.0 million equivalent; December 16, 1982 (Phase II)

The project is part of a comprehensive program for the establishment of health facilities to benefit the rural population. The program involves 356 health complexes, of which 150 are old rural centers to be converted and/or expanded, and 206 to be constructed. Each center will be equipped with a 25-bed hospital and out-patient clinics.

Meghna-Dhonagoda Irrigation Project.
- Allocation: US$4.932 million equivalent; December 16, 1982

The project is aimed at ensuring flood control in an area of 44,000 acres and the irrigation of 36,000 acres. It will help increase agricultural output, create employment opportunities and improve public health.

Common Fund

A grant in the amount of US$1.43 million was extended on November 16, 1982 to Bangladesh to cover its mandatory subscription of shares of directly contributed capital of the Common Fund for Commodities.

3 Burma

Project Loans

Telecommunications Project.
- Loan of US$3.14 million; 19-year maturity, including a 4-year grace period; October 6, 1977
- Co-financier: **IDA**
- Executing agency: Burma Posts and Communication Corporation
- Total cost: US$34.0 million

The project will meet part of the urgent demand for telecommunication facilities. The project involves the installation of (a) 17,000 line units of local automatic telephone exchange equipment as cables, telephone instruments trunk transmission and switching centres; (b) 120 telex and gentex exchange lines and 80 telex and subscriber units.

The expected economic rate of return is 22%. Expected benefits include a strong contribution to general economic and social development, as well as a contribution to the management of the economy and institution building.

Rangoon Water Supply System.
- Loan of US$1.28 million; 20-year maturity, including a 5-year grace period; October 6, 1977
- Co-financier: **ADB**
- Executing agency: Rangoon City Development Committee
- Total cost: US$74.1 million

The purpose of the project is to improve the water supply system of Rangoon, a city of more than 2 million inhabitants, having an annual population growth rate of 3.5%, by doubling the present capacity to meet projected demand up to 1989.

The project involves the construction of two earth dams at Pugy, 32 miles north of Rangoon. Two new pumping stations and a prestressed concrete pipeline will carry the water from the reservoir to the city.

The OPEC Fund loan will partly finance a cost overrun of US$8.0 million incurred over original cost estimates made in 1973.

The project is expected to have an internal rate of return of 7%. Indirect benefits include improved health standards as a result of a decrease in dependence on costly and unsafe sources of water and better control of the problem of ground water salination.

Pyinmana Integrated Sugar Project.
- Loan of US$6.5 million; interest free; 20-year maturity, including a 5-year grace period; October 3, 1979
- Co-financier: **ADB**
- Executing agency: Ministry of Agriculture and Forestry (MAF) and Foodstuff Industry Corporation (FIC)
- Total cost: US$74.7 million

The main objective of the project is to increase the annual production of white sugar from 18,000 to 51,000 tons and to increase the supply of cane commensurately. This integrated project covers several aspects of sugar production from agriculture, with the necessary irrigation and drainage works, to transport, with the construction of a network of farm and feeder roads, to industry, with the provision of a new sugar factory, ancillary works and laboratories. Existing facilities will also be rehabilitated.

The benefits of the project are increased output and employment. The agricultural component will benefit some 10,000 farmers and the other components are also expected to create significant employment opportunities. The economic rate of return is estimated at 18%.

Sedawgyi Hydropower Project.
- Loan of US$2.0 million; interest-free; 20-year maturity, including a 5-year grace period; July 27, 1979
- Co-financier: **ADB**
- Executing agencies: Electric Power Corporation (EPC), Ministry of Industry; and Irrigation Department (ID), Ministry of Agriculture and Forests
- Total cost: US$28.5 million

The project is an integral part of the Sedawgyi Multi-purpose Development Scheme which envisages irrigation for agriculture, water supply and power development, utilizing the waters of the Chaungmagyi River by means of a storage dam and related facilities. The project involves the construction of a hydropower station of 25 megawatts and a 65-km-long 132 kV single circuit transmission line; distribution equipment; and consultancy services.

Outports Project.
- Loan of US$6.32 million; interest free; 20-year maturity, including a 5-year grace period; April 10, 1980
- Co-financiers: **ADB** and BPC
- Executing agency: Burma Ports Corporation (BPC)
- Total cost: US$49.32 million

The project is to rehabilitate and improve facilities at eight outports: Bassein, Moulein (to be financed by ADB), Mergui, Taboy, Akyab, Kyaupyu, Sandoway, and Kawthaung (to be financed by the OPEC Fund). The outports play an important role in the transportation sector of Burma as they cover almost the country's entire coastline (about 1,700 miles) and serve areas which are not otherwise linked to the national road network.

Mandalay Water Supply.
- Loan of US$7.0 million; interest-free; 17-year maturity, including a 5-year grace period; January 19, 1983
- Co-financier: **ADB**
- Executing agency: Mandalay City Development Committee (MCDC)
- Total cost: US$33.0 million

The aim of the project is to improve the existing water supply, provide a drilling rig, establish a network of transmission pipelines about 4.3km in length, construct new chlorinators, a 2000 m^3 contact tank, booster pumping station and operations center, and three storage tanks with total capacity of about 20,000 m^3, provide two trenching machines, lay 80km of primary pipeline and 190km of secondary pipeline, and instal 40,000 water meters, 785 public faucets, 440 fire hydrants, workshops, and testing laboratories. Mandalay, the second largest city of Burma, has an annual growth rate of 3%. The project will extend the service coverage from the present level of 39% to 83% in 1987 and to 90% in 1990.

Program Loan

Crop Intensification Program.
- Loan of US$15.0 million; interest free; 15-year maturity, including a 5-year grace period; January 12, 1982
- Co-financier: **ADB**
- Executing agency: Agriculture Corporation, Ministry of Agriculture and Forests
- Total cost: US$29.0 million

The program loan will help import fertilizer in support of the country's Whole Township Paddy Production Development Program (WTPPDP), which involves twelve townships in Burma's main paddy growing areas. The objective of the WTPPDP is to achieve a rapid and sustained increase in paddy yields through the intensive use of fertilizer and introduction of high yielding seed varieties, and the improvement of farm practices.

Balance of Payments Support Loan

- *Loan of US$2.25 million*; interest free; 15-year maturity, including a 5-year grace period; January 11, 1977
- Utilization: edible palm oil

Local Counterpart Funds

Sedawgyi Multi-Purpose Dam and Irrigation.
- Allocation: US$2.25 million equivalent; August 10, 1977
- Total cost: US$78.08 million

The purpose of the project is to increase agricultural output of paddy, cotton and groundnuts through the provision of a year-round irrigation water supply by constructing a storage dam across the Chaungmagyi River and related irrigation works. These new irrigation facilities will permit double cropping on an area of 51,000 hectares in the dry zone of Central Burma and are expected to increase cropping intensity from the present 113% to 195%. The project will be of considerable benefit to the economy of the country. It will directly contribute to rice self-sufficiency for the Mandalay Division and thereby indirectly support the country's rice export capacity. The project is expected to at least double the net income of some 33,000 farm families in the area. The project will also provide opportunities for settlement of 3,600 in new communities to be established. The economic rate of return of the project is 21%.

Common Fund

A grant in the amount of US$1.06 million was extended on January 14, 1983 to Burma to cover its mandatory subscription of shares of directly contributed capital of the Common Fund for Commodities.

4 India

Project Loans

Bombay High Offshore Development.
- Loan of US$14.0 million; 20-year maturity, including a 4-year grace period; December 16, 1977
- Co-financier: **IBRD**
- Executing agency: Oil and Natural Gas Commission
- Total cost: US$571.0 million

India is engaged in a major development effort in the energy sector. The Bombay High Offshore Development Project will significantly increase the production of crude petroleum. The works include development drilling at Bombay High North and Bassein and the erection of the necessary well platforms, 209 km subsea gathering lines connected to the 3 main processing platforms, an onshore terminal, supply lines and a supply base for the offshore installations, telecommunications and a control system to cover the entire Bombay High Program. The project is intended to assist India in becoming self sufficient in petroleum. The economic rate of return of the project is estimated at 66% with benefits quantified at present market prices.

Ramagundam Thermal Power Project.
- Loan of US$20.0 million; interest free; 20-year maturity, including a 5-year grace period; October 24, 1980
- Co-financiers: **IBRD** and IDA
- Executing agency: National Thermal Power Corporation Ltd.
- Total cost: US$638.0 million

The project comprises the construction of a large thermal power station near the South Godavari coal fields in the Karimnagar district of Andhra Pradesh. It consists of three 200 MW turbo generating units, three boilers, and a 400 kV transmission system. The project will help meet the country's growing demand for energy while reducing dependence on imported energy through the utilization of domestically produced coal.

Korba Thermal Power Project.
- Loan of US$20.0 million; interest free; 20-year maturity, including a 5-year grace period; May 18, 1979
- Co-financiers: **IDA** and Government of India
- Executing agency: The National Thermal Power Corporation (NTPC)
- Total cost: US$448.3 million

The NTPC, a corporation established by the Government of India for the purpose of building and operating power stations, envisages in its program the construction of four thermal power stations to be located near coal fields. The Korba Thermal Power Station constitutes the second station, and will have eventually a total generating capacity of 2,100 MW. The proposed project will provide for the installation of the first three generating units of 200 MW each; it will supply electricity to the western region of India and could operate as an independent unit.

Second Bombay High Offshore Development Project.
- Loan of US$30.0 million; interest free; 20-year maturity, including a 5-year grace period; March 16, 1981
- Co-financier: **IBRD**

- Executing agency: Oil and Natural Gas Commission
- Total cost: US$823.2 million

The project has as its objective the further development of the Bombay High fields, the largest oil field discovered in India, in order to achieve a plateau production potential of 240,000 bbl/day (12 million tons/year) by mid-1982. The project consists of the drilling of 64 directional development wells; construction and installation of fifteen simple four-leg well platforms; one three-deck, eight leg-processing platform with 180,000 bbl/day capacity, and a four-leg two-deck living quarters platform; installation of 133km of 8"-20" subsea flow lines; additional shore facilities; telemetry and telecontrol facilities, and consulting services.

Second Ramagundam Thermal Power Project.
- Loan of US$30.0 million; interest free; 20-year maturity, including a 5-year grace period; May 21, 1982
- Co-financier: **IBRD** and KfW
- Executing agency: National Thermal Power Corporation
- Total cost: US$1,650.4 million

The project represents the second stage of the Ramagundam development scheme. The second phase comprises three 500 MW generating units and associated transmission lines, totalling about 1,400km of 400 kV lines. The project will bring the Ramagundam Power plant to its final evisaged installed capacity of 2,100 MW and thus help meet the rising demand for electricity in India's southern region.

Balance of Payments Support Loan
- *Loan of US$21.8 million*; interest free; 15-year maturity, including a 5-year grace period; January 11, 1977
- Utilization: various chemical products (sulphur, zinc, antimony, tin, stainless steel, potash, rock phosphate), crude oil

Local Counterpart Funds

Singrauli Thermal Power Project.
- Allocation: US$21.8 million equivalent; August 11, 1977
- Total cost: US$397.0 million

The project will provide an additional capacity of 200 MW to the northern region of India where power supply has fallen heavily in recent years. Located in Rambari, Uttar Pradesh, the plant will be fueled by domestic coal from the extensive Singrauli coalfields. The counterpart funds will be used to finance the first stage of the project which consists of three 200 MW generating units with transmission lines along with boilers and ancillary plant. The overall economic benefits of the project are very significant as the cost of power shortage to industry is incalculable. Eighty-five percent of the output will be sold to selected states in the northern region, thereby substantially assisting in the economic development of the states receiving power. The project will also lessen the dependence of India on imported energy. The economic rate of return is expected to be 10%.

5 Jordan

Project Loans

North East Ghor Irrigation.
- Loan of US$1.65 million; 20-year maturity, including a 5-year grace period; October 6, 1977
- Co-financiers: USAID and **IDA**
- Executing agency: Jordan Valley Authority
- Total cost: US$29.7 million

The Northeast Ghor Irrigation Canal Project covers an area of 7700 ha in the northern part of the Jordan Valley. It is essentially an irrigation and rural development project which involves the construction of two diversion weirs and siltation reservoirs, 55km of pipelines and a distribution network for sprinkler irrigation of 2760 ha, 30km of farm roads, and rehabilitation works on the existing East Ghor Canal. A population of 25,000 persons will benefit from this project.

Minor works include domestic water supply for 10 villages, 3 new health centers, some 159 classrooms and a vocational training center which will benefit the population in the project area.

Upon project completion, agricultural production would double and the standard of living of the population would be raised. The economic rate of return is 24% and the production of high value fruits and vegetable is expected to annually earn US$6.0 million in foreign exchange.

Arab Potash.
- Loan of US$7.0 million; interest rate of 4%; 20-year maturity, including a 5-year grace period; October 2, 1978
- Co-financiers: **KFAED**, IBRD, IsDB, AF, Libyan Government, commercial banks, USAID
- Executing agency: Arab Potash Company
- Total cost: US$424.6 million

Potash is one of the major natural resources available to Jordan. It is found in the Dead Sea brine which is also rich in minerals and salts. The project will aim for an annual output of 1.2 million tons of potash to be extracted by solar evaporation. The investment involved makes it the largest industrial undertaking in Jordan. The export potential is high.

The works include solar evaporation ponds, a refinery and a township initially for construction staff and later for the permanent workforce.

The economic rate of return is estimated at 12.5%. Benefits will accrue in the form of foreign exchange earnings, fiscal revenues to the government and job creation.

Aqaba Thermal Power Station.
- Loan of US$10.0 million; interest rate of 6%; 14-year maturity, including a 4-year grace period; January 19, 1983
- Co-financiers: **AF**, KFAED, SF, Iraqi Fund, KfW, World Bank
- Executing agency: Jordan Electricity Authority (JEA)
- Total cost: US$311.5 million

A complete power station with two steam-turbine-driven generating sets, each of 130 MW; 325km of double-circuit, 400 kV transmission lines. Technical assistance for design, tendering, bid evaluation, and supervision of construction.

6 Laos, PDR

Project Loan

Nam Ngum Hydroelectric Project.
- Loan of US$4.0 million; interest free; 20-year maturity, including a 5-year grace period; August 24, 1981
- Co-financier: **IDA**
- Executing agency: Electricité du Laos (EDL)
- Total cost: US$20.0 million

The project comprises the installation of a fifth turbine-generator unit (40 MW capacity) at the Nam Ngum hydroelectric plant, the strengthening of the institutional capacity of EDL, and assistance to the Government of Laos and EDL in formulating long-term energy strategy. In addition to adding to the electricity generation capacity of Laos, the project will enable it to export energy to neighboring Thailand, thus strengthening regional economic cooperation between the two countries. Agreement has already been reached between Laos and Thailand on the purchase of electricity to be generated under the project.

Program Loan

Vientiane Plain Development Program.
- Loan of US$5.0 million; interest free; 15-year maturity, including a 5-year grace period; July 28, 1978
- Loan administrator: U.N. Committee for Coordination of Investigations of the Lower Mekong Basin (Mekong Secretariat)

The loan proceeds were used to import bulldozers, wheeled loader, tractors trucks, small generators, etc for the construction of reservoirs and development of the Vientiane Plain. The main beneficiaries are the estimated 100,000 displaced persons being settled in the Vientiane Plain.

Heavy Equipment and Maintenance Program.
- Loan of US$1.5 million; interest free; 15-year maturity, including a 5-year grace period; October 24, 1980
- Loan administrator: U.N. Committee for Coordination of Investigations of the Lower Mekong Basin (Mekong Secretariat)

The loan proceeds will be used to purchase spare parts and maintenance installations needed for the construction of reservoirs in the Vientiane Plain (above). This loan complements an earlier BOP support loan of US$5.0 million extended by the Fund for the Vientiane Plain Development Program.

Balance of Payments Support Loan
- *Loan of US$2.15 million*; interest free; 15-year maturity, including a 5-year grace period; February 3, 1977
- Utilization: glutinous food and paddy

Local Counterpart Funds

Agriculture and Livestock Development Project.
- Allocation: US$1.3 million equivalent; July 27, 1978

This project will develop Laos' water resources, irrigation systems and agricultural supporting services to increase rice production; in a concurrent effort to increase the country's food production, the project will establish livestock breeding farms. The allocation of US$1.3 million equivalent will meet all the local financing requirements of the project.

Agriculture and Livestock Development Projects.
• Allocation: US$850,000 equivalent; November 5, 1980
The three financed projects comprise: (i) fisheries development; (ii) production of vaccine; and (iii) processing of powdered milk. All three form an integral part of projects approved by the Fund in 1978 consisting of: (i) development of an irrigation system; (ii) supporting services for rice production; and (iii) livestock breeding.

7 Maldives

Project Loans

Hulule Airport.
• Loan of US$1.0 million; interest free; 20-year maturity, including a 5-year grace period; July 31, 1978
• Co-financiers: KFAED, SF, ADF
• Executing agency: Ministry of Transport
• Total cost: US$19.1 million
The project includes the preparation of a master plan for an international airport, the repair and resurfacing of the existing runway together with a 350 meter extension, the construction of a control tower, a terminal building and other ancillary structures as well as the provision of the necessary equipment.

An efficient system of air transport is essential to the Maldives, an archipelago spread over a thousand islands. The airport is expected to encourage tourism and facilitate movement of commodities.

Inter-Island Transport Project.
• Loan of US$880,000; interest-free; 20-year maturity; including a 5-year grace period; July 16, 1981
• Co-financier: ADB
• Executing agency: Ministry of Transport
• Total cost: US$2.0 million
The project represents Phase I of a plan to expand the inter-island transport system. Of the roughly 1,200 islands of the Republic of the Maldives, which extend 900km from North to South, about 210 are inhabited. By providing regular, reliable and efficient cargo and transport facilities between the outer atoll islands and the main island of Male, the project will encourage the development of agricultural products in the outer islands for consumption in Male and the tourist islands. It will also release vessels for fishing.

Balance of Payments Support Loans

• *Loan of US$0.5 million*; interest free; 13-year maturity, including a 5-year grace period; May 16, 1977
• Utilization: foodstuffs
The Maldives has availed itself of the option not to have counterpart funds deposited

against withdrawal of Fund Loan proceeds, accepting a shorter period of loan maturity.
- *Loan of US$0.8 million*; interest free; 15-year maturity, including a 5-year grace period; July 11, 1979
- Utilization; foodstuffs
- *Loan of US$1.0 million*; interest free; 10-year maturity, including a 3-year grace period; October 24, 1980
- Utilization; foodstuffs
- *Loan of US$600,000*; interest free; 10-year maturity, including a 3-year grace period; July 20, 1981
- Utilization: foodstuffs
- *Loan of US$520,000*; interest free; 10-year maturity, including a 3-year grace period; July 28, 1982
- Utilization: foodstuffs

Local Counterpart Funds

Inter-Island Transport Project.
- Allocation: US$120,000 equivalent; February 23, 1981

The local counterpart funds will go towards meeting the local costs of the Inter-Island Transport Project, described above.

Hulule Airport/Civil Aviation Project.
- Allocation: US$800,000 equivalent; February 23, 1981

The local counterpart funds will help meet the costs of the Hulule Airport/Civil Aviation Project, which is designed to develop domestic air transportation and associated air navigation facilities through the establishment of three additional domestic airports and the training of civil aviation personnel.

8 Nepal

Project Loans

Sagarnath Forestry Development.
- Loan of US$3.0 million; interest free; 20-year maturity, including a 5-year grace period; April 26, 1978
- Co-financier: **ADB**
- Executing agency: Forestry Division, Ministry of Forests
- Total cost: US$13.2 million

The project, located in the Sarlabi and Mahottari Districts of the Janakpur Forest Division in central region of Nepal, enables the planting of 10,000 ha with fast growing tree species. It involves provision of material and equipment, works for forest clearance, the establishment of small sawmills and workshops as well as the necessary road and community infrastructures. Training and consultant services are also provided for in the project. Completion is expected to take ten years. The economic rate of return is estimated at 41%.

Tribhuvan International Airport.
- Loan of US$5.0 million; interest free; 20-year maturity, including a 5-year grace period; February 9, 1979
- Co-financier: **ADB**

- Executing agency: The Department of Civil Aviation of the Nepalese Ministry of Works and Transport
- Total cost: US$20.0 million

The project is aimed at expanding airport terminal facilities in order to meet traffic needs up to 1985, and will help the growth of the tourist industry, a significant contributor to foreign exchange earnings in Nepal; it will also increase employment opportunities in the area.

Third Power.
- Loan of US$1.3 million; interest free; 20-year maturity, including a 5-year grace period; February 1, 1980
- Co-financiers: **ADB**, UNDP
- Executing agency: Electricity Department of the Ministry of Water and Power and the Eastern Electricity Corporation
- Total cost: US$23.68 million

The project comprises the two parts: (i) interconnection of the central and eastern power systems, which will provide a reliable power supply; and (ii) rehabilitation of the Biratnagar distribution system, which is of particular importance to jute mills and other industrial and commercial enterprises.

The project will allow Nepal to benefit from the economies of scale derived from the operation of a single system.

Mini Hydropower Project.
- Loan of US$4.0 million; interest free; 20-year maturity, including a 5-year grace period; September 15, 1981
- Co-financiers: **ADB**, UNDP
- Executing agency: Small Hydro-Development Board
- Total cost: US$15.15 million

The project comprises the construction of eight mini hydroelectric power stations, including associated transmission, distribution, service connections, and provision of an associated central maintenance workshop, training facilities and consulting services. The project is expected to eventually benefit around 250,000 people living in 15 major potential growth centers in hill districts and 46 adjoining villages. The project will lead to savings in imported fuel and will provide for the irrigation of 1,600 hectares. It is part of a Government program to modernize underdeveloped areas of the country and bring about a balanced regional development.

Kulekhani Hydroelectric Project.
- Loan of US$7.0 million; interest free; 20-year maturity, including a 5-year grace period; September 15, 1981
- Co-financiers: **KFAED**, IDA, Overseas Economic Cooperation Fund of Japan and UNDP
- Executing agency: The Electricity Department
- Total cost: US$119.13 million

The project consists of the construction of a dam on the Kulekhani river and electrical generation and transmission works. It will provide 60 MW of dependable peaking capacity and generate 165 GWh of primary and 46 GWh of secondary energy annually, equivalent to about 65,000 tons of oil. It is part of a Government program to exploit the country's hydroelectric potential to meet its increasing energy needs.

Balance of Payments Support Loan
  - *Loan of US$4.15 million*; interest free; 15-year maturity, including a 5-year grace period; January 10, 1977
  - Utilization: crude oil, sugar, dairy products

Local Counterpart Funds

Three Micro Hydro Power Plants.
  - Allocation: US$0.809 million; August 11, 1977
  - Total cost: US$1.5 million

These three Micro Hydro Power Plants all located in the mountainous regions of the country, are part of a wider rural electrification program involving the erection of 9 hydro power plants which form part of the Government's continuing policy to develop the country's hydro resources. The three plants will be located at Jomson, Jumla and Phidim and will each have an output in the range of 200-300 kW. The implementation of these 3 power plants will ensure a better regional distribution of power in areas which often are deprived of power facilities. The supply of inexpensive hydro electric power will also promote and enable expansion of small scale and cottage industries, as well as encourage the flow of tourists to these districts. The economic rate of return is expected to average 9.5%.

Kulekhani Hydroelectric Project.
  - Allocation: US$3.33 million equivalent; October 20, 1977

Existing generating capacity in Nepal is insufficient to meet current demand and frequent shortages are having a detrimental impact on industrial, commercial and agricultural development. The project involves the construction of a 107 meter high rock-fill dam, two 30 MW generating units and associated 66 kV transmission line and switchyard facilities.

When fully implemented the project will replace the use of energy in one form or another equivalent to 65,000 tons of oil annually, thereby saving some US$8.0 million yearly in foreign exchange annually. The project will further provide training to Nepalese engineers and technicians in the handling of a modern hydroelectric plant and build up a staff able to undertake similar future projects.

9 Pakistan

Project Loans

Multan Fertilizer Project.
  - Loan of US$11.0 million; 20-year maturity, including a 5-year grace period; October 6, 1977
  - Co-financiers: ADB, **IBRD** and Abu Dhabi National Oil Company Equity Participation
  - Executing agency: Pakarab Fertilizer Limited
  - Total cost: US$194.6 million

The project which puts a valuable national asset, natural gas, to profitable use will expand and modernise the existing fertilizer industry in order to meet growing domestic demand. The works comprise the construction of an ammonia plant with a capacity of

910 tons/day, a nitric acid plant for 1200 tons/day, plants for 1020 tons/day of nitrophosphate and 1500 tons/day of calcium ammonium nitrate.

Tarbela Hydropower Project.
- Loan of US$13.0 million; interest-free; 20-year maturity, including a 5-year grace period; October 2, 1978
- Co-financiers: **ADB**, CIDA
- Executing agency: Water and Power Development Authority
- Total cost: US$281.0 million

The project provides for an extension of the Tarbela Powerhouse with two hydro-electric generating units of 175 MW each. The plant will thus reach a capacity of 1,050 MW. The expansion of generating capacity in Pakistan is necessary to meet the growing demand of both agriculture and industry. The project is also expected to increase food production and incomes of poor farmers. During construction, some 21,600 jobs will be created. Permanent employment for operation and maintenance is estimated at 7,000.

The financial rate of return is of the order of 20%.

Pipri Thermal Generation Project.
- Loan of US$5.5 million; interest free; 20-year maturity, including a 5-year grace period; August 28, 1979
- Co-financiers: SF, **ADB**, and Government of France
- Executing agency: Karachi Electric Supply Corporation Ltd (KESC)
- Total cost: US$319.5 million

The project is the next scheduled addition to the Karachi Power System, and its implementation is given high priority by the government. It will provide the framework for an orderly expansion of the Karachi power system to keep pace with the industrialization and population growth of the city. It will include the construction of a conventional thermal power station with an initial capacity of 200 MW, designed for phased expansion to an ultimate total capacity of 1000 MW. The surplus power from the project will help offset projected power shortages in Northern Pakistan.

Pipri Thermal Generation Project.
- Loan of US$10.2 million; interest free; 20-year maturity, including a 5-year grace period; January 14, 1980
- Co-financiers: **ADB**, SF, French State Credit and Government of Pakistan
- Executing agency: Karachi Electric Supply Corporation Ltd.
- Total cost: US$319.6 million

The project includes the construction of a conventional thermal power station with an initial capacity of 200 MW, designed for a phased expansion to an ultimate total capacity of 1,000 MW. It is the next scheduled addition to the Karachi power system. The surplus power from the project will offset projected power shortages in Northern Pakistan.

Tarbela Hydropower Extension (Units 9 & 10).
- Loan of US$32.0 million; interest free; 20-year maturity, including a 5-year grace period; January 19, 1983
- Co-financiers: **ADB**, CIDA

• Executing agency: Water and Power Development Authority (WPDA)
• Total cost: US$159.0 million

Civil engineering needed to extend Tarbela power house to accommodate two 175 MW hydroelectric generating units (Nos. 9 & 10) including a new penstock from the portal of tunnel 2. Installation of the two generating units including switchyard extension.

Balance of Payments Support Loan
• *Loan of US$21.45 million*; interest free; 15-year maturity, including a 5-year grace period; December 23, 1976
• Utilization: spare electrical and mechanical parts for power and water supply projects.

Local Counterpart Funds

Secondary Transmission and Grid Stations.
• Allocation: US$12.8 million equivalent; August 11, 1977
• Total cost: US$720.0 million

The program works consist of establishing a network of 4,600 miles of 132 and 66 kV secondary transmission lines and 158 grid stations to disperse power available at primary load centers. This project, which has high priority in the Government's 5th Five Year Plan, aims at meeting the power requirements of 4 markets in which power availability is inadequate hindering the region's industrial and agricultural development.

Benefits include the reduction in line losses on the secondary system and improvement in the voltage conditions in the far flung areas of the system. The program will boost the village electrification program, raise the standard of living of the rural poor and provide new opportunities for employment. It will strengthen the regional and national economies by value added to the agricultural and industrial sectors, by enhancing prospects for manufacturing and exporting goods and increasing Government tax revenues.

Distribution of Power.
• Allocation: US$8.65 million equivalent; August 11, 1977
• Total cost: US$550.5 million

This program involves establishing an adequate and reliable electrical power distribution system. The primary objective is to provide electrical connection for intending consumers in the agricultural and industrial sector of all Pakistan with the exception of Karachi. The required facilities include 21,000 miles of 33 kV lines, 7,500 miles of LT lines and 54,500 transformer substations. This program will add 800,000 new users of electricity.

The enhanced supply of electricity will add to the productivity of the industrial and agricultural sectors within the country. As the availability of power is expected to lead to the establishment of new industries, the project will also reduce unemployment and raise the general standard of living. The project is expected to have an economic rate of return of 12.3%.

10 Papua New Guinea

Project Loans

Technical Education.
- Loan of US$4.0 million; 2% interest rate; 20-year maturity, including a 5-year grace period; January 12, 1982
- Co-financier: **ADB**
- Executing agency: Department of Education
- Total cost: US$5.3 million

The project is part of the Government's 10-year technical education development plan. Its objective is to upgrade technical education and apprenticeship.

Technical Assistance in the Energy Sector.
- Loan of US$1.7 million; interest rate of 5%; 14-year maturity, including a 4-year grace period; January 19, 1983
- Co-financier: **IDA**
- Executing agency: Petroleum Resources Assessment Group
- Total cost: US$5.3 million

The project would provide a preparatory study to explore petroleum potentiality in the Papua basin in the south of Papua New Guinea. This would include (i) a geological/geophysical assessment consisting of a detailed review of the four main sedimentary basins of PNG, with the objective of preparing basin studies designed to identify new exploration targets and hence enhance industry interest; (ii) the strengthening of geological survey; (iii) to provide promotional trips overseas and training of PNG nationals in the field of petroleum development.

11 Philippines

Project Loans

Cotabato-General Santos Road.
- Loan of US$8.25 million; 20-year maturity, including a 3-year grace period; October 7, 1977
- Co-financier: **ADB**
- Executing agency: Department of Public Highways
- Total cost: US$36.0 million

The Cotabato-General Santos Road Project will upgrade the 209km road connecting two main port cities which lend the project its name, and will improve access to and mobility in the rich agricultural lands of the Mindanao River Basin. This basin is the major agricultural area of Mindanao island accounting for over 60% of the island's rice and corn production.

The project will also improve the level of access to the agricultural and forestry resources of Southern Mindanao and will facilitate marketing of surpluses both domestically and abroad. Other agricultural development and port expansion projects will complement the road project to facilitate the integrated development of a region of the country which is economically depressed. The economic rate of return of the project is expected to be 18%.

Laguna de Bay Fish Pen Development.
- Loan of the US$4.5 million; interest rate of 4%; 20-year maturity, including a 5-year grace period; December 19, 1978
- Co-financier: **ADB**
- Executing agency: Development Bank of the Philippines (DBP) and Laguna Lake Development Authority (LLDA)
- Total cost: US$23.0 million

The objectives of the project are increased fish production and supply to the Laguna de Bay region including Manila. The project provides for extension of credit to fishermen for the development of 2,500 ha of fish pen modules and for the construction of a fish hatchery/nursery complex.

Bukidnon Irrigation Project.
- Loan of US$3.5 million; interest rate of 4%; 20-year maturity, including a 5-year grace period; July 20, 1979
- Co-financiers: **ADB**, Government of the Philippines
- Executing agency: National Irrigation Administration (NIA)
- Total cost: US$39.4 million

The project, which has been given a high priority by the Government of the Philippines under its 5-year (1978-1982) Irrigation Development Program, will help make available a dependable water supply for irrigation. Its main objectives are to increase agricultural production, promote employment, and improve the incomes and living standards of the rural population. This will be achieved through: provision of irrigation facilities, soil conservation measures, rural water supply, public health services, a Schistosomiasis control program, and consulting services.

The project will involve, inter-alia, construction of two main diversion dams across the Manupali and Muleta rivers, and 3 main canal systems and access roads to the dam sites.

Second Laguna de Bay Development Project.
- Loan of US$7.5 million; interest rate of 4%; 20-year maturity, including a 5-year grace period; March 16, 1981
- Co-financier: **ADB**
- Executing agency: National Irrigation Administration (NIA)
- Total cost: US$50.8 million

The project will provide infrastructural facilities required for increasing paddy and vegetable production and as such will complement an earlier project financed by ADB. It will provide irrigation for about 14,000 ha in the wet season and 10,000 ha in the dry season. In addition to pumping facilities, the project consists of a 30km-long feeder canal and a diversion dam, rehabilitation and improvement of the existing irrigation system and an agricultural development program.

Rural Electrification.
- Loan of US$20.0 million; interest rate of 4%; 20-year maturity, including a 5-year grace period; May 6, 1982
- Co-financiers: **ADB**, Government of Norway
- Executing agency: National Electrification Administration (NEA)
- Total cost: US$218.7 million

The project involves mini-hydropower development. It is primarily designed to assist the Government in attaining its objectives of achieving nationwide electrification by 1987, rehabilitating the distribution systems, and benefitting the rural poor. The project will also be instrumental in evaluating NEA's dendro-thermal power generation program.

Local Counterpart Funds

Feeder Roads Project.
- Allocation: US$8.25 million equivalent; November 17, 1978

The Government of the Philippines has agreed to utilize these local funds to finance the construction and improvement of 10 secondary and tertiary roads contiguous to the Cotabato-General Santos Road. These roads, which have a total length of 110km, traverse agricultural lands on which rice and corn are grown. Construction and improvement of these feeder roads will stimulate agricultural production by providing faster and safer transport facilities.

12 Solomon Islands

Project Loans

Lungga Hydropower Project.
- Loan of US$1.5 million; interest free; 20-year maturity, including a 5-year grace period; April 30, 1981
- Co-financiers: **ADB**, IDA, Commonwealth Development Corporation, Australian Development Assistance Bureau, and EIB
- Executing agency: Ministry of Works and Public Utilities
- Total cost: US$35.0 million

The project is designed to increase the country's total installed capacity through the development of hydropower rather than diesel-based electricity generation. It will meet the needs of the capital city of Honiara and the Guadalcanal Plain, the center of commercial agricultural activity in the Solomon Islands, until the year 2003. It will also reduce the country's need to import fuel for diesel generation.

The project consists of the construction of a crushed rock/earthfill dam; a power tunnel; a reservoir of ultimate capacity of about 155 million cubic meters; a power station of 21 MW maximum capacity: a 33/11 kV substation; and an 8-km-long 33 kV double circuit transmission line. Miscellaneous equipment and consultancy services will also be provided.

Balance of Payments Support Loans

- *Loan of US$1.0 million*; interest free; 15-year maturity, including a 5-year grace period; October 2, 1978
- Utilization: equipment
- *Loan of US$1.0 million*; interest free; 10-year maturity, including a 3-year grace period; August 24, 1981
- Utilization: not yet determined

Local Counterpart Funds

Plant and Vehicle Replacement Fund.
- Allocation: US$1.0 million equivalent; November 29, 1979

The local counterpart funds are to be allocated to the Plant and Vehicle Replacement Fund established by the Government of the Solomon Islands in order to ensure the availability of an adequate pool of equipment and vehicles for construction and maintenance of main and feeder roads in the rural areas.

13 Sri Lanka

Project Loans

Bowatenna Power Project.
- Loan of US$3.15 million; 20-year maturity, including a 3-year grace period; October 6, 1977
- Co-financier: **ADB**
- Executing agency: Ceylon Electricity Board
- Total cost: US$32.8 million

Construction of a 40 MW hydropower station to be fed from the Bowatenna reservoir in the Mahaweli Ganga Basin which was built for irrigation purposes and is now used for power generation. The output of this new station is expected to be in the order of 180 GWh.

The project includes the construction of an intake structure, power tunnel and ancillary structures, a power station and switchyard and installation of a turbine and generator with a 16 mile long transmission line to connect the power station with the main grid.

Rural Electrification Project.
- Loan of US$6.0 million; interest free; 20-year maturity, including a 5-year grace period; April 12, 1980
- Co-financier: **ADB**
- Executing agency: Ceylon Electricity Board
- Total cost: US$31.8 million

The project comprises the electrification of 1,150 villages and includes the installation of 670km of 33 kV and 210km of 11 kV transmission lines, 5,140km of low voltage (415 volt) lines, 910 substations, and 57,500 consumer connections. Other project components include construction equipment and vehicles, and consultancy services. This project is part of a larger program to upgrade existing networks and bring electrification to new areas. It will provide electricity to about 1.5 million people, and serve agro-based industries, handicrafts, irrigation pumping and commercial activities.

Integrated Tea Development Project.
- Loan of US$5.0 million; interest free; 20-year maturity, including a 5-year grace period; January 27, 1981
- Co-financier: **ADB**
- Executing agency: Janatha Estates Development Board and Tea Small Holdings Development Authority
- Total cost: US$36.7 million

The project comprises the rehabilitation of 19 public estates in the Badulla District covering 7,380 ha; construction of three tea processing factories and provision of related support services for small-holders in Galle District. The project is part of a five-year government program to revitalize the tea sector, the country's most important source of foreign exchange. The project will increase the productivity of existing tea plantations and factories and improve the quality of tea. It will also help promote socio-economic links between the tea estate sector, which mostly employs immigrant labor, and the surrounding areas, by attracting indigenous villagers to work on the plantations.

Mahaweli Power Transmission Project.
- Loan of US$11.0 million; interest free; 20-year maturity, including a 5-year grace period; January 12, 1982
- Co-financier: **IDA**
- Executing agency: Ceylon Electricity Board
- Total cost: US$76.3 million

The main objective of the project is to distribute efficiently and at a minimum cost, the electricity generated by power stations located in the Mahaweli Basin to the principal load centers in and around Colombo. A secondary objective is to enable the existing system to function at acceptable levels of reliability, voltage control and energy losses.

Balance of Payments Support Loans

- *Loan of US$8.1 million*; interest free; 15-year maturity, including a 5-year grace period; December 23, 1976
- Utilization: flour and sugar
- *Loan of US$9.0 million*; interest free; 10-year maturity, including a 3-year grace period; April 9, 1981
- Partial utilization: imports of foodstuffs

Local Counterpart Funds

Bowatenna Power Project.
- Allocation: US$3.1 million equivalent; March 29, 1978

The counterpart funds generated under the Fund's first balance of payments support loan extended to Sri Lanka in 1976 complemented the Fund's project loan to this project (above).

This project, and the two projects mentioned below, will importantly contribute to the industrial extension planned in the area. The project will electrify the rubber and tea factories in the area and provide for the development of cottage industries.

Canyon Power Project.
- Allocation: US$3.44 million equivalent; March 29, 1978

The project represents the final stage of the development of the hydropower potential of the Maskeliya Oya River. The project comprises, inter-alia, a power station located on the Canyon Reservoir including a single generating unit of 30 MW capacity with transformer switchgear and auxiliaries as well as a 132kV transmission 11km in length to the Laxapana switchyard. The project will have an annual firm energy output of 114 GWh.

Samanalawewa Power Project.
- Allocation: US$1.56 million equivalent; March 29, 1978

This hydro-electric project is located on the Walawe Ganga River and its tributaries. It will have an annual output of 444 million units. The project comprises two 60 MW power plants and auxiliaries, a dam and reservoir at Samanalewewa with a 280 million cubic meter capacity, and a dam and reservoir at Diawini with 9.6 million cubic meter capacity.

Maduru Oya Irrigation.
  ● Allocation: US$9.0 million equivalent; February 24, 1982
The Maduru Oya Irrigation project is part of the Accelerated Mahaweli Development Program. Its objective is to provide irrigation water to the area lying along the left bank of the Maduru Oya River, to increase agricultural production, generate employment opportunities, develop the hydropower potential, and provide resettlements for landless poor estimated at about 35,000 families.

14 Syria

Project Loans

Aleppo Water Supply Project.
  ● Loan of US$2.0 million; interest rate of 4%; 20-year maturity, including a 4-year grace period; December 14, 1979
  ● Co-financiers: **IsDB**, IBRD
  ● Executing agency: Etablissement Public des Eaux d'Alep (EPEA)
  ● Total cost: US$116.8 million
The Aleppo Water Supply project's objectives are to extend the water source and transmission facilities in order to meet an increasing demand for water in the city of Aleppo. It will also provide for technical assistance designed to improve project implementation and operational capacity of the EPEA. The project includes a 75-km long aqueduct and pumping mains which will deliver 220,000 m^3/d and 110,000 m^3/d of water, respectively; pumping facilities at Lake Assad; service reservoirs; and distribution mains to serve the high level area of the city inhabited by the urban poor.

Damascus Refuse Composting Project.
  ● Loan of US$10.0 million; interest rate of 4%; 20-year maturity, including a 5-year grace period; April 9, 1981
  ● Co-financier: **Arab Fund**, IsDB
  ● Executing agency: Governorate of Damascus
  ● Total cost: US$21.0 million
The project consists of the construction of a compost plant to process the increased volume of refuse in Damascus over the next decade. The plant will process the refuse in a hygienic way, thus minimizing the kind of unhygienic conditions that have in the past led to health hazards as serious as epidemics. The processed refuse will also be sold to farmers in surrounding areas for use as soil conditioners.

15 Thailand

Project Loans

Accelerated Rural Electrification Project.
- Loan of US$7.0 million; 20-year maturity, including a 5-year grace period; October 7, 1977
- Co-financiers: **IBRD**, CIDA
- Executing agency: Provincial Electricity Authority (PEA)
- Total cost: US$118.0 million

The Accelerated Rural Electrification Program covers 3,825 villages in 16 north east provinces and 742 villages in 4 other provinces, affecting a population of 5 million. The project, which is the first phase of the program, involves the erection of some 12,500 kilometers of lines and the provision of all ancillary equipment from meters to voltage regulators and street lights.

The project relates to current concerns for a more equitable income distribution within developing countries and for the development of the poorest sections of the community. The benefits of this project will largely accrue to the population with the lowest per capita income in Thailand.

Mae Moh (Unit 4) Power Project.
- Loan of US$7.0 million; interest free; 20-year maturity, including a 5-year grace period; December 14, 1979
- Co-financiers: **ADB**, SF, Government of Switzerland, and EGAT
- Executing agency: Electricity Generating Authority of Thailand (EGAT)
- Total cost: US$253.0 million

The project is part of the five year development program (1977-1981) of EGAT. It will provide an additional 150 MW lignite-fired generation unit at Mae Moh in Northern Thailand, and 230 kV transmission facilities between Mae Moh and the main grid at Phitsanulok. The unit, which constitutes the fourth in a series of 5, will enhance the country's capacity to rely on its indigenous energy resources and reduce its dependence on imports of fuel oil.

Second Accelerated Rural Electrification Project.
- Loan of US$8.0 million; interest rate of 4%; 20-year maturity, including a 5-year grace period; October 24, 1980
- Co-financiers: **IBRD**, SF, Government of Norway
- Executive agency: Provincial Electricity Authority (PEA)
- Total cost: US$270.0 million

The project constitutes the second phase of the PEA Accelerated Rural Electrification Program. It comprises the electrification of 7,878 villages, as well as a feasibility study on mini-hydro schemes and consultancy services for the PEA. The project will benefit an estimated 6 million rural poor through increased agricultural productivity and an improved quality of life and will reduce the country's dependence on imported energy through diversification away from kerosene and diesel oil.

Chiew Larn Hydroelectric Project.
- Loan of US$21.8 million; interest rate of 1%; 20-year maturity, including a 5-year grace period; September 18, 1981

- Co-financiers: **IBRD**, KFAED
- Executing agency: Electricity Generating Authority of Thailand (EGAT)
- Total cost: US$181.3 million

The project is part of a government power development program designed to reduce the country's dependence on imported oil through the development of its indigenous energy resources.

The project consists of the construction of a rockfill dam, and open spillway, an intake structure, a surface powerhouse (with three 80 MW generating units); the installation of 230 kV and 115 kV double circuit transmission lines; and a resettlement program for 315 families living in the reservoir area.

Liquefied Petroleum Gas Project.
- Loan of US$15.0 million; interest rate of 6%; 14-year maturity, including a 4 year grace period; January 24, 1983
- Co-financiers: **IBRD**, CDC, Export Credit, OECF, Commercial Sources, Government of Thailand
- Executing agency: Petroleum Authority of Thailand (PPT)
- Total cost: US$455.0 million

The main objectives of the project are to separate ethane and heavier hydrocarbons from the gas stream and then market these products. The main components are the following: (i) A gas separation plant to recover ethane, propane, LPG and natural gasoline. The liquid hydrocarbon (propane, LPG and natural gasoline) will be transported to the Laem Chabang terminal; (ii) bulk storage and distribution installations to distribute propane and LPG in the domestic market; and (iii) studies and technical assistance relating to LPG marketing, petroleum sector investments, energy policy and other aspects of PTT.

16 Tonga

Balance of Payments Support Loan
- *Loan of US$1.0 million*; interest free; 10-year maturity, including a 3-year grace period; August 28, 1981
- Partial utilization: imports of oil

Local Counterpart Funds

Second Multi-purpose Project.
- Allocation: US$850,000 equivalent; December 16, 1982

The project consists of a number of sub-projects in the sectors of agriculture and agro-industry, health, transportation and tourism, as follows: (i) Development of vanilla plantings — US$695,000 equivalent; (ii) Construction and equipment of a fish marketing, processing and storage complex — US$27,000 equivalent; (iii) Construction and equipment of two rural Health Centers US$73,000 equivalent; (iv) Road construction and upgrading — US$33,000 equivalent; and (v) Construction of a Tourist and Handicraft Center — US$22,000 equivalent.

17 Turkey

Balance of Payments Support Loans

- *Loan of US$15.0 million*; interest rate of 5%; 15-year maturity, including a 5-year grace period; December 14, 1979
- Utilization: oil
- *Loan of US$25.0 million*; interest rate of 6%; 10-year maturity, including a 3-year grace period; October 16, 1981
- Utilization: oil

Local Counterpart Funds

Integrated Afsin-Elbistan Thermal Power Project.
- Allocation: US$15.0 million equivalent; January 30, 1980

The project, to be located near Elbistan in East-Central Turkey, comprises the development of an open-cast lignite mine by the Turkish Coal Enterprises, and a mine-based power station (four 300-MW units) and associated transmission lines by the Turkish Electricity Authority.

Integrated Afsin-Elbistan Thermal Power Project.
- Allocation: US$25.0 million equivalent; December 21, 1981

The project comprises the development of an open-cast lignite mine (planned capacity; 20.7 million tons per annum), construction of a mine based thermal power station (with four 300 MW lignite-fired units) and installation of associated transmission lines (380 kV transmission lines, about 540km long).

18 Vietnam

Project Loans

Fisheries Development.
- Loan of US$7.0 million; interest free; 20-year maturity, including a 5-year grace period; April 26, 1978
- Co-financier: Socialist Republic of Vietnam
- Loan Administrator: ADB
- Executing agency: Ministry of Marine Products
- Total cost: US$16.0 million

This project is part of a wider fisheries development program involving, *inter alia*, the expansion and modernization of the fishing fleet. The project will modernize 600 vessels with provision of marine diesel engines, fishing gear and navigation equipment, and provide spare parts for the rehabilitation of 4,600 fishing vessels currently idle.

The project will significantly increase fisheries, production and therefore exports. The estimated rate of return is 41%.

Dau Tieng Irrigation.
- Loan of US$10.0 million; interest free; 20-year maturity, including a 5-year grace period; October 2, 1978
- Co-financiers: **KFAED**, IDA, Government of Netherlands
- Executing agency: Ministry of Water Conservancy
- Total cost: US$110.0 million

The project involves the construction of a storage dam and an irrigation system for 42,000 ha in the south-western part of Vietnam. Two crops of paddy would be grown on 31,000 ha and three crops of groundnuts on the remaining 11,000 ha. Project works include the construction of an earth dam on the Saigon River with storage of 1,000 million cubic meters and a gravity irrigation system for the area concerned. Provisions are made for equipment and vehicles as well as training of personnel.

The economic rate of return is estimated at 17%. The project will benefit directly some 120,000 persons. It will create 26,000 jobs and increase the production of tradable crops thus leading to significant foreign-exchange savings.

19 Western Samoa

Balance of Payments Support Loans

- *Loans of US$1.6 million*; interest free; 15-year maturity, including a 5-year grace period; December 23, 1976
- Utilization: crude oil and foodstuffs
- *Loan of US$1.0 million*; interest free; 15-year maturity, including a 5-year grace period; October 3, 1978
- Utilization: imports of oil products
- *Loan of US$750,000*; interest free; 10-year maturity, including a 3-year grace period; January 14, 1980
- Utilization: imports of equipment and oil products
- *Loan of US$1.0 million*; interest free; 10-year maturity, including a 3-year grace period; May 27, 1981
- Utilization; imports of oil and equipment
- *Loan of US$1.0 million*; interest free; 10-year maturity, including a 3-year grace period; April 7, 1982
- Utilization: imports of oil products

Local Counterpart Funds

Highway Construction.
- Allocation: US$0.3 million equivalent; January 12, 1978

This project involves the reconstruction and improvement of 24km of the East Coast Road from Apia to Falefa Falls and 18km of the Central Cross Island Road from Vailima to Siumu.

Apart from the reduced vehicle running costs and savings in road maintenance, the project is expected to promote the agricultural development of the South Coast by providing ease of access to the Apia market and ports.

Western Samoa Telecommunications Project.
- Allocation: US$0.95 million equivalent; January 12, 1978

This project comprises installation of automatic telephone and telex exchange equipment, radio equipment and terminal facilities.

The project will effect basic improvements in the country's internal and overseas telecommunications abilities.

Western Samoa Workshop and Road Maintenance Project.
- Allocation: US$0.2 million equivalent; January 12, 1978

This project will improve the efficiency of repair plants and road maintenance. It will also provide employment opportunities for 200 individuals as well as improve the expertise of current personnel.

Apia National Hospital.
• Allocation: US$0.15 million equivalent; January 12, 1978
Under this project, the country's national hospital will be rebuilt and its treatment facilities expanded to improve medical care in the country.

Development Bank of Western Samoa.
• Allocation: US$1.0 million equivalent; October 3, 1978
The local counterpart funds to be mobilized under the Fund's second balance of payments support loan will be used to increase the Government's equity in the capital of the Development Bank of Western Samoa. The Bank plays a key role in the development of the economy. Strengthening the capital structure of the Bank will enable it to increase its developmental activities.

Samasoni (Magiagi) and Fale-Ole-Fee Hydropower Projects.
• Allocation: US$750,000 equivalent; April 21, 1981
The local counterpart funds will partially help meet the local costs of the Samasoni (Magiagi) and Fale-Ole-Fee hydropower projects, which will provide the country with additional generating capacity and help reduce its fuel oil imports.

Samasoni (Magiagi) and Fale-Ole-Fee Hydropower Projects.
• Allocation: US$1.0 million equivalent; February 23, 1982
The local counterpart funds will partially help meet the local costs of the Samasoni (Magiagi) and Fale-Ole-Fee hydropower projects, which will provide the country with additional generating capacity and help reduce its fuel oil imports.

Common Fund
A grant in the amount of US$1.0 million was extended on April 7, 1982 to Western Samoa to cover its mandatory subscription of shares of directly contributed capital of the Common Fund for Commodities.

20 Yemen AR

Project Loans

Third Highway Project.
• Loan of US$8.7 million; interest free; 20-year maturity, including a 5-year grace period; May 17, 1979
• Co-financiers: **IDA**, and Government of Yemen AR
• Executing agency: Highway Authority (HA)
• Total cost: US$60.3 million
The project is aimed at helping overcome the most important constraints to highway development in the country: deteriorating riding surfaces, significant overloading of paved roads by some vehicles, and crucial shortage of manpower at all levels of the

Highway Authority (HA). It focuses on institution building of the HA, highway maintenance and the consolidation and rational development of the highway sector.

Dhamar-Taiz Power Transmission Project.
- Loan of US$4.0 million; interest free; 20-year maturity, including a 5-year grace period; February 23, 1981
- Co-financiers: **AF**, ADF
- Executing agency: Yemen General Electric Corporation
- Total cost: US$34.2 million

The project is designed to distribute surplus electricity from Ras Katnib Power Station in the West to the cities of Ibb and Taiz in the South via the power distribution system of the cities of Sana'a and Dhamar. It comprises the construction of a 145km transmission line from Dhamar to Ibb and Taiz and two substations in the two cities. The socioeconomic benefits expected from the project include reduced oil imports, increased local employment and training opportunities, agricultural and industrial expansion through increased efficiency brought on by the use of electricity, and improved living conditions for the people in the project area.

Regional Electrification Project.
- Loan of US$4.35 million; interest free; 20-year maturity, including a 5-year grace period; August 24, 1981
- Co-financier: **IDA**
- Executing agency: Yemen General Electricity Corporation
- Total cost: US$21.5 million

The project consists of the rehabilitation and expansion of the electrical distribution network reaching 17 villages and the three principal farmers' markets at Sana'a, Taiz and Hodeida. It will in some cases involve the installation of generators and the construction of new distribution networks. The project represents the first phase (1981-1983) of the 18-year National Electrification Program, which will eventually extend publicly supplied electricity through the country.

The project comprises the installation of about 66km of 33 kV lines, 190km of 11 kV lines, 520km of 220 V wallmounted cables, 74 (3 phase) and 240 (single phase) distribution transformers (total capacity 15.5 MVA), 2,300 streetlights, 3 generating units (one 1,200 kW and two 100 kW), associated civil works and consulting services and pricing studies.

Mokha Power Station Project.
- Loan of US$10.0 million; interest free; 20-year maturity, including a 5-year grace period; July 28, 1982
- Co-financiers: **AF**, KFAED, SF, and Suppliers' Credit
- Executing agency: Yemen General Electricity Corporation
- Total cost: US$351.6 million

The objective of the project is to meet the increasing demand for electricity through the construction of a new steam power station in the southern part of the country, which will be connected to the national grid. The project will help ensure a reliable power supply to the region and will contribute to the development of a fast-growing area in terms of agriculture, industry and urbanization.

Balance of Payments Support Loan
- *Loan of US$2.25 million*; interest free; 15-year maturity, including a 5-year grace period; January 11, 1977
- Utilization: cold stores

Local Counterpart Funds

Cold Stores.
- Allocation: US$1.65 million equivalent; July 31, 1978

The project consists of the installation of six cold storage facilities. The capacity of the stores in Sana'a, Taiz and Hodaida is 250 tons each while the stores in Dhamar, Amran and Ibb have a capacity of 150 tons each.

The use of cold stores in the country will increase the availability of food products to consumers.

The allocation will meet the total local cost requirements of the project.

Third Highway Project.
- Allocation: US$0.6 million equivalent; May 17, 1979

For project description see above.

Common Fund

A grant in the amount of US$1.02 million was extended on July 28, 1982 to Yemen, A.R. to cover its mandatory subscription of shares of directly contributed capital of the Common Fund for Commodities.

21 Yemen PDR

Project Loans

Greater Aden Water Supply Project.
- Loan of US$4.0 million; interest free; 20-year maturity, including a 5-year grace period; October 24, 1980
- Co-financiers: **AF**, IDA, and IsDB
- Executing agency: Public Water Corporation
- Total cost: US$39.2 million

The project constitutes the first stage of a long-term master plan designed to meet the potable water requirements in Greater Aden until the year 2000. Greater Aden is currently supplied with water from some 50 wells sunk in the Wadi Tuban Aquifer. The project's basic objectives are to eliminate the current deficit in water supply to Greater Aden and to rehabilitate the existing water supply systems.

Naqabah-Nisab Road Project.
- Loan of US$10.5 million; interest free; 20-year maturity, including a 5-year grace period; August 24, 1981
- Co-financiers: **KFAED**, IDA
- Executing agency: Ministry of Construction
- Total cost: US$42.8 million

The project comprised the construction of a two-lane paved road from Naqaba to Nisab (92km) with a branch to As Said, the establishment of an independent construction unit to carry out road construction in Shabwah Governorate; provision of technical assistance to the Ministry of Construction to strengthen their project preparation and implementation capabilities and related training. The project is part of a Government plan to promote integration of different regions of the country and will strengthen national road construction capabilities.

East Mukalla Electrification Project.
- Loan of US$7.5 million; interest-free; 20 year maturity, including a 5-year grace period; July 13, 1982
- Co-financier: **IDA**
- Executing agency: Public Corporation for Electric Power
- Total cost: US$19.9 million

The project constitutes the first phase of an electrification scheme to supply electricity to five towns east of Mukalla and thirteen nearby villages. The objective of the project is to provide the towns with a central and more fuel-efficient power station, which will replace the existing independent generating sets. Thus, electricity losses will be reduced and demand presently in excess of supply will be met.

Balance of Payments Support Loans
- *Loan of US$2.4 million*; interest free; 15-year maturity, including a 5-year grace period; January 12, 1977
- Utilization; road construction vehicles
- *Loan of US$6.0 million*; interest free; 15-year maturity, including a 5-year grace period; July 16, 1979
- Utilization: tractors, trailers, foodstuffs

Local Counterpart Funds

Wadi Hadhramawt Agricultural Project.
- Allocation: US$0.7 million equivalent; January 8, 1979

The project's main objective is to increase agricultural production in the project area through the provision of fertilizers and insecticides, and agricultural and irrigation equipment. Other objectives are to: build feeder roads, establish a date fumigation and packing plant, supply potable water to 8 villages with 40,000 people and undertake a feasibility study to explore possibilities of underground water.

Education Project I.
- Allocation: US$1.1 million equivalent; June 7, 1979

The project is designed to support the Government's efforts to improve and develop the educational system in the Yemen PDR. It involves the construction of two teachers' institutions and housing facilities, a student hotel and three schools, an agriculture machinery and a rural development center, the rebuilding of 2 secondary schools, supply of workshop equipment, and the provision of specialists and training courses.

Agriculture Support Services.
- Allocation: US$3.0 million equivalent; January 27, 1981

The local counterpart funds will help meet the local costs of the Agricultural Support Services Project, which is designed to increase agricultural production and farmers' incomes through training of cooperative staff, improved irrigation, extension services and provision of necessary inputs, machinery and equipment.

Al Mukalla-Wadi Hadhramwat Road Project.
• Allocation: US$3.0 million equivalent; January 7, 1981
The local counterpart funds will be used to meet part of the costs of the Al Mukalla-Wadi Hadhramwat Road Project. The road will link Wadi Hadhramwat to the rest of the country, promoting increased agricultural production in the Wadi for trading purposes and providing the country with training and institution building in highway construction and maintenance.

Naqaba-Nisab Road Project.
• Allocation: US$600,000 equivalent; October 19, 1981
The local counterpart funds will help meet the local costs of the Naqaba-Nisab Road Project, described above.

Common Fund

A grant in the amount of US$1.02 million was extended on February 7, 1983 to Yemen, PDR to cover its mandatory subscription of shares of directly contributed capital of the Common Fund for Commodities.

LATIN AMERICA AND THE CARIBBEAN

1 Antigua and Barbuda

Balance of Payments Support Loan

• *Loan of US$1.0 million*; 6% interest; 10-year maturity, including a 3-year grace period; May 21, 1982
• Utilization: not yet determined

2 Barbados

Balance of Payments Support Loans

• *Loan of US$1.5 million*; 4% interest; 15-year maturity, including a 5-year grace period; June 25, 1979
• Utilization: hospital equipment, equipment and spare parts
• *Loan of US$1.5 million*; 4% interest; 10-year maturity, including a 3-year grace period; May 5, 1980
• Utilization: foodstuff, materials
• *Loan of US$2.0 million*; 8% interest; 10-year maturity, including a 3-year grace period; September 16, 1981
• Utilization: not yet determined

Local Counterpart Funds

Community Health Clinics.
• Allocation: US$1.5 million equivalent; May 25, 1979; US$0.5 million equivalent; July 5, 1982
This project is part of a program to develop a network of polyclinics which will provide community health care to the population of the island. Three new polyclinics will be developed and two existing health centers will be upgraded to polyclinic status.

Rural Development Program.
  • Allocation: US$1.5 million equivalent; May 5, 1980
This project is designed to promote agricultural diversification and increase food production in Barbados. It will help raise the productivity and incomes of the small farmer households. The project will consist of the development of approximately 30 rural development units in a total area of about 400 hectares and will affect some 1,500 families.

Spring Garden St. Barnabas Road Project.
  • Allocation: US$1.0 million equivalent; July 5, 1982
The project is directed at improving traffic conditions and transport facilities in the city of Bridgetown. It consists of the construction of the Spring Garden Road and the improvement of the St. Barnabas Road in the city of Bridgetown. The Spring Garden Road is a new facility which will provide a direct and fast link between Bridgetown, the West Coast and the North of Barbados. The St. Barnabas Road is an existing facility located on the periphery of the urban area of Bridgetown.

Scotland District Development Project.
  • Allocation: US$0.5 million equivalent; July 5, 1982
This project is designed to help in the research and application of adequate techniques to counter soil erosion and the resulting loss of land. Its implementation will enable the Government to adopt least-cost solutions in resolving soil conservation problems, to lower production cost and to improve productivity in the district. Additionally, improvements in basic information, measures to conserve soils and regenerate land, experimental planting, and better infrastructure should result in greater agricultural production, higher yields and lower cost of production.

3 Bolivia

Project Loan

Urban Water Supply and Sewerage Project.
  • Loan of US$5.0 million; interest free; 20-year maturity, including a 4-year grace period; July 3, 1979
  • Co-financiers: **IDB**, Central Bank of Bolivia
  • Executing agency: Servicio Autonomo Municipal del Agua Potable y Alcantarillado (SAMAPA) in La Paz; Servicio de Agua Potable, Alcantarillado y Desagues Pluviales (SEMAPA) in Cochabamba
  • Total cost: US$45.2 million
The objectives of the program are to expand and improve the existing water supply facilities in La Paz, and the sewerage system in Cochabamba. These two cities have the greatest population concentration in Bolivia. The program will help ameliorate the prevailing poor sanitary conditions caused by insufficient water and sewerage services. The investments in the sanitation sector, which reflect the basic priorities set by the Bolivian Government, are to benefit mainly the poorest people in the two cities of La Paz and Cochabamba.

4 Costa Rica

Project Loans

San Jose-Siquirres Highway Project.
- Loan of US$3.0 million; interest-free; 19 year maturity, including a 4-year grace period; September 13, 1977
- Co-financier: **IBRD**
- Executing agency: Ministry of Public Works and Transport
- Total cost: US$74.0 million

This project, which involves the construction of two main highways, San Jose-Rio Sucio-Siquirres (about 96km) and Rio Sucio-Puerto Viejo (2.9km) was begun in April 1977. The OPEC Fund loan of US$3.0 million closes the gap between the estimated foreign cost component of US$50.7 million and the combined World Bank loan of US$39 million and the Government contribution of US$8.7 million. Access to new agricultural and forested areas will be facilitated, operating cost for road users reduced and all-weather services provided to areas isolated during part of the year. The project will accelerate the development of geographical areas and economic sectors previously hindered by the existence of transport bottlenecks.

Ventanas-Garita Hydroelectric Project.
- Loan of US$13.4 million; 7% interest; 20-year maturity, including a 5-year grace period; October 19, 1981
- Co-financier: **IDB**
- Executing agency: Instituto Costarricense de Electricidad
- Total cost: US$204.7 million

The project consists of the construction of a dam and installation of electricity generation and transmission facilities with total capacity of 90MW. It is part of a government program to develop indigenous sources of energy, mostly hydro and geothermal in order to reduce the need for energy imports.

5 Dominica

Project Loan

Road Maintenance and Rehabilitation Project.
- Loan of US$2.0 million; 1% interest; 20-year maturity, including a 5-year grace period; May 21, 1982
- Co-financier: **IDA**
- Executing agency: Ministry of Communications, Works and Tourism (MCWT)
- Total cost: US$7.2 million

The project provides for the rehabilitation and maintenance of priority road sections destroyed by hurricanes, and for the strengthening of the MCWT's road maintenance organization. The project consists of the rehabilitation of three road sections totalling 26km: Roseau-Loubiere-Pointe Michel, Loubiere-Grand Bay, and Bois Diable-La Plaine; the pavement patching and drainage restoration of over 320km of main roads; the procurement of about 22 units of road maintenance equipment and vehicles and spare parts, and the provision of about 160 man-months of consultancy services.

Balance of Payments Support Loans

- *Loan of US$0.5 million*; 4% interest; 10-year maturity, including a 3-year grace period; May 5, 1980
- Utilization: foodstuff
- *Loan of US$1.0 million*; interest free; 10-year maturity, including a 3-year grace period; July 20, 1981
- Utilization: material for soap and foodstuff

Local Counterpart Funds

Bulk Shipment of Water Project.
- Allocation: US$0.25 million equivalent; May 21, 1982

The project consists of the construction of water storage facilities which will be used to supply water to tankers and barges. The facilities will also supply additional water to the capital city, Roseau, during emergencies.

Construction of Industrial Shed.
- Allocation: US$1.13 million equivalent; May 21, 1982

The project's objective is to stimulate the industrial sector and consists of the construction of 40,000 square feet of additional factory space at Canefield.

6 Dominican Republic

Project Loans

Bao Dam and Associated Works.
- Loan of US1.0 million; interest free; 20-year maturity, including a 5-year grace period; December 16, 1977
- Co-financier: **IDB**
- Executing agency: Corporacion Dominicana de Electricidad
- Total cost: US$57.4 million

The Bao Dam project is a multi-purpose project which will provide irrigation for the Valley of the Yaque del Norte River, electrical power, flood control and furnish potable water for the city of Santiago. The project includes construction of a rockfill dam 435 meters long with a crest 110 meters above foundation, two dikes and a channel connecting the new Bao Reservoir with the Tavera Reservoir. The water storage capacity that will be created by the Bao Reservoir is 280 million cubic meters.

Program for the Development of Fisheries and Cooperatives.
- Loan of US$1.935 million; interest free; 20-year maturity, including a 3 year grace period; December 16, 1977
- Co-financier: **IDB**
- Executing agency: Instituto de Desarrollo y Credito Cooperativo de la Republica Dominicana (IDECOOP)
- Total cost: US$4.0 million

The project will assist the development of artisan-type fishing in the coastal waters of the Dominican Republic. The provision of credit to six fishing cooperatives and to a central federation of cooperatives is involved. The funds will finance such components as a fishing base for each cooperative including the necessary equipment, boats, refrigeration, fishing gear, tools and vehicles.

Balance of Payments Support Loans

- *Loan of US$5.0 million*; 4% interest; 15-year maturity, including a 5-year grace period; December 14, 1979
- Utilization: fertilizer
- *Loan of US$10.0 million*; 4% interest; 10-year maturity, including a 3 year grace period; July 20, 1981
- Utilization: material

Local Counterpart Funds

Yaque del Norte Irrigation Project.
- Allocation: US$5.0 million equivalent; November 20, 1980

The project is to provide a modern irrigation and drainage system to a region located in the northwestern part of the country (Valley of the Yaque del Norte River) and thus will help increase agricultural production. It will ensure a full water supply to an area of 27,500 ha and will include:

- — a diversion and de-silting structure
- — an irrigation and drainage system
- — on-farm development
- — support for agricultural extension services, research and credit, and
- — equipment and facilities for operations and maintenance

Expansion and Improvement of Haina Port Project.
- Allocation: US$5.0 million equivalent; July 29, 1982

Haina Port, located 15km from Santo Domingo, serves that city's industrial zone. The project's main purpose is to upgrade the port facilities at Haina. It is further aimed at correcting deficiencies in cargo handling operations, with the consequent reduction in operating costs. The project consists essentially of the construction of five new wharves, one of which is to be used to handle container cargo and the other four for general cargo.

Agricultural Credit Program.
- Allocation: US$5.0 million equivalent; July 29, 1982

The main objective of the program is to provide credit to about 7,000 small and medium sized agro-livestock farmers. The purpose is (i) to increase agro-livestock production to supply the needs of domestic consumption; and (ii) to improve the income and consumption levels of the poorest agro-livestock producer families in the country.

7 El Salvador

Project Loan

Completion of the San Lorenzo Hydroelectric Project.
- Loan of US$10.0 million; 1% interest; 20-year maturity, including a 5-year grace period; April 15, 1983

- Co-financiers: **IDB**, Comision Ejecutiva Hidroelectrica del Rio Lempa (CEL)
- Executing agency: CEL

The objective of the overall project is to expand the electrical generation capacity of the CEL system through the construction of a hydroelectric plant on the Rio Lempa of 180 MW nominal capacity. The project will contribute to replacing expensive thermal energy by cheaper hydroelectric energy and to meeting the increasing demand.

Balance of Payments Support Loan

- *Loan of US$1.75 million*; interest free; 25-year maturity, including a 5 year grace period; May 16, 1977
- Utilization: oil

Local Counterpart Funds

Grain Storage and Gathering Facilities Program.

- Allocation: US$1.28 million equivalent; August 8, 1978

The Government's program for improving grain and cereal storage plants and gathering sites figures prominently in the country's drive to modernize the agricultural marketing system. The program involves the purchase of essential equipment for the unloading transportation, processing and packing of cereals and grains. The program will lower plant operating cost, facilitate the unloading and packing of grains, minimize waste and damage of grains as well as lower warehouse maintenance costs. The program is expected to encourage the production of basic foods by removing bottlenecks in the processing of grains and cereals which have dampened incentives to increase production.

8 Grenada

Balance of Payments Support Loans

- *Loan of US$0.35 million*; interest free; 25-year maturity, including a 5-year grace period; May 16, 1977
- Utilization: equipment, trucks, landrovers
- *Loan of US$1.0 million*; 4% interest; 15-year maturity, including a 5-year grace period; November 16, 1978
- Utilization: imports of road construction equipment and spare parts
- *Loan of US$1.0 million*; 4% interest; 10-year maturity, including a 3-year grace period; May 5, 1980
- Utilization: equipment
- *Loan of US$2.0 million*; 1% interest; 10-year maturity, inclding a 3-year grace period; July 15, 1981
- Utilization: equipment
- *Loan of US$2.0 million*; 2% interest; 10-year maturity, including a 3-year grace period; May 21, 1982
- Partial utilization: material and equipment for road construction

Local Counterpart Funds

Point Salines International Airport Project.

- Allocation: US$4.35 million equivalent; February 19, 1982

The objective of the project is to develop and expand Grenada's tourism and trading opportunities through the establishment of an adequate and efficient air transport system. The project consists of the construction of a modern international airport with a runway 9,000 ft long and night-landing facilities, capable of accommodating wide-bodied jet aircraft.

9 Guatemala

Balance of Payments Support Loan

- *Loan of US$1.75 million*; interest free; 25-year maturity, including a 5-year grace period; January 10, 1977
- Utilization: spare parts and foodstuff

Local Counterpart Funds

Fertilizer Supply Program.
- Allocation: US$1.75 million equivalent; September 15, 1980

The project involves the construction of 15 warehouses for the storage and distribution of fertilizers. Part of the local counterpart funds will also be used to finance the operational cost of the warehouses and to cover the administrative costs incurred by the Banco Nacional de Desarrollo (BANDESA).

10 Guyana

Project Loan

Tapakuma Irrigation Project.
- *Loan of US$4.0 million*; 4% interest rate; 20-year maturity, including a 5-year grace period; July 28, 1978
- Co-financiers: **IBRD**, CDB, UK Overseas Development Ministry
- Executive agency: The Ministry of National Development and Agriculture
- Total cost: US$40.4 million

The objective of the project is to increase rice production in an area of 41,750 acres through double cropping, better drainage, on-farm development and the use of improved seed varieties. Project works involve the rehabilitation and improvement of irrigation and drainage systems on the existing Tapakuma scheme, and the construction of new systems elsewhere. The project will benefit some 5,000 farmers raising their productivity and improving the country's distribution of income. It will also increase rice exports.

Balance of Payments Support Loans

- *Loan of US$1.6 million*; interest free; 25-year maturity, including a 5-year grace period; January 10, 1977
- Utilization: foodstuff
- *Loan of US$2.0 million*; 4% interest; 15-year maturity, including a 5-year grace period; July 28, 1978
- Utilization: imports of equipment and foodstuff
- *Loan of US$5.0 million*; 4% interest; 10-year maturity, including a 3-year grace period; May 5, 1980
- Utilization: imports of foodstuffs and tractors

- *Loan of US$10.0 million*; 4% interest; 10-year maturity, including a 3-year grace period; April 9, 1981
- Utilization: imports of foodstuff and chemicals

Local Counterpart Funds

Guyana Glassworks Company.
- Allocation: US$1.6 million equivalent; April 3, 1978

The project involves the construction of a factory to produce sheet and container glass in sufficient quantities to fully meet local demand plus create a surplus to be exported within the region. The project will add to the nation's trained manpower and provide employment opportunities to 470 workers.

Upper Demerara Forestry Project.
- Allocation: US$2.0 million equivalent; July 21, 1982

The project's aim is to increase exports of marketable wood products and gradually to introduce lesser known species to the international markets. It will also improve the present supply of lumber for domestic construction, particularly housing. For these purposes, the project will utilize the timbers in an area of approximately 152,000 ha located between the Demerara and Essequibo Rivers, to produce sawn lumber, piles and poles.

Tapakuma Irrigation Project.
- Allocation: US$5.0 million equivalent: July 21, 1982

For project description see above.

Mahaica-Mahaicony-Abary Water Control Project.
- Allocation: US$10.0 million equivalent: July 21, 1982

The project's objectives are to (i) increase agricultural exports; (ii) supply local markets and reduce imports requirements; and (iii) diversify production in order to establish a broader agricultural base. The project will provide flood control for the agricultural development of 115,000 acres of land. It consists of a reservoir dam and a drainage and irrigation system. About 3,800 farmers will directly benefit from the project.

11 Haiti

Project Loans

Port-au-Prince Storm Drainage Project.
- Loan of US$4.0 million; interest-free; 20-year maturity, including a 5-year grace period; May 17, 1979
- Co-financiers: **IDB**
- Executing agency: Ministry of Public Works, Transportation and Communication

This project is intended to deal with storm drainage as well as erosion control. Given a high priority by the Government of Haiti, it is aimed at rehabilitating the existing storm-sewer system, expanding its capacity, installing machinery for the disposal of solid waste, and initiating erosion control. Other objectives of the project are to improve the environment of the metropolitan area of Port-au-Prince; reduce floods, thus benefitting the 700,000 inhabitants in the area, improve public health, and generate 10,600 new jobs in a period of 5 years for the low-income sectors of the population.

Line of Credit to the Institut de Developpement Agricole et Industriel (IDAI).
- Loan of US$3.5 million; interest free; 20-year maturity, including a 5-year grace period; December 15, 1980
- Co-financier: **IDB**
- Executing agency: IDAI

The Government of Haiti will on-lend the proceeds of this loan to IDAI, the main source of government financing for the agricultural sector and the only public institution which lends directly to industry. The proceeds of this line of credit will be allocated to farmers and small-scale manufacturing entrepreneurs and will also be used to finance the expansion of the state-owned Port-au-Prince Industrial Bank.

Balance of Payments Support Loans
- *Loan of US$3.15 million*; interest free; 25-year maturity, including a 5-year grace period; January 11, 1977
- Utilization: power plant

Local Counterpart Funds

Rural Development of the Northern Plain.
- Allocation: US$1.0 million; August 11, 1977

The aim of the project is to increase agricultural production in the Northern Plain of Haiti. Project works include necessary agricultural support services and infrastructural inputs.

The annual foreign exchange savings resulting from this project are US$8.2 million. The project is expected to increase the income, basic food supplies and general standard of living of some 50,000 people in the project area.

Port-au-Prince Storm Drainage.
- Allocation: US$1.80 million equivalent; November 4, 1982

For project description see above.

Fifth Transportation Project-Road and Bridge Component.
- Allocation: US$0.24 million equivalent; November 4, 1982

The project aims at (i) upgrading and paving 54km of priority roads around Cap Haitien in the Northern Plain of Haiti; (ii) the reconstruction of the Hyppolite Bridge connecting the north-eastern region with Cap Haitien and the Northern Road; (iii) replacing the Trois Rivieres Bridge connecting the northwestern region with the Northern Road; (iv) upgrading 12.8km of access roads; and (v) conducting pre-investment bridge and road studies.

Community Health Post and Rural Water Supply Program.
- Allocation: US$0.11 million equivalent; November 4, 1982

The program's objective is to provide an adequate and safe supply of water and thus improve the living conditions of the population mainly in the rural areas. The water supply system will serve approximately 100 rural communities with a total population of 100,000 inhabitants.

12 Honduras

Project Loans

Fifth Power Project.
- Loan of US$1.70 million; interest-free; 19-year maturity, including a 4-year grace period; October 7, 1977
- Co-financier: **IBRD**
- Executing agency: Empresa Nacional de Energia Electrica (ENEE)
- Total cost: US$17.8 million

The Fifth Power Project accounts for some 11.5% of a seven-year program for the development of a main power system in Honduras. The project comprises a diesel power station (four units of 6MW, 400-500 rpm each, burning bunker oil) at La Ceiba; a 150km long single-circuit 230kV transmission line, linking Suyapa to Paroma and the Nicaraguan border; a 47km long 138 kV transmission line, between La Ceiba and the Aguan Valley; a number of substations; 150 km of 34.5 kV sub-transmission lines; and a variety of consulting and training services. An interconnection will be provided between power grids in Honduras and Nicaragua.

El Cajon Hydroelectric Project.
- Loan of US$3.5 million; interest free; 20-year maturity, including a 5-year grace period; May 17, 1979
- Co-financiers: **IDB**, IDA, VIF, CABEI, Govt. of Great Britain
- Executing agency: Empresa Nacional de Energia Electrica (ENEE)
- Total cost: US$582.69 million

One of the project's objectives is to expand the electric generating capacity in Honduras to meet the country's requirements by 1985. With its 4 generating units, the project will have a nominal capacity of 292 MW. In addition to providing economical energy, the project will regulate the Humuya River flow, thus allowing for the development of irrigation.

El Cajon Hydroelectric Project (Additional Loan).
- Loan of US$5.0 million; 4% interest; 20-year maturity, including a 5-year grace period; July 29, 1980

For project description see above.

Puerto Castilla Port Project.
- Loan of US$7.25 million; 1% interest; 20-year maturity, including a 5-year grace period; January 19, 1983
- Co-financiers: **IBRD**, VIF
- Executing agency: National Port Authority (ENP)
- Total cost: US$31.84 million

General cargo handling facilities at a 150 meters long wharf are to be provided, along with supporting infrastructure, at Puerto Castilla. These facilities are needed in 1984, when considerable export/import traffic is expected from investments in agricultural and forest products in the neighboring areas of the Aguan Valley and the Olancho Forest.

Balance of Payments Support Loan

> • *Loan of US$1.75 million*; interest free; 25-year maturity, including a 5-year grace
>   period; January 11, 1977
> • Utilization: seeds, equipment, insecticides and foodstuff

Local Counterpart Funds

Puerto Castilla Port Project.
> • Allocation: US$1.75 million equivalent; January 19, 1983
For project description see above.

13 Jamaica

Project Loan

Second Power Project.
> • Loan of US$3.3 million; 4% interest; 20-year maturity, including a 5-year grace
>   period; December 19, 1978
> • Co-financier: **IBRD**
> • Executing agency: The Jamaica Public Service Company Ltd.
> • Total cost: US$39.4 million
The objective of the project is to improve the quality of power supplies by balancing
installed capacity with the requirements of the system. The power system in Jamaica has
proved unreliable because of inadequate maintenance, insufficient capital expenditures on transmission and distribution. The project provides for both maintenance and
investment in the network.

Balance of Payments Support Loans

> • *Loan of US$3.0 million*; interest free; 20-year maturity, including a 5-year grace
>   period; October 7, 1977
> • Utilization: foodstuff
> • *Loan of US$4.0 million*; 4% interest; 15-year maturity, including a 5-year grace
>   period; October 2, 1978
> • Utilization: foodstuff
> • *Loan of US$7.0 million*; 4% interest; 10-year maturity, including a 3-year grace
>   period; May 2, 1980
> • Utilization: foodstuff
> • *Loan of US$10.0 million*; 5% interest; 10-year maturity, including a 3-year grace
>   period; July 28, 1981
> • Partial utilization: foodstuff

Local Counterpart Funds

Black River/Upper Morass Development Project.
> • Allocation: US$3.0 million equivalent; October 7, 1977
The project consists of providing drainage, irrigation and flood control of 11,500 acres
of the Upper Morass area of the Black River. This will enable the settlement of some
1,500 family farm units with community and agricultural extension services, a network
of roads and ancillary infrastructure inputs. The project is expected to generate
annually some US$9.6 million in foreign exchange. Other benefits include the hiring of
2,000 full time laborers and the establishment of farmers' cooperatives.

Rural Market Construction Project.
● Allocation: US$2.977 million equivalent; October 28, 1981
The major objective of this program is to improve the supply of domestically produced agricultural commodities streamlining and improving present marketing systems and channels for agricultural produce in the country. The project is aimed at establishing and improving the physical facilities and operational procedures of 16 rural markets in six parishes in Jamaica.

Agricultural Research Project.
● Allocation: US$1.1 million equivalent; October 28, 1981
This project is aimed at establishing a Research and Development Institution to reorganize and carry out the research required for the improvement of agricultural production in the country.

Kingston Sewerage and Water Supply Project — Castleton Scheme.
● Allocation: US$1.423 million equivalent; December 16, 1982
The project consists of the construction of a pumping station at Castleton, the laying of supply pipelines and the erection of a break pressure tank and other facilities to provide 6 million gallons of additional water per day to the Constant Spring Filter Plant.

Kingston Sewerage and Water Supply Project.
● Allocation: US$6.0 million equivalent; December 16, 1982
The project is basic to the development of a long-range program to augment and improve the water supply and to provide adequate sewerage service for Kingston. It consists of the following parts: (i) the construction of well fields near the Tulloch Springs Pumping Station and in the Rio Magno Valley, including pipelines; a number of wells and related connections in the Liguana Plains; and intake works, pumping station and pipeline at Hall's Green; (ii) the treatment of water and the improvement of the distribution system; (iii) the provision of sewerage services; (iv) evaluation studies; and (v) management advisory services and staff training program.

Third Education Project.
● Allocation: US$4.5 million equivalent; December 16, 1982
The project is related to the technical and vocational education system of Jamaica. It has three objectives; selective expansion, quality improvement and improved management. It includes the following specific items: (i) construction, equipping and furnishing of a College of Arts, Science and Technology, a Vocational Training Development Institute, and Industrial Production Centers; (ii) provision of technical assistance; and (iii) pre-investment study for the development of learning materials.

14 Nicaragua

Balance of Payments Support Loans
● *Loan of US$10.0 million*; 4% interest; 15-year maturity, including a 5-year grace period; September 28, 1979
● Utilization: cotton, oil, steel products, food and equipment

- *Loan of US$10.0 million*; 4% interest; 10-year maturity, including a 3-year grace period; November 10, 1980
- Utilization: foodstuff
- *Loan of US$10.0 million*; 4% interest; 10-year maturity, including a 3-year grace period; July 15, 1982
- Utilization: not yet determined

Local Counterpart Funds

Second Educational Project.
- Allocation: US$3,752,500 equivalent; October 28, 1981
The local counterpart funds will help finance the construction of 16 educational centers in the rural areas, comprising 585 classrooms; the construction and equipping of 21 basic secondary education centers, and emergency repairs of 22 centers of intermediate education. The project also includes staff training, technical assistance and the provision of scholarships.

School Rehabilitation Program.
- Allocation: US$880,000 equivalent; December 3, 1981
The program consists of the rehabilitation of forty schools severely damaged during the civil strife which occurred in the country in the period 1978/79.

15 Paraguay

Project Loans

Water Supply Project in the Cities of Coronel Oviedo and Villarrica.
- Loan of US$1.45 million; 4% interest; 20-year maturity, including a 4-year grace period; March 1, 1979
- Co-financiers: **IDB** and Corporacion de Obras Sanitarias of Paraguay (CORPOSANA)
- Executing agency: CORPOSANA
- Total cost: US$9.25 million
The project consists of the installation of water supply systems to improve the quality of potable water in the cities of Coronel Oviedo and Villarrica and will lead through better sanitary conditions to a great improvement in public health. It will help control water-borne diseases, thereby reducing the high rate of morbidity and mortality, and in the long run, will affect positively the productivity and incomes of the inhabitants.

Storm-Water Sewerage System of Asuncion-Stage II.
- Loan of US$1.45 million; 4% interest; 20-year maturity, including a 5-year grace period; July 16, 1979
- Co-financiers: **IDB** and CORPOSANA
- Executing agency: CORPOSANA
- Total cost: US$20.33 million
The purpose of the storm water sewerage system is to serve an area of 490 ha in the center of the capital city of Paraguay. Furthermore, the project will directly benefit the entire metropolitan population by preventing a complete standstill in the city's activities whenever heavy or even moderate rainfalls occur. The first stage of the storm water sewerage system was completed in 1976.

Line of Credit to Fondo Ganadero for Livestock Development.
- Loan of US$10.0 million; 4% interest; 20-year maturity, including a 5-year grace period; October 14, 1981
- Co-financier: **IBRD**
- Executing agency: Fondo Ganadero
- Total cost: US$60.0 million

The proceeds of the line of credit will be on-lent by the Government to the Fondo Ganadero, which is the principal source of long-term credit to the livestock sub-sector in Paraguay. The line of credit will be used to extend credit to mixed farms involved in both livestock and crops and it is estimated to benefit 1,400 small producers in the country.

16 St. Vincent & the Grenadines

Balance of Payments Support Loan
- *Loan of US$1.0 million*; interest free; 10-year maturity, including a 3-year grace period, August 24, 1981
- Utilization: not yet determined

LOANS AND GRANTS SIGNED UP TO APRIL 15, 1983

Benin

Common Fund

A grant in the amount of US$1.02 million was extended on January 19, 1983 to Benin to cover its mandatory subscription of shares of directly contributed capital of the Common Fund for Commodities.

The Gambia

Balance of Payments Support Loan

- *Loan of US$1.0 million*; interest free; 8-year maturity, including a 3-year grace perod; February 16, 1983
- Utilization: not yet determined

Haiti

Project Loan

Artibonite Valley Development Project.
- Loan of US$1.8 million; interest free; 17 year maturity, including a 5-year grace period; April 15, 1983
- Co-financiers: **IDB**
- Executing agency: The Artibonite Valley Development Agency (ODVA)
- Total cost: US$22.12 million
The project comprises the second stage of development of the Artibonite Valley for irrigation, and extends over 5,400 ha. Canals, intake works, drainage roads, land grading, technical advice and assistance and a land registration survey.

Common Fund

A grant in the amount of US$1.05 million was extended on April 15, 1983 to Haiti to cover its mandatory subscription of shares of directly contributed capital of the Common Fund for Commodities.

India

Project Loan

Railway Modernization Maintenance Project.
- Loan of US$22.5 million; 3% interest; 14-year maturity, including a 4-year grace period; April 15, 1983
- Co-financiers: IDA; **IBRD**
- Executing agency: Indian Railways (IR)

•Total cost: US$1,212.7 million
The project has the following objectives:

(1) Improvement of repair and maintenance for diesel-electric locomotives, by establishing at Patiala, in Punjab State, a workshop based on the unit exchange concept, and by procuring axles for use in unit-exchange maintenance at Patiala and at running repair shops.

(2) Acquiring prototype electric locomotives for testing under operating conditions on Indian railways.

(3) Procuring components and materials for the construction of 11,300 high capacity, bulk-handling wagons.

(4) Acquisition of testing equipment; technical advisory services; and staff training. These items to be applied to technical control at the new workshop, to improving train operations and to energy efficiency.

Lesotho

Project Loan

Four Towns Water Supply Project.
- •Loan of US$3.0 million; interest-free; 17-year maturity, including a 5-year grace period; April 15, 1983
- •Co-financiers: **AfDF**
- •Executing agency: Ministry of Water, Energy and Mines, Water and Sewerage Branch
- •Total cost: US$14.495 million

The project involves: improvement of the water supply system serving the four urban centers of Mafeteng, Mohale's Hoek, Mokhotlong, and Quthing. Raw water intakes at all four centers will be improved; water treatment capacity increased at Mafeteng, Mokhotlong and Quthing; pump houses constructed and equipped, and works for the storage, transmission and distribution of water constructed; workshops and offices will be built; engineering design and supervisory services will be provided; and operational assistance provided by the purchase of vehicles and equipment for communications and accounting, and the provision of technical assistance.

Mali

Balance of Payments Support Loan

- • *Loan of US$7.5 million*; interest free; 8-year maturity, including a 3-year grace period; February 16, 1983
- •Utilization: not yet determined

Mauritania

Project Loan

Manantali Hydroelectric Dam Project.
- •Loan of US$3.3 million; interest free; 17-year maturity, including a 5-year grace period; April 15, 1983
- •Co-financiers: SF, KFAED, ADF, **IsDB**, KfW, EDF, AfDB, USAID, UNDP

•Executing agency: Organisation pour la Mise en Valeur du Fleuve Senegal (OMVS)
•Total cost: US$583.8 million
The project, which is part of OMVS' overall program for the development of the Senegal River Basin, consists of the construction of a dam at Manantali to store water for irrigation of about 255,000 ha of land in the territory of the Borrower and in the Republic of Mali and the Republic of Senegal; to regulate the flow of the Senegal River making it navigable by large tonnage vessels at all times; and to generate, in a second phase, electricity for consumption in the region. The project comprises the following components:

(a) civil works;
(b) provision and installation of electromechanical equipment;
(c) construction of a feeder road;
(d) deforestation of the area to be flooded;
(e) resettlement;
(f) training of personnel;
(g) technical assistance to OMVS;
(h) works control and supervision;
(i) railway; and
(j) institutional support to OMVS.

Mauritius

Balance of Payments Support Loan

•*Loan of US$2.0 million*; 6% interest; 7-year maturity, including 3-year grace period; April 15, 1983
•Utilization: not yet determined

Sao Tome & Principe

Balance of Payments Support Loan

•*Loan of US$1.0 million*; interest free; 8-year maturity, including a 3-year grace period; February 16, 1983
•Utilization: not yet determined

Senegal

Project Loan

Manantali Hydroelectric Dam Project.
•Loan of US$9.3 million; 3% interest; 15-year maturity, including a 5-year grace period; April 15, 1983
•Co-financiers: SF, KFAED, ADF, **IsDB**, KfW, EDF, AfDB, USAID, UNDP
•Executing agency: OMVS
•Total cost: US$583.8 million
The project, which is part of OMVS' overall program for the development of the

Senegal River Basin, consists of the construction of a dam at Manantali to store water for irrigation of about 255,000 ha of land in the territory of the Borrower and in the Republic of Mali and the Republic of Mauritania; to regulate the flow of the Senegal River making it navigable by large tonnage vessels at all times; and to generate, in a second phase, electricity for consumption in the region. The project comprises the following components:

(a) civil works;
(b) provision and installation of electromechanical equipment;
(c) construction of a feeder road;
(d) construction of the area to be flooded;
(e) resettlement;
(f) training of personnel;
(g) technical assistance to OMVS;
(h) works control and supervision;
(i) railway; and
(j) institutional support to OMVS.

Tanzania

Project Loan

Kimbiji Oil and Gas Exploration Project: II.
 • Loan of US$5.0 million; interest free; 17-year maturity, including 5-year grace period; April 15, 1983
See details of first loan for project description.

Yemen AR

Project Loan

Mokha Power Station Project: II.
 • Loan of US$10.0 million, interest free, 17-year maturity, including a 5-year grace period; April 15, 1983
 • Co-financiers: **AFESD**, KFAED, SFD
 • Executing agency: Yemen General Electricity Corporation (YGEC)
 • Total cost: US$353.5 million
The project involves the construction of a complete power station, with four steam-turbine-powered generating sets, each of 40 MW nominal capacity. The boilers will burn heavy oil, and the sets will be cooled by sea water.

Additionally, the project includes works for the transmission and distribution of electricity: 320 km of 132 kV double circuit lines linking with the cities of Mokha and Bajil; 10 km of single-circuit 132 kV line; 86 km of 33 kV and 11 kV single-circuit lines; three 132/33 kV switching stations; four substations; enlargement of three main switching stations; a control and supervisory center; other transmission line expansion; and installation of transformers.

The project has two further components: technical assistance and consultancy services covering bidding and supervision of construction; and the construction of 200 housing units for the staff who will operate the station.

GRANTS FOR TECHNICAL ASSISTANCE, RESEARCH, ETC. (SIGNED UP TO APRIL 15, 1983)

		Allocation (US$ thousand)
I *World Food Program — International Food Reserve and Cooperation in Food Activities.*		25,000.0
II *Technical Assistance and Similar Activities.*		
UNDP-assisted projects		
1	Caribbean Regional Food Plan	2,000.0
2	Central American Energy Program	1,500.0
3	Development of the Niger Basin	5,000.0
4	Development of the Red Sea and Gulf of Aden Fisheries — first grant	4,200.0
5	Development of the Red Sea and Gulf of Aden Fisheries — second grant	3,441.7
6	Emergency Desert Locust Assistance	1,000.0
7	Energy Fund	6,000.0
9	Industrial Vocational Training Center in Egypt	1,500.0
10	International Center for Diarrhoeal Disease Research in Bangladesh — first grant	641.0
11	International Center for Diarrhoeal Disease Research in Bangladesh — second grant	950.0
12	Labour-intensive Public Works Program	1,300.0
13	Onchocerciasis (River Blindness) Control Program	2,000.0
14	Regional offshore prospecting in East Asia	2,000.0
12	Labour-Intensive Public Works Program	2,000.0
14	Regional Offshore Prospecting in East Asia	2,000.0
15	UNCTAD Research and Training Program	650.0
CGIAR — I		
1	International Center for Agricultural Research in Dry Areas — first grant	1,000.0
2	ICARDA — second grant	3,165.5
3	International Rice Research Institute	400.0
4	International Services for National Agricultural Research	200.0
5	West Africa Rice Development Association — first grant	400.0
CGIAR — II		
1	ICARDA — third grant	650.0
2	International Center for Potato Research	190.0
3	International Center for the Improvement of Maize and Wheat	740.0
4	International Center for Tropical Agriculture	600.0
5	International Crop Research Institute for the Semi-Arid Tropics	165.0
6	International Institute of Tropical Agriculture	440.0
7	WARDA — second grant	190.0
8	Contingencies	25.0

Agency for the Safety of Aerial Navigation in Africa	1,000.0
Latin American Energy Organization	5,000.0
Refinery Orientation Program	50.0
UNFPA-administered family welfare centers in Pakistan	1,500.0
UNICEF Rural water supply and sanitation program in:	
1 Benin	1,000.0
2 Cape Verde	500.0
3 Sudan	1,500.0
UNIFSTD-assisted projects	
1 Wood for Energy — technological program in Honduras	305.0
2 Development of solar energy and biogas production in Lesotho	240.0
3 Sago starch hydrolysis and fermentation in Papua New Guinea	61.4
United Nations Relief and Works Agency — first grant	2,470.9
UNRWA — second grant	1,263.0
West African Economic Community	5,000.0
African Fertilizer Development Center	500.0
International Development Law Institute	200.0

Grants for Research and Other Intellectual Activities

	Allocation (US$)
Asian Institute for Technology	45,600
Center for Arab Unity Studies	35,000
Center for Research on the New International Economic Order (NIEO) — first grant	50,000
Center for Research on the NIEO — second grant	50,000
Center for Research on the NIEO — third grant	50,000
Eastern African Universities Research Project	50,000
Independent Commission on International Development Issues (the Brandt Commission)	200,000
Institute for Development Studies, University of Sussex	30,000
International Center for Public Enterprises in Developing Countries	50,000
International Center for Theoretical Physics — first grant	100,000
International Center for Theoretical Physics — second grant	19,550
International Committee on the Management of Population Programs, Kuala Lumpur	26,500
International Economic Association	5,000
International Institute for Advanced Studies, Caracas, Venezuela	50,000
International Ocean Institute — first grant	45,000
International Ocean Institute — second grant	45,000
Latin American Faculty for Social Sciences	50,000
National Development Fund of Mauritania	20,000
OPEC Fund/OPEC Secretariat/UNCTAD — Workshop on Energy and Development	30,000
Oxford Energy Seminar — first grant	10,000

	Allocation (US$)
Oxford Energy Seminar — second grant	12,000
Oxford Energy Seminar — third grant	8,000
Regional Arab Federation of Associations for Voluntary Fertility Control	23,000
Seminar on the Financing of New and Renewable Energy Sources	20,000
St John's Ophthalmic Hospital, Jerusalem	50,000
The Brandt Commission — second grant	20,000
Third World Foundation	10,000
United Nations Children's Fund	27,500
Workshop on Petrochemistry co-sponsored by OPEC Fund/OPEC Secretariat/UNIDO	30,000
Workshop on Long Term Energy Projections	5,600
Investment Corporation for African Development	20,000
Inter Press Services	30,000

Total Amounts to March, 1983

	US$ million approved
Technical assistance and similar activities* (including World Food Program)	86.89
Research and other intellectual activities	1.22
Common Fund for Commodities	37.16
IFAD	20.0

* Includes two cancelled grants, not yet reallocated.

ANNEX 2: TABLES 9-20

Detailed Statistical Data Referred to in Chapters 3 and 5

Table 9: Agricultural Projects Financed by the OPEC Fund for International Development (at December 31, 1982)

Region/country	Name of project	Type of agriculture	Amount of financing (US$'000)	Co-financiers
AFRICA				
Burundi	East Mpanda Agricultural Project	Irrigation/settlement	2,000	AfDB, IFAD, EDF, WFD
Burundi	Mosso Sugar	Drainage/irrigation	7,000	AfDB, ADF, BADEA
Chad	Mamdi Polder	Drainage/irrigation	2,450	IsDB, BADEA
Kenya	Line of Credit to Support Small Scale Enterprises and Farmers	Agriculture Credits to small-scale farmers	3,000	
Kenya	Tea Industries	Agro-industry	5,300	IBRD
Kenya	Bura Irrigation and Settlement	Irrigation	12,000	IDA, KFAED, EDF, Government of UK, NL, WFD
Morocco	Tamzaourt Dam	Irrigation	5,000	KFAED
Mozambique	Tea Rehabilitation	Plantation	6,000	AfDB
Somalia	Juba Sugar	Agro-industry	5,500	SF, Government of UAE
Tunisia	Sidi Salem Multipurpose	Irrigation, regulation and control of Medjerda River	6,000	Government of Iran, IBRD, KFAED, EEC, Government of China, KfW
Sub-total			54,250	
ASIA				
Bangladesh	Ashuganj Fertilizer	Fertilizer	10,000	IDA, ADB, USAID, KfW, Governments of Iran, UK, Switzerland
Burma	Pyinmana Integrated Sugar	Drainage, irrigation, agro-industry	6,500	ADB
Jordan	Northeast Ghor Irrigation and Rural Development	Irrigation	1,650	IDA

Table 9 *(continued)*

Country	Project	Sector	Amount	Funding
Jordan	Arab Potash	Fertilizer	7,000	KFAED, IBRD, IsDB, AF, Libyan Government, Commercial Bank, USAID
Nepal	Sagarnath Forestry Development	Forestry	3,000	ADB
Pakistan	Multan Fertilizer	Fertilizer	11,000	ADB, IBRD, ADNOCO
Philippines	Fish Pen Development	Fisheries	4,500	ADB
Philippines	Bukidnon Irrigation	Irrigation	3,500	ADB
Philippines	Second Laguna de Bay Development	Irrigation/fisheries	7,500	ADB
Sri Lanka	Integrated Tea Development	Plantation	5,000	ADB
Vietnam	Fisheries Development	Fisheries	7,000	
Vietnam	Dau Tieng Irrigation	Irrigation	10,000	KFAED, IDA, Government of Netherlands
Sub-total			76,650	
LATIN AMERICA				
Dominican Republic	Program for the Development of Fisheries and Cooperatives	Fisheries	1,935	IDB
Dominican Republic	Bao Dam and Associated Works	Irrigation	1,000	IDB
Guyana	Tapakuma Irrigation	Irrigation	4,000	IBRD, CDB, Government of UK
Haiti	Line of Credit to Institut de Developpement Agricole et Industriel (IDAI)	Agriculture credit to small-scale farmers	3,500	IDB
Paraguay	Livestock Development	Animal husbandry	10,000	World Bank
Sub-total			20,885	
Grand Total			151,785	

Table 10: Program and Balance of Payments Support Loans Utilized for Importation of Food and Agricultural Inputs (at December 31, 1982)

Region/country	Amount of loan (US$ million)	Utilization of loan proceeds	Year of loan signature
AFRICA			
Benin	1.00	Foodstuffs	1977
	1.00	Insecticides	1977
Botswana	2.00	Vaccine	1979
Burundi	2.25	Foodstuffs	1979
Cameroon	4.95	Fungicide	1977
Cape Verde	0.775*	Foodstuffs	1977
	1.00	Foodstuffs	1978
	1.00	Foodstuffs	1979
	1.50	Foodstuffs	1980
	1.00	Foodstuffs	1981
Chad	2.40	Fertilizer	1977
Comoros	0.25*	Foodstuffs	1977
	0.50	Foodstuffs	1978
Congo	2.00*	Foodstuffs	1978
Djibouti	1.50	Agricultural equipment	1980
	1.00	Agricultural equipment	1981
Egypt	7.225*	Foodstuffs	1977
Equatorial Guinea	0.50	Agricultural products	1977
Ethiopia	4.80	Foodstuffs	1977
Gambia	1.00	Foodstuffs	1979
	0.75*	Foodstuffs	1981
Guinea	2.35	Foodstuffs	1976
	2.25*	Foodstuffs	1977
	1.00*	Foodstuffs	1979
Guinea Bissau	0.825*	Foodstuffs	1977
	1.00	Foodstuffs	1978
Kenya	4.00	Agricultural capital goods	1980
Lesotho	1.90	Grain dryers	1977
Madagascar	3.10	Foodstuffs	1977
	5.00	Foodstuffs	1980
	10.00	Foodstuffs	1981
	10.00	Foodstuffs	1982
Mali	3.55	Bags for agricultural crops/foodstuffs	1977
	2.50	Foodstuffs	1978
	6.00	Foodstuffs	1980
	10.00	Foodstuffs	1981
	5.00	Foodstuffs	1982
Mauritania	1.60	Foodstuffs	1977
	5.50	Foodstuffs	1980
	8.00	Foodstuffs	1981
Mauritius	2.00	Foodstuffs	1980
Mozambique	3.275*	Foodstuffs	1977
Niger	1.45*	Foodstuffs	1977
	3.00*	Foodstuffs	1981
Rwanda	2.25*	Foodstuffs	1979
	1.50	Foodstuffs	1980
Sao Tome & Principe	0.50*	Foodstuffs	1981
Senegal	3.40	Foodstuffs	1977
	4.00	Foodstuffs	1978
	4.50	Foodstuffs	1980
Seychelles	0.30	Foodstuffs	1978
	0.20	Foodstuffs	1979
	0.50	Foodstuffs	1980
	0.50*	Foodstuffs	1981
	1.00	Foodstuffs	1982

Table 10 *(continued)*

Sierra Leone	1.025*	Foodstuffs	1977
Somalia	2.05	Coconut oil/edible oil	1977
Tanzania	2.50*	Foodstuffs	1980
Togo	1.75*	Insecticide	1979
Upper Volta	0.563**	Foodstuffs	1977
	0.75**	Foodstuffs	1978
	0.375**	Foodstuffs	1979
	3.00*	Foodstuffs	1980
	5.00*	Foodstuffs	1981
Sub-total	174.363		
ASIA			
Bangladesh	3.50*	Fertilizer import	1978
	12.50*	Fertilizer import	1981
Burma	15.00	Crop intensification program	1982
Laos PDR	2.15	Foodstuffs	1977
	5.00	Irrigation/agricultural support services	1978
	1.50	Agricultural equipment/irrigation	1980
Maldives	0.50	Foodstuffs	1977
	0.80	Foodstuffs	1979
	1.00	Foodstuffs	1980
	0.60	Foodstuffs	1981
	0.52	Foodstuffs	1982
Nepal	2.075*	Foodstuffs	1977
Western Samoa	0.533**	Foodstuffs	1976
Yemen AR	2.25	Cold storage	1977
Yemen PDR	2.40	Graders, tractors, loaders	1977
	6.00	tractors, foodstuffs	1979
Sub-total	56.328		
LATIN AMERICA			
Barbados	0.75	Foodstuffs	1980
Dominica	0.50	Foodstuffs	1980
Dominican Republic	5.00	Fertilizer	1979
Guatemala	1.17*	Foodstuffs	1977
Guyana	1.60	Foodstuffs	1977
	1.00*	Foodstuffs	1978
	2.50*	Foodstuffs	1980
	10.00	Foodstuffs	1981
Honduras	0.875*	Foodstuffs	1977
	0.875*	Insecticides	1977
Jamaica	3.00	Foodstuffs	1977
	4.00	Foodstuffs	1978
	7.00	Foodstuffs	1980
	5.00*	Foodstuffs	1981
Nicaragua	10.00	Cotton oil/foodstuffs	1979
	10.00	Foodstuffs	1980
Sub-total	63.270		
Grand Total	293.961		

Notes:
  * Represents half of the BOP loan extended by the OPEC Fund.
  ** Represents a quarter of the BOP loan extended by the OPEC Fund.

Source: The OPEC Fund for International Development, various annual reports, 1976-82.

Table 11: Agricultural projects financed with local counterpart funds generated under balance of payments support loans (at December 31, 1982)

Region/country	Name of project	Agricultural sub-sector	Amount approved for financing (US$',000 equivalent)
AFRICA			
Botswana	Foot and Mouth Diseases	Animal vaccine	2,000
Burundi	Coffee Improvement	Plantation	1,110
Cape Verde	1 Emergency program 1977/1978	Agro-industry	1,550
	2 "Bolacha" and Pasta Factory	Agro-industry	2,000
Chad	Mamdi Power Project	Irrigation	2,400
Egypt	Talkha Fertilizer	Agro-industry	14,450
Ethiopia	Second Minimum Package Program	Credit, technical training to farmers	4,800
Ghana	1 Twifo Palm Oil	Agro-industry	4,090
	2 Kpong Resettlement	Crop cultivation	2,080
Guinea	Siguiri Rural Development	Irrigation	6,350
Guinea Bissau	1 Cumere Factory	Agro-industry	2,650
	2 Reclaiming of Land for Rice Cultivation	Grain cultivation	222.40
	3 Rural Extension Pilot in Bachil	Grain cultivation	313.47
	4 Development of Department of Soils	Soil research	307.30
Kenya	1 Nzoia Sugar	Agro-industry	2,500
	2 The Int'l Center of Insect Physiology and Ecology	Insecticide, research	1,500
	3 Mbita Point Capital Development, Phase 1	Pest research	500
Madagascar	1 Birni N'Koni Irrigation III	Agro-industry	3,100
Niger	2 Livestock	Animal husbandry	4,450
	3 Land Ploughing	Irrigation, ploughing	250
Senegal	1 Feasibility Studies for Agricultural Development of Soungrougrou Valley	Irrigation	500
	2 National Company for Meat Production	Soil research	1,000
	3 Debi Lampsar Irrigation	Agro-industry	2,000
	4 Agricultural Storage	Irrigation	950
	5 M'Bour and Louga Rural Development	Agro-industry	2,400
	6 Damba Solar Pumping Station	Grain cultivation, soil research	1,500
		Irrigation	1,000

Table 11 *(continued)*

Sierra Leone	1 Integrated Agricultural Development	Agro-industry	534
	2 Gambia-Mattry Oil Palm Project	Plantation	367
Somalia	Juba Sugar	Agro-industry	5,000
Sudan	Rahad Irrigation	Irrigation, crops cultivation	4,250
Upper Volta	Extension of Forestry Zone in Ouagadougou	Forestry	2,240
Sub-total			78,260
ASIA			
Bangladesh	1 Ashuganj Fertilizer	Fertilizer	7,000
	2 Meghna-Dhonagoda Irrigation	Irrigation	4,900
Burma	Sedawgyi Multipurpose Dam and Irrigation	Irrigation, grain and cotton production	2,250
Lao PDR	1 Agriculture and Livestock Development	Irrigation, grain cultivation, animal husbandry	1,300
	2 Agriculture and Livestock Development	Fisheries, animal husbandry and vaccine	850
Sri Lanka	Maduru Oya Irrigation	Irrigation	9,000
Tonga	Second Multipurpose	Crop cultivation	850
Yemen AR	Cold Store program	Crop storage	1,650
Yemen PDR	1 Wadi Hadhramawt Agriculture	Fertilizer, insecticides, irrigation research	700
	2 Agriculture Support Services	Irrigation, grain cultivation	3,000
Sub-total			31,532
LATIN AMERICA			
Barbados	1 Scotland District Development	Irrigation	500
	2 Rural Development Program	Grain production	1,500
Dominican Republic	1 Yaque del Norte Irrigation	Irrigation, drainage, soil research	5,000
	2 Agricultural Credit Program	Credits to farmers	5,000
El Salvador	Grain Storage and Gathering Facilities Program	Agro-industry	1,280
Guatemala	Fertilizer Supply	Fertilizer	1,750
Guyana	1 Upper Demerara Forestry	Forestry	2,000
	2 Tapakuma Irrigation	Irrigation, drainage	5,000
	3 Mahaica-Mahaicony-Abary Water Control	Irrigation, drainage	10,000
Haiti	1 Restoration of Irrigation Canals and Agricultural Development of the Artibonite Valley	Grain cultivation	900
	2 Rural Development of the Northern Plain of Haiti	Irrigation, drainage	1,000
Jamaica	1 Upper Morass Area of Black River	Irrigation, drainage	3,000
	2 Improvement of Rural Parish Markets	Agro-industry	2,977
	3 Agricultural Research	Soil research	1,100
Sub-total			40,107
Grand-total 1976-82			149,774

Table 12: Grants Extended to the Agriculture Sector
(at December 31, 1982)

Program	Amount in US$'000
Grants channelled through:	
UNDP	
Development of the Red Sea and Gulf of Aden Fisheries, 1st grant	4,200
Development of the Red Sea and Gulf of Aden Fisheries, 2nd grant	3,441.7
Caribbean Regional Food Plan	2,000
Sub-total	9,641.7
CGIAR	
International Center for Agricultural Research in Dry Areas, 1st grant	1,000
International Center for Agricultural Research in Dry Areas, 2nd grant	3,165.5
International Center for Agricultural Research in Dry Areas, 3rd grant	650
International Rice Research Institute	400
West Africa Rice Development Association, 1st grant	400
West Africa Rice Development Association, 2nd grant	190
International Services for National Agricultural Research	200
International Center for Tropical Agriculture	600
International Center for the Improvement of Maize and Wheat	740
International Crops Research Institute for the Semi-Arid Tropics	165
International Institute of Tropical Agriculture	440
International Center for Potato Research	190
Contingency	25
Sub-total	8,165.5
UNIFST	
Papua New Guinea — sago starch	61.5
World Food program	25,000
IFAD	20,000
Grand Total	62,868.7

Table 13: Energy Projects Financed by The OPEC Fund for International Development (at December 31, 1982)

Region/country	Name of project	Type of energy	Ammount of financing (US$'000)	Co-financiers
AFRICA				
Djibouti	Boulaos Power Extension	Diesel	2,500	AF, KFAED, CCCE, IsDB
Ghana	VRA Systems Improvement Package	Power	6,000	IBRD
	Kpong Hydroelectric	Hydro	3,700	IBRD, Saudi Fund, CIDA, KFAED, BADEA
Liberia	Bushrod Power Expansion	Diesel	5,000	IBRD
Madagascar	Andakeleka Hydroelectric	Hydro	6,500	KFAED, IDA, CIDA, BADEA, Saudi Fund
Mali	Biomass Power Scheme	Biomass	6,450	IDA
Mauritius	Champagne Hydroelectric	Hydro	2,000	KFAED, BADEA, CCE, EIB
Morocco	Sidi Cheho Al-Massira Hydro Power	Hydro	3,000	IBRD
Mozambique	Mucanha-Vuzi Coal Development	Coal	2,300	Government of Brazil
Rwanda	Mukungwa Hydroelectric	Hydro	2,350	BADEA
Sierra Leone	Third Power	Diesel	1,600	IDA, BADEA
	Power Engineering and Technical Assistance	Power	5,000	IDA
Sudan	Power II	Hydro, diesel	9,500	IDA
Tanzania	Kitadu Mufindi Power	Transmission	5,000	AfDB, NIB, CDC
	Kimbiji Hydrocarbon Exploration	Oil and gas	10,000	SONATRACH
	Second Songo Songo Petroleum Exploration	Oil and gas	12,000	IDA,EIB
Zaire	Shaba Power Rehabilitation	Power	5,000	IDA
Sub-total			87,900	

	Project	Type	Amount	Funders
ASIA				
Bangladesh	Greater Khulna Electrification	Distribution	8,500	IDA
	East-West Electrical Interconnection	Transmission	10,000	KFAED, IsDB, Abu Dhabi Fund
	Bakhrabad-Chittagong Gas	Gas	21,000	IDA, Government of Japan
	Ashuganj Thermal Power	Gas/thermal	30,000	IDA, KFAED, ADB, KfW
Burma	Sedawgyi Hydro Power	Hydro	2,000	ADB
India	Bombay High Offshore Development	Oil and gas	14,000	IBRD
	Second Bombay High Offshore Development	Oil and gas	30,000	IBRD
	Korba Thermal Power	Coal	20,000	IDA
	Ramagundam Thermal Power	Coal	20,000	IBRD, IDA
	Second Ramagundam Thermal Power	Coal	30,000	IBRD, KfW
Laos PDR	Nam Ngum Hydroelectric	Hydro	4,000	IDA
Nepal	Third Power	Transmission and distribution	1,300	ADB, UNDP
	Mini Hydropower	Hydro	4,000	ADB, UNDP
	Kulekhani Hydropower	Hydro	7,000	KFAED, IDA, OECP, UNDP
Pakistan	Tarbela Hydro Power	Hydro	13,000	ADB, CIDA, IsDB
	Pipri Power Generation	Gas/thermal	10,200	ADB, SF, French State Credit
	Pipri Power Generation	Gas/thermal	5,500	SF, ADB, Government of France
Philippines	Rural Electrification	Power/Hydro	20,000	ADB, Government of Norway
Solomon Islands	Lungga Hydropower	Hydro	1,500	ADB, IDA, CDC, Australian Dev. EIB
Sri Lanka	Bowatenna Power	Hydro	3,150	ADB
	Rural Electrification	Transmission	6,000	ADB
	Mahaweli Power Transmission	Transmission	11,000	IDA
Thailand	Rural Electrification	Distribution	7,000	IBRD, CIDA, Swiss Government
	Mae Moh Unit 4 Power	Lignite/thermal	7,000	ADB, SF
	Second Rural Electrification	Distribution	8,000	IBRD, SF, Government of Norway
	Chiew Larn Hydroelectric	Hydro	21,800	KFAED, IBRD

Table 13 *(continued)*

Yemen AR	Regional Electrification	Transmission	4,350	IDA
	Dhamar Taiz Power	Distribution	4,000	AF, Abu Dhabi Fund
	Mokha Power Station	Thermal	10,000	AF, KFAED, Saudi Fund, Supplier's Credit
Yemen PDR	East Mukhalla Electrification	Distribution	7,500	IDA
Sub-total			341,800	
LATIN AMERICA				
Costa Rica	Ventanas-Garita Hydro	Hydro	13,400	IDB
Dominican Republic	Bao Dam and Associated Works	Hydro	1,000	IDB
Honduras	Power Project	Diesel	1,700	IBRD
	El Cajon Hydro Power	Hydro	3,500	IDB, IBRD, Great Britain, CABEI, IDA, VIF
	El Cajon Hydro Power	Hydro	5,000	IDB, IBRD, Great Britain, CABEI, IDA, VIF
Jamaica	Power Project II	Power	3,300	IBRD
Sub-total			27,900	
Grand Total			457,600	

Table 14: The OPEC fund's Balance of Payments Support Loans
utilized for Energy Related Imports (at December 31, 1982)

Region/country	Amount of loan (US$ million)	Utilization of loan proceeds	Year of loan signature
AFRICA			
Central African Republic	1.75	oil, school, books	1977
Comoros	0.25*	cement, oil	1977
Comoros	1.00	oil	1980
Equatorial Guinea	1.00	oil	1979
Guinea	1.00*	crude oil	1979
Guinea Bissau	0.82*	gas oil, butane	1977
Guinea Bissau	0.50*	crude oil	1978
Guinea Bissau	1.00	oil/crude oil	1979
Guinea Bissau	2.00	oil	1980
Guinea Bissau	0.75*	oil	1981
Mozambique	3.28*	crude oil	1977
Mozambique	5.00	crude oil	1979
Mozambique	3.50	oil	1980
Niger	3.85	crude oil	1979
Niger	2.00*	oil	1980
Niger	3.00	oil	1981
Rwanda	1.50*	oil	1980
Seychelles	0.30	oil	1977
Somalia	5.00	crude oil	1979
Somalia	4.50*	oil	1981
Sudan	6.00*	oil	1981
Sudan	3.73*	oil equipment	1976
Tanzania	5.45	oil	1977
Tanzania	2.50*	oil	1980
Tanzania	10.00	oil	1981
Togo	1.75*	motor fuel	1979
Sub-total	71.43		
ASIA			
Bangladesh	13.90	oil/crude oil	1977
India	10.90*	crude oil	1977
Nepal	4.15	oil/foodstuffs	1977
Tonga	1.00	oil	1981
Turkey	15.00	oil	1979
Turkey	25.00	oil	1981
Western Samoa	1.60	oil/foodstuffs	1976
Western Samoa	1.00	oil products	1978
Western Samoa	0.37*	oil	1980
Western Samoa	1.00*	oil equipment	1981
Western Samoa	1.00	oil	1982
Sub-total	74.92		
LATIN AMERICA			
El Salvador	1.75	oil	1977
Haiti	3.15	power plant	1977
Nicaragua	5.00*	cotton, oil, steel products	1979
Sub-total	9.90		
Grand Total	156.25		

Note: * Amount represents half the BOP loan extended by the OPEC Fund.

Source: OPEC Fund for International Development.

Table 15: Energy Projects Financed with Local Counterpart Funds
Generated under Balance of Payments Support Loans
(at December 31, 1982)

Region/country	Name of project	Amount of financing (US$'000)
AFRICA		
Ghana	1 Bui Hydroelectric Power	
	2 Feasibility Study	1,630
Mozambique	Coal Development	0,800
Rwanda	Mukungwa Hydroelectric	0,460
Tanzania	Songo Songo Petroleum	5,000
Upper Volta	Voltelec Feasibility and Prefinancing for	
	Kapienga Hydroelectric	1,500
Sub-Total		9,390
ASIA		
Bangladesh	Ashuganj Thermal Power	10,000
India	Singrauli Super Thermal Power Station	
	Project	21,800
Nepal	1 Jamson Hydropower Plant	0,346
	2 Jumla Hydropower Plant	0,305
	3 Kulekhani Hydropower Plant	3,330
	4 Phidim Hydropower	0,170
Pakistan	1 Second Transmission Lines and Grid	
	Station	12,800
	2 Distribution of Power	8,650
Sri Lanka	1 Bowatenna Power Project	3,100
	2 Canyon Power Project	3,440
	3 Samanalawewa Power Project	1,560
Turkey	1 Integrated Afsin Elbistan Thermal Power	15,000
	2 Integrated Afsin Elbistan Thermal Power	25,000
Western Samoa	1 Samasoni (Magiagi) Hydropower	0,500
	2 Fale-ole-Fee Hydropower	0,250
	1 Samasoni (Magiagi) Hydropower	0,500
	2 Fale-ole-Fee Hydropower	0,500
Sub-Total		107,251
Grand total		116,641

Table 16: The OPEC Fund's Technical Assistance Grants to the Energy Sector (at December 31, 1982)

Grant programs channelled through:	Amounts (in US$)
UNDP	
1 Central American Energy Program	1,500,000
2 Regional Offshore Prospecting in East Asia	2,000,000
3 Energy Revolving Fund (US$2.0 million per year)	6,000,000
Sub-total	9,500,000
OLADE*	
1 Program of Studies on the Use of Alternative Sources of Energy in Latin America	5,000,000
OEMV**	
1 Refinery Orientation Program	50,000
UNIFSTD**	
1 Honduras — Wood for Energy Program	305,000
2 Lesotho — Solar Energy & Biogas Project	240,000
CEAO***	
1 Solar Energy Regional Project	5,000,000
Grand total	20,095,000

Notes:
* OLADE — Organizacion Latinamericana de Energia.
** OEMV — Oesterreichische Mineraloelverwaltung.
*** United Nations Interim Fund for Science and Technology for Development.
**** CEAO — West African Economic Community.

Source: OPEC Fund for International Development.

Table 17: Total ODA to the LLDCs from OPEC Member Countries, 1974-81 (net disbursements in US$ million)

Country	1974	1975	1976	1977	1978	1979	1980	1981
Afghanistan	28.6	21.6	14.7	25.4	24.7	8.3	1.5	20.5
Bangladesh	34.8	61.1	10.9	179.7	27.9	23.8	54.3	80.2
Benin	4.5	2.4	3.6	4.2	3.4	3.4	4.1	4.2
Bhutan	–	–	–	–	–	–	–	–
Botswana	–	5.4	0.1	1.5	0.1	0.6	2.2	0.5
Burundi	4.0	1.0	10.8	2.9	3.1	6.2	8.2	4.1
Cape Verde	–	0.1	–	1.8	0.7	1.0	4.0	1.0
Central African Republic	1.4	1.4	1.4	1.2	6.0	1.3	2.1	–
Chad	13.8	8.1	14.1	3.6	1.2	–	–	–
Comoros	–	–	–	3.9	5.2	3.1	15.1	14.6
Ethiopia	1.3	15.4	–	3.9	2.7	–	4.8	14.5
Gambia, The	1.5	0.4	2.1	3.7	8.8	6.6	14.2	13.1
Guinea	21.0	5.9	0.2	5.4	12.0	5.9	4.5	2.0
Guinea-Bissau	3.1	3.2	3.5	1.8	2.4	3.0	3.9	1.6
Haiti	–	–	–	3.2	–	–	–	1.3
Laos PDR	–	–	–	2.2	–	4.2	0.7	–
Lesotho	–	2.8	–	1.9	0.1	0.3	0.1	1.0
Malawi	–	–	–	–	–	–	1.3	0.5
Maldives	–	0.2	2.8	0.6	3.5	4.0	15.9	8.0
Mali	13.6	29.4	3.0	15.8	11.2	12.8	27.6	19.3
Nepal	–	0.3	0.1	8.8	1.6	3.5	6.8	11.4
Niger	1.0	16.8	3.9	5.8	21.7	6.0	8.7	36.8
Rwanda	1.0	9.5	0.1	5.4	4.1	2.9	7.3	8.6
Somalia	49.6	80.4	37.5	224.3	119.2	79.2	145.6	52.3
Sudan	80.0	188.2	253.2	121.9	94.0	298.8	189.1	197.5
Tanzania	7.1	7.3	–	12.8	2.1	4.8	11.5	14.7
Uganda	18.8	25.7	5.0	8.1	4.3	1.0	1.5	0.2
Upper Volta	6.1	2.9	1.0	3.0	1.5	4.9	6.9	8.7
Western Samoa	–	–	0.8	1.6	0.5	0.5	0.8	1.0
Yemen AR	90.6	141.0	203.2	197.6	196.1	148.4	304.4	246.9
Yemen PDR	35.4	34.3	141.8	86.8	42.4	20.3	51.8	61.2
Total	417.2	664.8	713.8	934.9	600.5	654.8	898.9	825.7

Source: *Development Cooperation*, various issues, OECD/DAC, Paris.

Table 18: Bilateral ODA to the LLDCs from OPEC Member Countries, 1974-81 (net disbursements in US$ million)

Country	1974	1975	1976	1977	1978	1979	1980	1981
Afghanistan	28.6	21.6	14.7	21.6	24.7	8.3	1.5	20.5
Bangladesh	34.8	61.1	10.9	165.8	26.8	13.3	50.1	47.5
Benin	4.5	—	3.6	0.6	—	2.1	1.8	1.3
Bhutan	—	—	—	—	—	—	—	—
Botswana	—	—	—	—	—	—	—	—
Burundi	3.0	—	0.1	0.4	2.1	1.7	3.7	2.1
Cape Verde	—	0.1	1.3	1.3	—	—	2.0	—
Central African Republic	—	0.2	—	—	—	—	2.1	—
Chad	9.4	3.7	1.4	—	6.0	1.3	—	—
Comoros	—	—	3.6	2.7	4.0	2.8	14.5	13.6
Ethiopia	1.3	1.2	—	1.5	0.3	—	4.8	14.5
Gambia, The	1.1	—	2.1	2.0	7.5	4.2	7.0	11.0
Guinea	21.0	5.9	0.2	2.9	7.1	2.8	0.1	-0.3
Guinea-Bissau	2.8	3.2	3.5	0.1	1.9	1.9	1.4	0.1
Haiti	—	—	—	—	—	—	—	—
Laos PDR	—	—	—	—	—	—	—	—
Lesotho	—	—	—	—	0.1	0.3	—	—
Malawi	—	—	—	—	—	—	0.1	0.2
Maldives	—	0.2	2.8	0.3	3.2	3.6	15.1	6.3
Mali	9.7	25.5	3.0	11.2	4.7	9.3	17.3	6.4
Nepal	—	0.3	0.1	4.6	1.6	3.5	6.8	8.8
Niger	1.0	14.1	4.1	2.9	16.2	0.1	1.7	27.8
Rwanda	—	8.5	0.1	4.5	1.2	0.6	1.3	0.7
Somalia	42.4	72.9	33.3	217.5	110.9	68.6	130.2	31.5
Sudan	42.6	174.1	224.7	106.3	75.5	283.2	166.4	163.1
Tanzania	13.1	0.2	5.0	6.9	1.0	3.6	7.4	5.8
Uganda	6.1	20.0	1.0	3.0	4.0	0.9	1.4	0.1
Upper Volta	—	0.2	—	—	—	—	—	—
Western Samoa	—	—	—	—	—	—	—	—
Yemen AR	79.7	139.4	190.6	187.0	189.2	136.2	292.5	215.8
Yemen PDR	23.5	34.1	135.1	82.3	28.5	11.4	39.9	42.6
Total	324.6	586.5	641.2	825.4	516.5	559.7	769.1	619.4

Source: *Development Cooperation*, various issues, OECD/DAC, Paris.

Table 19: The OPEC Fund's Project Lending Operations in the LLDCs to January 19, 1983, Sectoral Distribution (amounts in US$ million)

Country	Energy	Transportation	Agriculture & agro-industry	National Development banks	Industry	Water supply sewerage	Telecommunications	Total
Afghanistan		3.55						3.55
Bangladesh	69.50	3.50	10.00					83.00
Benin	2.50	7.60	4.00	4.50				18.60
Botswana		4.00						4.00
Burundi			9.00			3.00		12.00
Cape Verde							1.50	1.50
Central African Republic		5.10						5.10
Chad			2.45					2.45
Comoros		3.00						3.00
Guinea					11.00			11.00
Haiti				3.50		4.00		7.50
Laos PDR	4.00							4.00
Lesotho		3.00						3.00
Malawi		1.80						1.80
Maldives		1.88						1.88
Mali	6.45	7.00						13.45
Nepal	12.30	5.00	3.00					20.30
Rwanda	2.35							2.35
Somalia			5.50			2.66		8.16
Sudan	9.50	10.95						20.45
Tanzania		27.00			5.00			32.00
Uganda				15.00				15.00
Upper Volta		4.50						4.50
Yemen AR	18.35	8.70						27.05
Yemen PDR	7.50	10.50				4.00		22.00
Total	132.45	107.08	33.95	23.00	16.00	13.66	1.50	327.64
(in per cent)	(40.4)	(32.7)	(10.4)	(7.0)	(4.9)	(4.2)	(0.4)	100.0

Table 20: The OPEC Fund's Use of Local Counterpart Funds in the LLDCs to January 19, 1983, Sectoral Distribution (amounts in US$ million)

Country	Agriculture and industry	Transportation	Energy	Health	Water supply & sewerage	Industry	National development banks	Education	Other	Total
Afghanistan							3.75			3.75
Bangladesh	11.93		10.00	19.90						41.83
Benin							2.00			2.00
Botswara	2.00	1.00								3.00
Burundi	1.11	4.37			0.72					6.20
Cape Verde	2.55								1.00	3.55
Central African Republic								0.70		0.70
Chad	2.40									2.40
Comorcs		2.00								2.00
Ethiopia	4.80									4.80
Gambia, The		4.65								4.65
Guinea	6.35					1.50				7.85
Guinea-Bissau	4.35			0.10				0.37	0.83	5.65
Haiti	1.00	0.24			1.91					3.15
Laos PDR	2.15									2.15
Lesotho		1.90								1.90
Maldives		0.92								0.92
Mali		7.05								7.05
Nepal			4.15							4.15
Niger	5.20	2.90			2.73					10.83
Rwanda			0.46							0.46
Somalia	5.00				2.05					7.05
Sudan	4.25	3.20								7.45
Tanzania			5.00			5.45				10.45
Upper Volta	2.24		1.50		9.00					12.74
Western Samoa		0.70	1.75	0.15			1.00		0.75	4.35
Yemen AR	1.65	0.60								2.25
Yemen PDR	3.70	3.60						1.10		8.40
Total	60.68	33.13	22.86	20.15	16.41	6.95	6.75	2.17	2.58	171.68
(in per cent)	(35.3)	(19.3)	(13.3)	(11.7)	(9.6)	(4.1)	(3.9)	(1.3)	(1.5)	(100.0)

ANNEX 3: Acronyms

AAAID	Arab Authority for Agricultural Investment and Development
ADB	Asian Development Bank
ADNOCO	Abu Dhabi National Oil Company
ADF	Abu Dhabi Fund for Arab Economic Development
AfDB	African Development Bank
AfDF	African Development Fund
AFESD } AF	Arab Fund for Economic and Social Development
ASECNA	Agency for the Safety of Aerial Navigation in Africa and in Madagascar
BADEA	Arab Bank for Economic Development in Africa
BOP	Balance of payments or balance of payments support
CABEI	Central American Bank for Economic Integration
CCCE	Caisse Centrale de Coopération Economique
CDB	Caribbean Development Bank
CDC	Commonwealth Development Corporation
CEAO	West African Economic Community
CGIAR	Consultative Group on International Agricultural Research
cif	cost, insurance, freight
CIDA	Canadian International Development Agency
CILSS	Permanent Inter-State Committee for Drought Control in the Sahel
DAC	Development Assistance Committee (of OECD)
DMI	Dar Al-Maal Al-Islami (Islamic Finance House)
EDF	European Development Fund
EEC	European Economic Community
EIB	European Investment Bank
ENA	Executing national agency
FAO	Food and Agriculture Organization of the United Nations

GDP	Gross domestic product
GNP	Gross national product
GODE	Gulf Organization for Development in Egypt
Group of 77	Negotiating group of developing countries
IBRD	International Bank for Reconstruction and Development (World Bank)
ICARDA	International Center for Agricultural Research in the Dry Areas
ICO	International commodity organization
IDA	International Development Association (World Bank Group)
IDB	Inter-American Development Bank
IDLI	International Development Law Institute
IEFR	International Emergency Food Reserve
IFAD	International Fund for Agricultural Development
IFC	International Finance Corporation (World Bank Group)
IMF	International Monetary Fund
IsD	Islamic dinar
IsDB	Islamic Development Bank
KFAED	Kuwait Fund for Arab Economic Development
KfW	Kreditanstalt für Wiederaufbau
LCF	Local counterpart funds
LDC	Less developed country
LLDC	Least developed country (UN definition)
MSA	Most seriously affected country (UN definition)
NIB	Nordiska Investeringa Banken
NICs	Newly industrialized countries
NIEO	New International Economic Order
NL	Netherlands
NRE	New and renewable energy (sources)
OAPEC	Organization of Arab Petroleum Exporting Countries
ODA	Official Development Assistance
OECD	Organization for Economic Cooperation and Development
OECF	Overseas Economic Cooperation Fund (of Japan)
OLADE	Latin American Energy Organization (Organisacion Latinoamericano de Energia)
OPEC	Organization of Petroleum Exporting Countries
OPECNA	OPEC News Agency

SAAFA	Special Arab Aid Fund for Africa
SDR	Special Drawing Rights (IMF unit of credit)
SF	Saudi Fund for Development
SIDA	Swedish International Development Agency
SONATRACH	National Oil Company of Algeria
UAE	United Arab Emirates
UN	United Nations
UNCTAD	UN Conference on Trade and Development
UNDP	UN Development Programme
UNFPA	UN Fund for Population Activities
UNICEF	UN Children's Fund
UNIDO	UN Industrial Development Organization
UNIFSTD	UN Interim Fund for Science and Technology for Development
UNRWA	UN Relief and Works Agency for Palestine Refugees in the Near East
USAID	United States Agency for International Development
VIF	Venezuelan Investment Fund
WARDA	West African Rice Development Association
WFP	World Food Programme (UN)

INDEX

Note: names, data etc in the annexes
are not indexed except in a few cases
where cross-references were
appropriate.